T0345821

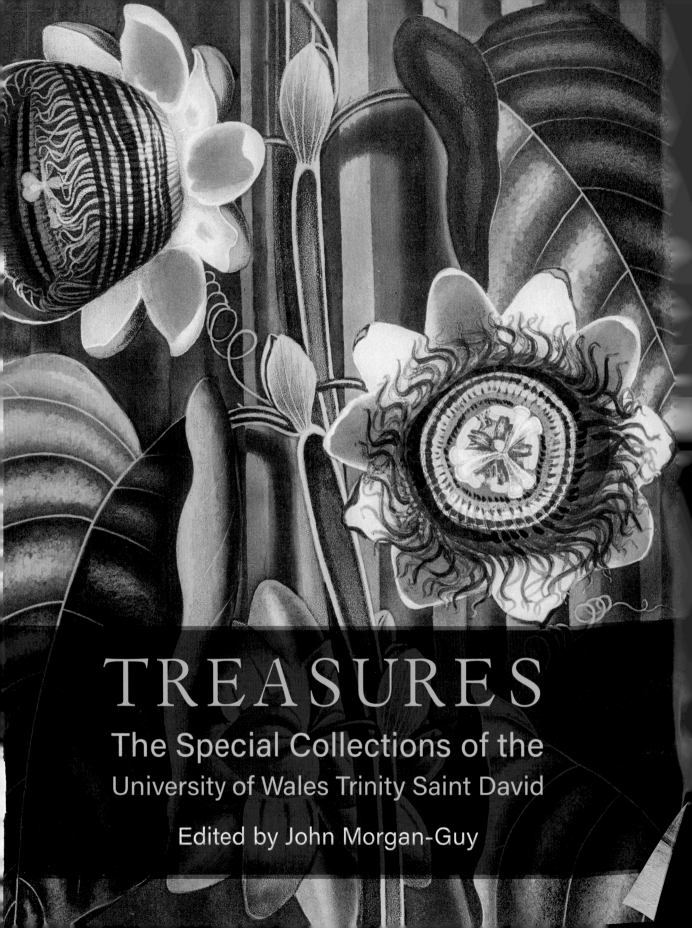

TREASURES

The Special Collections of the

University of Wales Trinity Saint David

Edited by John Morgan-Guy

TREASURES

The Special Collections of the
University of Wales Trinity Saint David

Edited by John Morgan-Guy

Photography and design by Martin Crampin

University of Wales Press

2022

British Library Cataloguing-in-Publication Data

A catalogue record for this book is available from the British Library.

ISBN 978-1-78683-901-5
eISBN 978-1-78683-903-9

Front cover
Initial from the Lampeter Bible

Back cover
Sarah Stone, *Superb warblers*, 1789, from John White, *Journal of a voyage to New South Wales with sixty-five plates of non descript animals, birds, lizards, serpents, curious cones of trees and other natural productions*

Half-title page
Peter Charles Henderson, *The Quadrangular passion-flower*, 1802, engraved by J. Hopwood the elder, from R. J. Thornton, *A new illustration of the sexual system of Linnæus*

Frontispiece
John Frederick Lewis, *Door of the hall of ambassadors*, 1835, engraved by W. Gauci, from J. F. Lewis, *Lewis's sketches and drawings of the Alhambra, made during a residence in Granada in the years 1833–4*

Contents page
From Maria Sibylla Merian, *Der rupsen begin, voedzel en wonderbaare verandering*, 1714

Contributors page
From Boddam Book of Hours

Facing page 1
A suggested plan and elevation for the College, by C. R. Cockerell

Unless otherwise indicated, all images are from the RBLA collections.

Contents

Acknowledgements

Although it is my name which appears on the title page of this book, it is far from being 'all my own work', which will be immediately apparent to the reader. Without the active and enthusiastic collaboration of my colleagues in the university, *Treasures: The Special Collections of University of Wales Trinity St David* would never have seen the light of day. Especial thanks are due to my colleagues in the Roderic Bowen Library and Archives; the Special Collections Librarian, Ruth Gooding; and the Special Collections Archivist, Nicky Hammond, both of whom are contributors to this book, for their knowledge of our outstanding collections, and their willingness to deploy that knowledge, so that a fascinating and visually rich selection of our *Treasures* could be made.

Then there are the contributors from among the past and present members of the academic staff of University of Wales Trinity St David here on the Lampeter Campus: Professor Janet Burton, Dr William Marx, Dr Harriett Webster and Dr Peter Mitchell, all of whom have placed their expertise at my disposal, as did Dr Allan Barton, who succeeded me as Chaplain on the Lampeter Campus, and permitted me to garner fruits of his research here in the library on two of our early printed liturgical books. All submitted to the strict time limit that I imposed for their contributions, and, to my joy and relief, fulfilled their promises with only the very gentlest of promptings. Research may sometimes be a lonely activity but it is rarely insular; the help of others is required more often than not, and here I would acknowledge that of Dr Philip Gooding for locating and scanning material more easily available in Montréal than in the United Kingdom.

In many ways a book such as this stands or falls not only on the authority and accessibility of its text, but also on its design and illustration. Here I have been extremely fortunate in being able to work with the outstanding photographer, designer and artist Dr Martin Crampin, a friend and collaborator for more than twenty years. A scholar and art historian in his own right, his knowledge and understanding of what was needed to bring text and illustration together have been of enormous benefit.

The decision was made at the very beginning that this book, based as it is on the collections of a university library set in the heart of Wales, should be published both in Welsh and English. This would not have been possible without the collaboration and support of Professor Elin Haf Gruffydd Jones, Director of the Centre for Advanced Welsh and Celtic Studies at Aberystwyth (where I was formerly, for three enriching and happy years, a Research Fellow) and the skill and dedication of the translators: Catrin Beard, Gwenllïan Dafydd, George Jones, Osian Rhys and Lowri Schiavone.

Bringing all this work together in its final form has been the task of the University of Wales Press, and here I have been fortunate to work with a patient and enthusiastic team including, Sarah Lewis, Head of Commissioning; Steven Goundrey, Production Manager; and Natalie Williams, Director of the Press. Copy-editing was by Marian Beech Hughes and Mike Gooding. Ruth Gooding compiled the index.

One advantage of having an association with an institution that stretches back over many years is the opportunity of working with, and learning from, colleagues whose fields of study and expertise greatly enrich one's own. The first port of call for anyone delving into the 200-year history of St David's College is the two-volume *History* by Canon Dr William Price. It has been my good fortune to have known William for over fifty years, succeeding him here as University Archivist, and he will recognize from the pages of this book how much as editor I have relied upon his research. Of those whose work has been with our Special Collections, I acknowledge, with gratitude the contributions to my knowledge and understanding of them, the late Robin Rider, the Revd Dr David Selwyn (who also supervised my doctoral research), Peter Hopkins and Sarah Roberts.

A project such as this also relies upon the support of many others who make up the 'college', and here I would especially acknowledge the help and support of the Executive Head of Library and Learning Resources, Alison Harding, herself a contributor to this volume; Sarah Goodwin, of the University's Audio-Visual Media Service; and the Vice-Chancellor, Professor Medwin Hughes; and his Chief of Staff, Shone Hughes. Finally, on a personal level, my thanks and gratitude are due to my wife Valerie – herself a graduate twice over of this venerable institution – for patiently encouraging – and putting up with – a husband whose mind and energies were so often directed into the past.

It is my hope that this volume amply fulfils the intention to bring before the readership some understanding of the rich holdings of the Roderic Bowen Library and Archives within University of Wales Trinity St David at Lampeter, and by so doing make a small contribution to the commemoration of its 200-year history.

John Morgan-Guy
February 2022

quoniam multiplicati sunt

odio iniquo oderunt me.

ustodi animam meam et e

non erubesca qm speram in

nnocentes et recti adhes

michi: quia sustinui te.

iberit deus istael: ex om

tribulationibz suis an. De

inuentutis mee et ignorantia

as ne memineris v̊. Credo.

O minus illuminatio

et salus mea que tim

ominus protector bite m

aquo trepidabo.

um apropiant super

centes: vt edant carnes me

m tribulant me inimic

ipsi infirmati sunt et cecade

i consistant aduersum

castra: non timebit cor me

i exurgat aduersum m

tuum: in hoc ego sperabo.

nam petii adomino han

quiram: vt inhabitem in d

List of Contributors

Allan Barton is an independent scholar, lecturer and art historian, and formerly Chaplain on the Lampeter Campus of University of Wales Trinity St David.

Janet Burton is Professor of Medieval History at University of Wales Trinity St David.

Ruth Gooding is Special Collections Librarian at the Roderic Bowen Library and Archives, University of Wales Trinity St David.

Nicky Hammond is Special Collections Archivist at the Roderic Bowen Library and Archives, University of Wales Trinity St David.

Alison Harding is Executive Head of Library and Learning Resources, University of Wales Trinity St David.

William Marx is Reader in Medieval Literature at University of Wales Trinity St David.

Peter Mitchell is Senior Lecturer in Early Modern English Literature at University of Wales Trinity St David.

John Morgan-Guy is Honorary Professor of Practice (Cultural History) at University of Wales Trinity St David.

Harriett Webster is Lecturer in Medieval History at University of Wales Trinity St David.

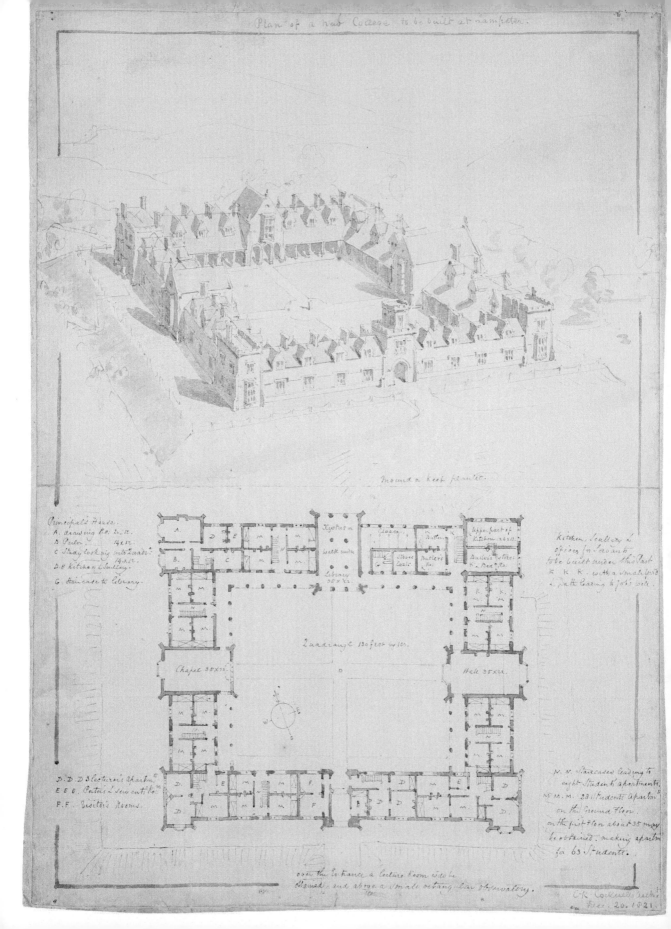

Plan of a new College to be built at Lampeter.

Mound a keep peruilt.

Principal's House.
A. drawing Ro. 2. 11.
B. Parlor   14 x 12.
C. Study looking into Quadt.
                14 x 12.
D.E Kitchen Scullery.
G. Staircase to Library.

Kystes in
walk under
Library
35 x 14

Closca.   Battery

Stores
Coalt.   Butler's
         Ho.

Upper part of
Kitchen 26 x 13.

Butler's Stores
&c. &c. &c.

Kitchen, Scullery &
offices for Servants
to be built under this Part
K. K. K. with a small yard
& path leading to Job's well.

Quadrangle 130 feet by 100.

Chapel 35 x 22.   Hall 35 x 22.

D. D. D 3 Lecturers' Apartmt.
E. E. E. Portals & servants Ho.
F. F. Visitor's Rooms.

N. N. Staircases leading to
eight Students apartments.
M. M. M. 28 Students apartmt.
on the Ground Floor.
on the first floor about 35 may
be obtained. making apartmt
for 63 Students.

over the Entrance a Lecture Room will be
obtained. and above a small octangular observatory.

C. R. Cockerell Archt.
Dec. 20. 1821.

'The Greatest Little Library in Wales' The Story of the College and its Library[1]

Books, according to Bishop Thomas Burgess's literary hero, John Milton, 'do preserve as in a vial the purest efficacy and extraction of that living intellect that bred them'. No doubt the bibliophile bishop of St Davids was familiar with and approved of that understanding, from Milton's *Tractate of Education*, which appeared in 1644. Thus, when he set about the founding of a college to provide a university-standard education for the men primarily from his diocese who sought entry into the Holy Orders of the Established Church of England, but who could not afford the fees charged by either of the English universities of Oxford and Cambridge, it was of books he first thought. Before he sought a suitable architect to design his college, or scholars to staff it, or, perhaps, where he was to find the money to build and endow it – even a site upon which to erect it – Bishop Burgess began to appeal for and collect books with which to fill the shelves of its library, books which would be vital in the education of those who would study within its walls, and equip them for life in a far wider world than that which they had known hitherto. Long before the foundation stone of the first college building was laid in 1822, on the birthday of the reigning monarch, George IV, the collection was growing. The first books arrived in 1809, housed, ready and waiting, within the walls of Burgess's Episcopal Palace at Abergwili, on the outskirts of the county town of Carmarthen. Here they rested, alongside the bishop's own extensive library – or part of it, as Burgess was also a canon of Durham Cathedral, and the remainder of his books were in his house there – until their final move to Lampeter.

Wax bust believed to be of Bishop Thomas Burgess, but may be of Samuel Horsley, Bishop 1788–93

These early donations, from supporters and well-wishers of the bishop's project, were to form the initial Foundation Collection of the college. Most, but not all, came from clergy, the most generous of whom was Dr Charles Poyntz, an aristocratic and well-connected colleague of Burgess's and a fellow canon of Durham. More books trickled in, and by the time the college opened it has been estimated some 4,000 were waiting to be shelved. The most important single donation was that of Dr Thomas Bowdler, a friend of Burgess and a resident of Swansea, the story of whose massive collection of seventeenth- and eighteenth-century tracts is outlined elsewhere in the pages of this book.[2] Largely put together by two earlier generations of Dr Bowdler's family, who were non-jurors, many of the tracts reveal that concern for orthodoxy and orthopraxis as the Established Church understood it which was also a preoccupation of Bishop Burgess. The collection had been first undertaken by Thomas Bowdler I in the seventeenth century, so as well as reflecting later political and religious life and controversies, it also contained a significant number of tracts from the era of the Civil Wars, Commonwealth and Protectorate of the 1640s and 1650s.[3] Far from being concerned only with theological and doctrinal matters, the tracts cover many aspects of daily life and interest. As Dr Bowdler died in 1825, his collection must have come to Abergwili whilst the college at Lampeter was still a building site.[4] Apart from the Bowdler Tract Collection, perhaps the most notable of these early donations is a first edition of Sir Walter Ralegh's (*c.* 1552–1618) *History of the World* (1614), the gift of St Edmund Hall, Oxford, and featured in this volume.

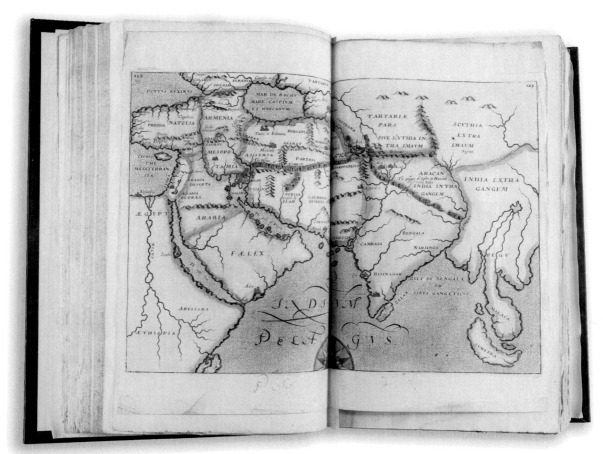

From Walter Ralegh, *The History of the World*, 1614

TREASURES

The Special Collections of the
University of Wales Trinity Saint David

Bishop Burgess, in his late sixties, with failing sight, and, according to the diary of the college architect Charles Cockerell, some diminution in his mental powers of concentration, accepted translation to the less demanding see of Salisbury in 1825. At Abergwili he left behind the accumulated books intended for the college; he added to these those from his own personal library previously housed in his canon's residence at Durham. Salisbury being a wealthier see than St Davids, he had on translation surrendered his canonry at that northern cathedral. His successor as bishop of St Davids, John Banks Jenkinson, was a cousin of the prime minister, the Earl of Liverpool. In some respects, Jenkinson was cast in a similar mould to his predecessor; he was rather shy and self-effacing, a scholarly bibliophile with a substantial library of his own. He quickly, and to the evident satisfaction of John Scandrett Harford, donor of the site, and Charles Cockerell the architect, interested himself in the fledgling college at Lampeter, and continued Burgess's practice of accumulating books for its library.

The hope was that the college would be ready for a formal opening in August 1826, again on the king's birthday. Bishop Burgess journeyed from Salisbury in late July in anticipation, but it was not to be. The building was not ready, and certainly not the library. Not all the shelving was in place to receive the books. The formal opening did not take place until St David's Day, 1 March 1827, and even then, the library was still in a state of chaos, with shelves incomplete and books awaiting unpacking and arranging. The newly appointed librarian, and Professor of Welsh, the Revd Rice Rees, had many hours of hard work ahead of him to bring about some semblance of order. Meanwhile, donations continued to arrive, and, as already instanced in St Edmund Hall's gift of Ralegh's *History*, they contained books of exceptional interest. From the Revd Edward Berens came a unique issue of Jeremy Taylor's *Vindication of Episcopacy*,[5] and in 1834 from the major Carmarthenshire and Pembrokeshire landowner

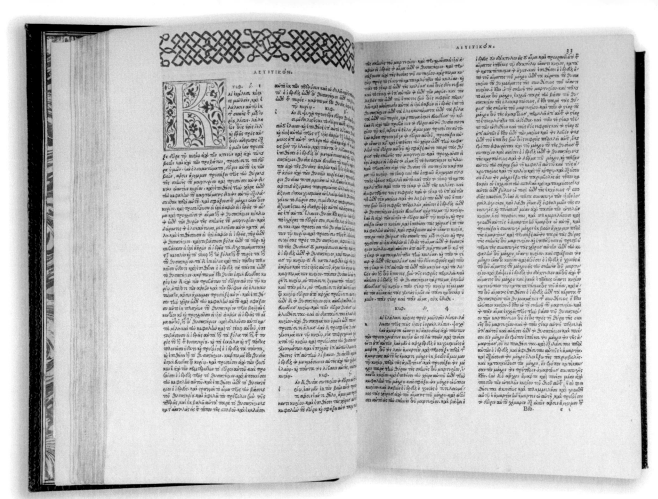

The Aldine Greek Bible of 1518, the gift of Lord Cawdor

Lord Cawdor a 1518 copy of the Aldine Greek Bible. For simple elegance it would be hard to surpass this book: the clear, readable, immaculate typeface is relieved only by more elaborate capital letters at the beginning of each biblical book, which are printed in red in the Old Testament and black in the New; it is a joy to handle and refer to.

In the year of the gift of this Bible, the library began a period of major expansion, largely due to the donations of the London Welshman and retired East India Company surgeon, Thomas Phillips. Then in 1837 on the death of Bishop Burgess, it received, under the terms of his will, the residue of his library. It has often been assumed that this was the sole benefaction of his books, but, as noted earlier, this was not the case. His Durham library had been earmarked for the college in 1825, and had no doubt been transferred with the other accumulated books at Abergwili once the library was equipped to receive them in 1828. Burgess therefore made two, not one, major donations, though it is now not possible to differentiate them. The Phillips benefaction

TREASURES
The Special Collections of the
University of Wales Trinity Saint David

of manuscripts, incunabula and books of later date continued for some eighteen years, with consignments being received at intervals until 1852, the year after his death. It was to completely transform the college library; it was also to cause major problems of space.

Something needs to be said here about these two principal donors to the Library, Thomas Burgess and Thomas Phillips. Burgess was born in Odiham, Hampshire in 1756, the son of a grocer, a trade which his brother John (d. 1820) was to carry on, greatly expanded, from premises in The Strand, London.[6] Educated at Winchester and then Corpus Christi College, Oxford, Thomas Burgess showed an early aptitude for scholarship, becoming a fellow and tutor at his college. He came to the notice of the bishop of Salisbury from 1782–91, the Hon. Shute Barrington (1734–1826), who appointed him as his Examining Chaplain, and then, on translation in 1791 to the Prince-Bishopric of Durham, took him with him. Burgess was given the country parish of Winston near Barnard Castle – his only parochial experience – and a prebend and residentiary canonry in Durham Cathedral. Burgess and Barrington shared a similar outlook; both were deeply interested in Christian education. At Salisbury Barrington had worked to establish a network of Sunday Schools in the parishes of his diocese, in which endeavour Burgess was to share – indeed he devoted time to compiling short and simple books for children, one of which was a guide to spelling. This was alongside his concern to raise the standards of those applying for admission to Holy Orders (he was known for his strictness), and his own, far from inconsiderable, devotion to scholarship. Fluent in Latin and Greek, and able to write in French and Italian, after ordination in 1784 Burgess devoted his energies to the study of Hebrew (a language which, later in life he was to say was easier to master than Welsh).[7]

Like Barrington, Burgess was not a party man; labels can be misleading and attempts for example to shoehorn both into the category of 'Evangelical' do justice to neither. Barrington, as Elizabeth Varley has pointed out, was no friend to Methodism, particularly of the Calvinistic variety, which flourished in Wales where he had been Bishop of Llandaff from 1769–82. He 'enjoyed an uneasy theological relationship with the evangelicals'.[8] He may have shared the practical philanthropy of evangelicals of the stamp of William Wilberforce and Hannah More, but at the same time had the conservatively orthodox theological outlook of the leaders of the 'Hackney Phalanx', men of the temper of Joshua Watson and Henry Handley Norris. The same can be said of Burgess. Like Barrington he opposed the slave trade on moral grounds (he was an honorary member of the Anti-Slavery Society) and came to number Wilberforce and More among his friends. They were also to be subscribers to his foundation of St David's College. Again, like Barrington, he was opposed to dissent from the teachings of the Established Church, be it Roman Catholic or Protestant, and in his diocese of St Davids he saw his college at Lampeter as a bulwark against Unitarianism, then prominent in that area of Cardiganshire (his first published sermon in 1790 had been on the Divinity of Christ). The broad but conservative theological outlook that characterized Burgess is easy to detect in the books which in 1825 and 1837 he donated to the library of St David's College.

It would be hard to find a greater contrast than that between Burgess and the other major donor – indeed, *the* major donor – to the library of St David's College, the one quiet and scholarly, the other physically strong and adventurous. Thomas Phillips (1760–1851) was a London Welshman, the son and namesake of an officer in His Majesty's Customs and Excise service. The family came from Llandegley in Radnorshire, and it was in this deeply rural county rather than in London that he spent most of his childhood, in the care of the rector of Cusop. Determined on a medical career, he was first apprenticed to a surgeon-apothecary at Hay-on-Wye. Before his twentieth birthday, he was back in London, studying surgery under John Hunter, probably the greatest comparative anatomist of his day. In 1780 he joined the Royal Navy as surgeon's mate on the frigate HMS *Danae*, later transferring to HMS *Hind*, on board which he experienced the rigours of a Canadian winter in the icebound waters of the St Lawrence, and enlarged his surgical skills in the hospitals of Quebec City and Montréal. Returning home in 1782, he gained the Certificate of the Corporation of Surgeons (which was later to qualify him for Membership of the Royal College of Surgeons), transferred from the Navy to the East India Company, and sailed for Calcutta. The remainder of his working life was spent in the service of the Company, originally as surgeon to a succession of native infantry and artillery regiments in its army at various stations. It was an active and varied life, and included in 1796 a voyage to Australia, to inspect and report on the hospital provision at the penal colony at Botany Bay. On this occasion he took the opportunity to return via China and Penang. He was to retain an interest in the 'Far East' throughout his life; in retirement he was active in the Royal Asiatic Society, and this abiding interest is reflected in some of his donations to the St David's College Library.

TREASURES

The Special Collections of the
University of Wales Trinity Saint David

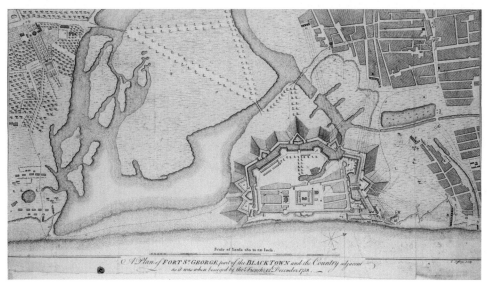

Plan of Fort St George, the Bengal Headquarters of the East India Company, from Richard Owen Cambridge's *An Account of the War in India*, 1760

Phillips's life during his East India Company service, which lasted until his retirement in 1817 from his final appointment as a member of the Calcutta Medical Board, was not without incident and hazard. In 1798, whilst sailing home on furlough in a Danish East India Company ship, the vessel was captured by a French privateer and Phillips was interrogated for two days at Bordeaux before being released. In 1810 he was on active service in the Java War; later he was in Nepal in a campaign against the Gurkhas in the Anglo-Nepalese War of 1814–16 under the command of Major-General Robert Gillespie. At the woefully mismanaged siege of Kalunga in the high Himalayas, Gillespie, personally leading an attack – an impulsive man, he was known as 'Rollicking Rollo' – was mortally wounded, and died in Phillips's arms. Although by this date Phillips was 53, and a senior surgeon, he was first and foremost a 'battlefield surgeon', active in the front line, as evidenced by the fact that one soldier was killed by a second shot whilst Phillips was actually treating him.

It is clear that Phillips was personally fearless; he was also compassionate. During his time with the Royal Navy, on board HMS *Hind*, he had given up his own berth to a sick sailor. At Kalunga, when the fort finally capitulated, he realized that many of the women who had helped in its defence, some wounded, were being left to their fate. He gave up his tent for them, and gave them the same medical and surgical treatment that he gave to the soldiery of both sides of the conflict. There are other examples of similar behaviour which could be recorded; he did not prioritize his own safety and comfort. Later in life he was known for his generosity to refugees from, for example,

Poland and Hungary, and to those who called on him for financial assistance. After his retirement to London, he purchased the lease on a house in Brunswick Square,[9] almost at the gates of the Foundling Hospital. He also acquired in December 1821 for an estimated sum of £40,000 from the heirs of Sir John Boyd and John Trevanion, the plantation of Camden Park on the volcanic island of St Vincent in the Caribbean.[10] It remained in his ownership until his death,[11] that is, both before and after the 1834 abolition of slavery. It is difficult to discern with any degree of certainty Phillips's personal feelings about the ownership of slaves. There were 164 enslaved persons at Camden Park under its previous owners, later augmented by a further eighty-five. His position may well have been close to that of Bishop Burgess. As mentioned earlier, in 1789 Burgess as a young Oxford don had published a well-received work condemning the slave trade, but the tenor of the work was that the time was not ripe for eman-

cipation. As John Scandrett Harford, said in his 1840 biography of Burgess, in 1789 he argued not for immediate emancipation, but for a ban on the further importation of enslaved persons, and, after a limited period, in which Christian instruction of those on the plantations could take place, eventual abolition of the condition. It was this standpoint which won him the approbation of the London Abolition Committee and honorary membership of the Anti-Slavery Society.[12] Or perhaps Phillips saw things in a similar light to Thomas Jefferson (1743–1826), third president of the United States from 1801–9, who accepted the moral arguments against the institution of slavery, but was not moved to liberate the enslaved persons who worked his own plantation in Virginia.[13] We shall never know; as Steven Brindle said of Phillips's younger contemporary, Isambard Kingdom Brunel (1806–59) he was 'paradox – rooted in

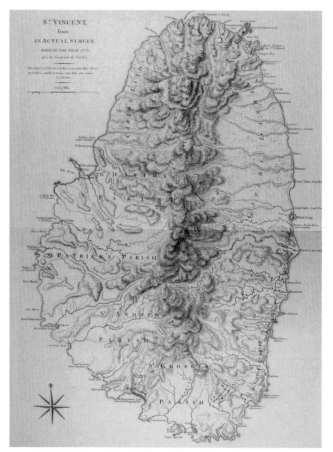

Thomas Jefferys, *St Vincent from an actual survey*, 1775, from T. Jefferys, *The West-India atlas*

TREASURES
The Special Collections of the
University of Wales Trinity Saint David

the old world, he imagines, and helps create, the new'.[14] All that can be said is that, although a non-resident proprietor, Phillips maintained an active concern for those who worked Camden Park; he encouraged churchgoing – as befitted the son-in-law of an Anglican rector – and required of those who managed the plantation on his behalf particular care of the aged, infirm and women. Emancipation came in 1833 with the Abolition of Slavery Act for the enslaved persons in the Caribbean, Mauritius and Cape Colony (but not in the territories controlled by the East India Company). The government raised £20 million to compensate the 47,000 eligible plantation owners, shareholders and other interested parties. Phillips received in due course £4,737 8s. 6d, which was added to his already considerable fortune, and used to further augment his educational philanthropy. He also invested in the East India Company's Dhobah Sugar Company, which endeavoured to use the techniques of the West India planta-tions in India itself, but without the employment of slave labour. The initiative failed in 1848, and Phillips lost thousands of pounds as a result.

It was during his long years of service with the East India Company that his interest in what might be called 'continuing education' first emerged, and it involved the foundation of libraries and the provision of books. From about 1813, when he was senior surgeon at Chunar,[15] overlooking the Ganges and close to the 'eternal city' of Varanasi, one of the most important pilgrimage sites in India, and only about six miles from where the Buddha had first preached, he began supplying mess rooms with small libraries for the common soldier. The impulse was both medical and educational. On the one hand, readily available and easily readable literature would broaden the horizons of the garrisons, and on the other help break the monotony of regimented peacetime duty, providing a constructive alternative to the temptations that were all-too-obviously available for those with time on their hands. Herein lie the seeds of his philanthropy once he was back home in England, where he supplied books and museum exhibits to libraries and literary and scientific institutions. St David's College was not the only recipient of his generosity in this respect; libraries at Hereford, Hay-on-Wye, Builth, and, after 1847 – when he was 87 – his foundation of Llandovery College were all beneficiaries, as was the Royal Institution in London, and a number of private individuals who received parcels of books for distribution in their neighbourhoods. He was actively involved in the Russell Institution for the Promotion of Literary and Scientific Knowledge, with its headquarters at 55 Coram Street, close to his home, and no doubt contributed to the building up of the 17,000 books in its library. More than 22,000 manuscripts, incunabula and books came to

St David's College alone, and it has been estimated that a staggering 50,000 awaited distribution at Brunswick Square on his death in 1851, along with the latest tools and appliances destined for Camden Park.

It was long thought that Phillips's consignments of books to Lampeter had no coherent pattern. William Price, for example, in his history of the college, speaks of Phillips's 'indiscriminate buying' and the sixty batches which arrived between 1834 and 1852 as a 'heterogeneous collection'.[16] It is certainly true that, as a former conservator of the library, Dr David Selwyn, pointed out,[17] Phillips was buying books at London sales from the 1820s, including the Kloss Sale at Sotheby's in 1825. In fact, the decades of the 1820s and 1830s were favourable to collectors, as the quantity of books on the market depressed prices. Inevitably, when at least some of the books were sold in 'lots', there would be duplicates – if such a designation can be used for books printed before about 1850 – and some of little interest. However, more recent analysis of the Phillips Collection shows that far from being indiscriminate, there was a purpose behind the purchases. It was Phillips's intention to equip the libraries that he supported and enhanced with books that would greatly extend the mental horizons of those who used and perused them. In an age that could not conceive of radio, television and the internet, it was through books, and especially illustrated books (in which the Phillips Collection is rich) that 'global' knowledge and understanding would be acquired. It was for such works that Phillips, and no doubt the agents he employed to visit the salerooms and bid, were seeking.

There is some evidence, albeit slight, that Phillips included works from his own library at Brunswick Square among his donations. In 1846 the Welsh Manuscript Society published Samuel Rush Meyrick's *Heraldic Visitations of Wales and Parts of the Marches*. It was a limited edition – only 240 copies were printed (by Rees of Llandovery, the family of the Revd Rice Rees, first Professor of Welsh at the college) – and issued to subscribers only. For this reason, within twenty years, it was described as 'extremely scarce'. One of the subscribers was Thomas Phillips, who passed it on to the college in 1849.[18] A curious feature of the two volumes is that, although concerned with the genealogy and heraldry of families entitled to use a coat of arms, all of the coats of arms printed are, in fact, blank.

Transportation of the books of the Phillips benefaction to Lampeter was not without its hazards. The usual route in this pre-railway era was by sea to the port of Carmarthen,

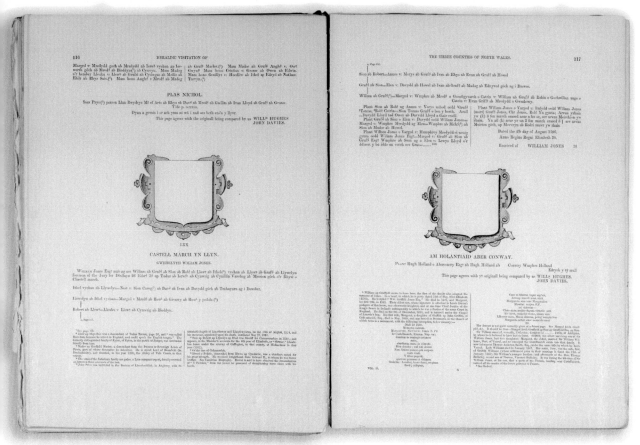

Samuel Rush Meyrick, *Heraldic Visitations of Wales and Part of the Marches,* 1846, showing the blank shields

Alfred Ollivant, Vice-Principal of the College 1827–1843

and then by carrier's cart to the college. There was always a risk of loss or damage, as seems to have happened in the case of Alfred Ollivant, appointed vice-principal in 1827. En route from Cambridge the vessel carrying at least part of his personal library to Carmarthen foundered, and many of his books were damaged and some lost. Whether or not any part of the Phillips benefactions met a similar fate is unknown, but, as noted earlier, what did arrive safely caused acute problems of shelving. The library space provided in Cockerell's original plan was too small, and by 1835 the problem was becoming acute. Cockerell was employed between 1835 and 1837 to extend the library northwards and eastwards – to its present dimensions – and both Bishop Burgess and his wife contributed to the cost of the new work. (His own munificent donations rather more than those of Phillips at this stage – these only started to arrive in 1834 – had after all, contributed in no small measure to the problem!)[19] With little change what is now known as the 'Founders' Library' continued in use as a working library for staff and students until the latter part of the twentieth century.

With the arrival of the last batch of the Phillips benefaction in 1852, the days of expansion were over, and it has to be admitted that the library had already entered an era of torpor and neglect. After the death of Rice Rees in 1839, the newly appointed Professor of Latin, the Revd William North, took over as librarian but seems to have taken little interest in the collection. By 1850 the building was in poor repair, books suffered damage from rainwater penetrating a leaking roof, and students were admitted only once a week. Not until the appointment of Rowland Williams as vice-principal in 1850 did matters improve. He found the collection in considerable disorder, with shelving that was inadequate for the number of books. The leaking roof was repaired (1852) and the galleries mentioned earlier were erected (1855), but there was no proper catalogue.[20] The library by now contained some 35,000 volumes and was thus the largest in Wales, and as William Price pointed out, larger than the majority of Oxford and Cambridge college libraries at that date.[21] However, it was little known, and, being uncatalogued, was little used even by those resident in the college itself. Not until the Revd Joseph Matthews, the first Phillips Professor of Science at the college (1853–72) became librarian in 1862 was an attempt made to compile a catalogue, and that remained unfinished when he left for a parish in Montgomeryshire.[22] The twentieth century had dawned before a full-time cataloguer, Alexander de Zandt, was appointed for three years in 1902. This was on the initiative of the principal, Llewellyn Bebb, who had been librarian of his Oxford college (Brasenose). Only then did the true extent and value of the collection become apparent.

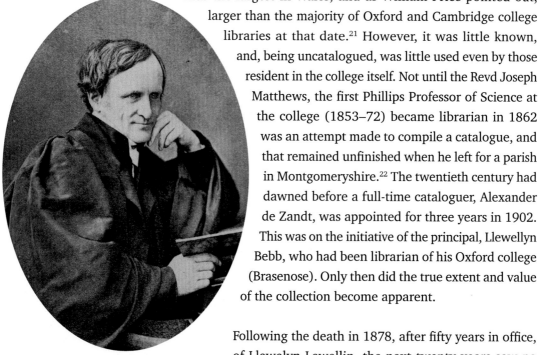

Rowland Williams, Vice-Principal of the College 1850–1862

Following the death in 1878, after fifty years in office, of Llewelyn Lewellin, the next twenty years saw no fewer than five short-lived occupants of the post of principal. Lewellin, holding simultaneously the vicarage

TREASURES
The Special Collections of the
University of Wales Trinity Saint David

of Lampeter and the Deanery of St Davids Cathedral with the office of principal, had been increasingly infirm for some years, and, as far as can be traced, taken little or no interest in the library. The same seems to have been largely true of his five immediate successors, but not true in respect of some at least of the academic staff, which included scholars of high calibre, including T. F. Tout (Professor of History 1881–90), Hugh Walker (Lecturer, then Professor, of English 1884–1939) and Edmund Tyrell Green (Lecturer, then Professor, of Hebrew and Theology 1890–1924). It was Tout, in association with his friend the distinguished seventeenth-century historian C. H. Firth (1857–1936), best remembered for his work on the period of the English Civil Wars, the Commonwealth and Protectorate, who rescued the precious Bowdler Tract Collection from the neglect into which it had fallen. With the advent of Llewellyn John Montfort Bebb as principal in 1898, the library emerges into a period of some stability and growth. Bebb – like Thomas Phillips – had Radnorshire roots, though he himself was born in Cape Town in 1862. Educated at Winchester and New College, Oxford, he had been a fellow of Brasenose since 1885, serving for a time also as librarian, and for five years – overlapping, in fact, his appointment to Lampeter – as a curator of the University's Botanic Gardens. (He was to take some pains in laying out the grounds of St David's College during his term of office as principal.)

Although he was not a Welsh-speaker, Bebb quickly realized that the library was notably deficient in works in the vernacular. In association with Evan Lorimer Thomas, appointed Professor of Welsh in 1903, he set about remedying this defect. As far back as 1850 it is possible to trace a hope that there could be established a national library for Wales.[23] Addressing the Cambrian Archaeological Society in August of that year, the bibliophile Sir Thomas Phillipps (not to be confused with the college bene-factor of the same name) expressed a hope that such an institution could be founded, and that it should be close to St David's College. He was merely re-expressing the hope and aspiration of some of the early proponents of Bishop Burgess's desire to found a college in the early years of the century, including Archdeacon Thomas Beynon and Herbert

Llewellyn Bebb, Principal of the College 1898–1915

Evans of Highmead. It was not to be. Principal Lewellin, although a Welsh-speaker, and his successors – several of whom were not – had no interest in pursuing the idea.[24] Bebb and Lorimer Thomas recognized the paucity of Welsh-language works, both books and periodicals, and determined to correct this deficiency. A Welsh library was established, and in 1904 Bebb authorized the considerable expenditure of £110 to purchase all the relevant books and the invaluable collection of Welsh Ballads which formed the core of the library of the Revd D. H. Davies, Vicar of Cenarth. Housed on the ground floor of Cockerell's 1835 extension, it remained as a separate library until the building of the new university library in 1966.

The acquisition of the Cenarth Collection stimulated further gifts and legacies, notably those of Canon Ellis Davies (1872–1962) for many years editor of *Archaeologia Cambrensis*. As Wyn Thomas in his history of the Welsh Library said:

> We may note that the Welsh Library was instituted as part of an intention to give the Welsh language and Welsh culture a higher profile in the College, and that this should be seen as a local aspect of the wider awakening of Welsh conscious-ness and sensibility at the end of the nineteenth century and the beginning of the twentieth century.[25]

Inevitably, the outbreak of the First World War in 1914 brought further developments of both libraries to an end. Lorimer Thomas left the college in 1915, and in the same year Principal Bebb died, prematurely, at the age of 53. Numbers of students in residence slumped, as many joined, or were recruited into, the armed forces. Admissions, for example, dropped from fifty-seven in 1912 to ten in 1918; there were only thirty-two students in residence in 1916, the number dropping still further to an almost vanishing point of twenty-three. Bebb was succeeded as principal by Gilbert Cunningham Joyce (1866–1942) whose 'reign' (1916–22) almost proved disastrous for the college. A former sub-warden of St Michael's College when it was still at Aberdare and before it moved to Llandaff, and the first warden of St Deiniol's Library at Hawarden, Joyce, scholarly but remote, was particularly interested in the training of men for Holy Orders. He came to the conclusion that the college, in the aftermath of the war and of the disestablishment of the Church in Wales in 1920, should confine itself to the postgraduate training of men for the Anglican ministry. This would inevitably involve the abandonment of the three-year BA degree course, as well as major changes in the College Charters. Suffice it to say here that ultimately Joyce's ideas, which it has to be

admitted had considerable support, were not accepted, and in 1922 he resigned. His successor, the 59-year-old Dr Maurice Jones, a fluent Welsh-speaker, had been for many years an army chaplain (something which endeared him to those students who had themselves served in the forces during the 1914–18 war). Jones proved to be an energetic and enthusiastic principal, in office until he was 75, but was not exactly a friend to the library. However, in 1924 an assistant librarian was first appointed – the archaic practice of appointing one of the professors as librarian continued for many years thereafter – which enabled opening hours to be extended. The annual library grant for the purchase of books remained small and in the late 1920s an indeterminate number of volumes were sold off. Jones himself is said to have disposed of many works of Victorian theology donated by former students, some given away as gifts, and others, so the 'folklore' would have it, used to feed the boilers of the heating system!

Once again, war, followed by protracted negotiations over the future of the college, detailed by William Price and also by J. R. Lloyd Thomas (Principal 1953–75) in his autobiography, effectively stalled all but minor changes and improvements.[26] For example, it was not until 1961 that a full-time sub-librarian, Robin Rider, was appointed, and even then evening opening was only maintained through the library being 'staffed' by volunteer final-year undergraduates.[27] A turning point was reached in 1964 when an allocation of £60,000 from the University Grants Committee enabled plans for the construction of a new library building to be drawn up. Designed by Verner Rees, work was largely complete by 1966 – though by no means all of the books of the 'working library' had been transferred when on 7 July it was

Robin Rider, Sub-Librarian and
first Keeper of Special Collections

officially opened by the Duke of Edinburgh, the first royal visitor to the college in its by then 144-year history. Unhappily, structural weaknesses and other faults in the design and construction soon became apparent, and major work was required on the building within twenty years; greatly enlarged, the new work was designed by Ivan Dale Owen of Percy Thomas Partnership. The building had in less than twenty years proved too small to house the 'working library'. The extension was formally re-opened by the Prince of Wales on 21 June 1984.

Whilst the Welsh Library had been transferred to the new building in 1966, the 'Foundation Collections' remained in the old library. Transferring the Welsh Library was something of a mixed blessing. It had, admittedly, been little used in its original home (many students were blissfully ignorant of its whereabouts and even of its existence). However, when it was transferred, it was integrated into the main collection, and therefore, though more accessible, lost its integrity. The Foundation Collections remained in their old home until the early years of the twenty-first century, carefully managed by Robin Rider, who on his retirement as sub-librarian in 1989 took on the role of honorary curator of the historic collections, now renamed the 'Founders' Library', and the Revd Dr David Selwyn, Lecturer in Ecclesiastical History as Conservator

The Old (now Founders') Library in the 1950s

of the collection. Under their care for the first time, the extent and historic value of the collection, and its potential for academic research were originally realized.

However, attractive though the old library was, it was certainly not suitable as a home for such an important collection. In 2000 the Historic Manuscripts Commission (HMC) inspected the building and declared it 'unfit for purpose'. The amount of woodwork, the inade-

TREASURES

The Special Collections of the
University of Wales Trinity Saint David

quacy of temperature and humidity control, uncertain electrics and absence of fire exits combined to make it 'fire-hazardous' and the conclusion was that however modified, the building could never be made suitable to house the collections it contained. The HMC said that they would be willing to guide, support and advise on any draft plans that might be drawn up for a new, dedicated, building for the collection.[28] Some years were to elapse before it was possible to act on the report, but it was clear that after 2000 the days of the old library were numbered.

The coincidence of two things enabled the HMC recommendation to become a reality. Funding was made available for a purpose-built research centre and library by the Higher Education Funding Council for Wales through its Science Research Infrastructure Fund, and by a munificent legacy from Roderic Bowen, QC, former MP for Cardigan and President of the Council of St David's University College from 1977 to 1992. Designed by Henry James of the Aberystwyth architectural practice James, Jenkins, Thomas, the new facility was constructed to meet all the stringent requirements for the housing of archives and early printed books laid down by the British Standards for such repositories. The library was officially opened on 17 October 2008 by the First Minister for Wales, the Rt Hon Rhodri Morgan, PC, AM, himself a graduate of Oxford and Harvard. In view of his legacy, the new facility was named the Roderic Bowen Library and Archives. What may now be termed the 'Special Collections' were moved from the old Founders' Library by Harrow Green, the firm which had been employed to move the collections of the British Library to their new home in St Pancras. In accordance with 'best practice', the books were arranged by donor, so, for example, the integrity of the Burgess and Phillips donations was restored.

The Revd Canon Dr D. T. W. Price, first University Archivist

Allied to the recent history of the library is the story of the University Archives. Principal Llewellyn Bebb, anxious to preserve material illustrative of the college's history, had appealed for donations of books and papers which could constitute the basis of an archive. Nothing systematic was to be done for the ensuing half-century until the Revd William Price, appointed Lecturer in History in 1970 (Senior Lecturer from 1987) as he undertook his history of the college, began the putting together of what was to become the University Archive with himself as the first archivist, albeit in an honorary capacity. Price remained in the college until he moved to be vicar of Cydweli in 1997, the archive in his time

AGORWYD Y
LLYFRGELL HON
A ENWYD AR ÔL

E·RODERIC
BOWEN QC·LLD
(Anrh)
CYN-LYWYDD Y
SEFYDLIAD HWN

GAN Y GWIR
ANRHYDEDDUS
RHODRI
MORGAN PC·AC
PRIF WEINIDOG
CYMRU

THIS LIBRARY
NAMED AFTER

E·RODERIC
BOWEN QC·LLD
(Hon)
FORMERLY
PRESIDENT
OF THIS
INSTITUTION

WAS OPENED BY

THE RIGHT HON
RHODRI
MORGAN PC·AM
FIRST MINISTER
FOR WALES

17·10·2008

Commemorative Plaque recording
the opening of the Roderic Bowen
Library by Rhodri Morgan, First
Minister for Wales, 17 October 2008

boxed and housed in the History Department. He was succeeded by the editor of this volume, who joined the academic staff in that year. During his tenure the archive was moved to the former Welsh Library, which had been vacated in 1966, and appropriate shelving provided. Robin Rider retired as Curator of Special Collections in 1994. The roles of curator and archivist were later combined for a short time, with Dr Nigel Yates (1944–2009), Professor of Ecclesiastical History (2005–9) and a former Kent County Archivist as Keeper of Special Collections. Yates compiled the first catalogue of the official records of the university in 2007; this was updated in 2018. Subsequently catalogues of the Library Archive (2017) and of the rich Photograph Archive (2018) were compiled by the Special Collections Archivist, Sarah Roberts, who had revised and updated the 2007 catalogue. Price, Morgan-Guy and Yates were all largely honorary and necessarily part-time, holding academic posts in the university. At the time of writing there is both a full-time Special Collections Librarian, Ruth Gooding, who succeeded Peter Hopkins, who did much work on the reappraisal of the Phillips benefaction and was largely responsible for the reassembling of the Burgess and Phillips collections; and a Special Collections Archivist, Nicky Hammond, who followed Sarah Roberts in the post.

Since 1966, and especially since the mid-1980s, those responsible for the Special Collections have curated many exhibitions drawing on the deposited material, and in recent years these have reached a wider audience, thanks to the World Wide Web. In the bicentenary year of the foundation of St David's College, the work of what has been since 2008 the Roderic Bowen Library and Archives on the Lampeter Campus of the University of Wales Trinity St David continues to develop and expand.

John Morgan-Guy

TREASURES
The Special Collections of the
University of Wales Trinity Saint David

From Edward Young,
*The complaint, and the consolation;
or, Night thoughts*, 1797,
illustrated by William Blake

Supporter sole of man above himself;
Even in this night of frailty, change, and death,
She gives the soul a soul that acts a God.
Religion! providence! an after-state!
Here is firm footing—here is solid rock—
This can support us—all is sea besides—
Sinks under us—bestorms, and then devours.
* His hand the good man fastens on the skies,
And bids earth roll, nor feels her idle whirl.

    As when a wretch, from thick polluted air,
Darkness and stench, and suffocating damps,
And dungeon-horrors by kind fate discharged,
Climbs some fair eminence, where ether pure
Surrounds him, and elysian prospects rise;
His heart exults, his spirits cast their load;
As if new-born he triumphs in the change;
So joys the soul, when, from inglorious aims
And sordid sweets, from feculence and froth
Of ties terrestrial set at large, she mounts
To reason's region, her own element,
Breathes hopes immortal and affects the skies.

    Religion! thou the soul of happiness;
And, groaning Calvary, of thee! there shine
The noblest truths; there strongest motives sting;
There sacred violence assaults the soul;
There nothing but compulsion is forborn.
Can love allure us? or can terror awe?
HE weeps!—the falling drop puts out the sun;
HE sighs!—the sigh earth's deep foundation shakes:
If in his love so terrible, what then

1   This introduction is greatly indebted to the researches of the Revd Canon Dr D. T. William Price when he was Senior Lecturer in History and University Archivist, the fruits of which were published in D. T. W. Price, *A History of Saint David's University College, Lampeter. Volume One: to 1898* (Cardiff: University of Wales Press, 1977), and D. T. W. Price, *A History of St David's University College, Lampeter. Volume Two: 1898–1971* (Cardiff: University of Wales Press, 1990).

2   Bowdler also donated a large set of the prints by William Hogarth, which remain in the library collection.

3   Ivan Roots (1921–2015), an acknowledged expert on the Cromwellian era, and Professor of History at Exeter University from 1967, to whom I showed this collection in the mid-1960s, expressed the view that it was one of the most significant such collections in the country.

4   Bowdler also gave a painting of the Virgin and Child, originally thought to be by Ludovico Carracci (1555–1619) but more likely to have been by Giovanni Battista Salvi de Sassoferrato (1609–85), to his parish church of St Mary in Swansea, to serve as an altarpiece. It may originally have been in the collection of the antiquarian Sir Robert Cotton, with whose family Dr Bowdler was connected. The painting was destroyed in the blitz of 1941, though an early photograph of it survives in the collection of the Royal Institution, Swansea.

5   Jeremy Taylor, *A vindication of the sacred order and offices, divine institution, apostolical tradition, and Catholick practice of episcopacy* (London: printed for Austine Rice, 1660). The work is not listed in Donald G. Wing, *Short-Title Catalogue of Books Printed in England, Scotland, Ireland, Wales and British America, and of English Books printed in other Countries, 1641–1700* (New York: Modern Language Association of America, 1998), familiarly known as ESTC, nor in standard bibliographies of Taylor's works.

6   Both John and Burgess's nephew William were early subscribers to the Building Fund of the college. It was John and Thomas's father, William, who had sent John to London to establish the business. Frank George, *Anchovy Paste by Appointment. The History of John Burgess & Son, and a Guide to Collecting Victorian Fish Paste Pot Lids* (published for the author, 1976).

7   His portrait, which has pride of place in the Old Hall of the St David's Building of the college, shows the bishop turning the pages of the Hebrew text of the Old Testament.

8   E. A. Varley, 'Barrington, Shute (1734–1826)', in *Oxford Dictionary of National Biography* (Oxford: Oxford University Press, 2009).

9   What became Brunswick Square was originally part of the grounds of the Foundling Hospital, land leased for housing to raise funds for the institution in 1790. The houses were built by James Burton between 1795 and 1802, and were thus relatively new when Phillips acquired No. 5. Today none of the original housing stock remains; the site of No. 5 now forms part of the University of London's International Hostel – which would probably have pleased Phillips. Devotees of the works of Jane Austen will recall that in *Emma* John and Isabella Knightley made their home in Brunswick Square.

10 The volcano remains active; witness the eruption in the spring of 2021.

11 With no children or close relatives of his own, Phillips willed the plantation to John Whirrall of Pipton, Radnorshire, and Richard Whirrall of the Bengal Medical Service.

12 John S. Harford, *The Life of Thomas Burgess* (London: Longman, Orme, Brown, Green and Longman, 1840), p. 135.

13 See for example Simon Schama, *The American Future* (London: Vintage Books, 2009), p. 182.

14 Steven Brindle, *Brunel: The Man Who Built the World* (London: Weidenfeld and Nicolson, 2005), p. 5.

15 Chunar Fort, captured by the East India Company in 1772, became its depot for artillery and ammunition.

16 Price, *A History, Volume One*, p. 182.

17 Personal communication, 13 August 2013.

18 I am grateful to Peter Hopkins, formerly Special Collections Librarian in the Roderic Bowen Library, who drew this work to my attention in 2010.

19 Cockerell's changes included the elegant staircase to the first-floor library – access had previously been by a utilitarian external stair – and what is now designated as the Rider Room, over what was originally envisaged as a lecture room, but which subsequently served as the Welsh Library, and a Common Room.

20 A series of galleries running across the tops of the original book-shelves was the only substantial change. The narrow galleries, with their vertiginous sets of seven shelves reaching to the ceiling, altogether proving a disincentive to use, largely housed the college's historic collections, the original shelving being utilized for the working library.

21 Price, *A History, Volume One*, p. 184.

22 The chair was endowed by Thomas Phillips under the terms of his will.

23 What follows is greatly indebted to Wyn Thomas, 'The Welsh Library: National Institution or Aladdin's Cave?' in K. Robbins and J. Morgan-Guy, and W. Thomas (eds), *A Bold Imagining. University of Wales Lampeter. Glimpses of an Unfolding Vision 1827–2002* (Lampeter: University of Wales Lampeter, 2002), pp. 67–76.

24 Even John Owen, Professor of Welsh 1879–85 and Principal 1892–7 and a fluent Welsh-speaker himself, did not encourage the use of the language in the college.

25 Wyn Thomas, 'The Welsh Library', pp. 75–6.

26 J. R. Lloyd Thomas, *Moth or Phoenix? St David's College and The University of Wales and The University Grants Committee* (Llandysul: Gomer Press, 1980).

27 Personal experience!

28 Report presented to the then Academic Registrar, Dr Thomas Roderick, and laid before the Founders' Library and Archives Group on 10 November 2000.

TREASURES

The Special Collections of the
University of Wales Trinity Saint David

An Elegant Georgian Gothic Quadrangle[1]

The Royal Charter of 1828

There are two foundation stones to what began life as St David's College, Lampeter, in the reign of King George IV (1820–30): one literal and the other metaphorical. The literal stone is that which was laid – with modified Masonic ceremony – by Thomas Burgess, Bishop of St Davids and Canon of Durham, on 12 August 1822, the king's birthday. The metaphorical stone is the Royal Charter, granted by the king on 6 February 1828, nearly a year after the first students had been admitted, though the building was not then quite complete. The site of the college, on the outskirts of the small market town of Lampeter in Cardiganshire, had been conveyed (for a consideration of £100) by the Lord of the Manor, John Scandrett Harford and his two brothers to Bishop Burgess, John Jones of nearby Derry Ormond, and another local landowner, Herbert Evans of Highmead, Llanwenog. It was itself a historic location, the Castle Field, containing what remained – as it still does – of the earth motte of the Norman castle. The literal foundation stone, quickly buried as the building rose above it, until uncovered in January, 1976, and revealed again in 2021, does not concern us. The story of 12 August 1822 and the excavation of 1976 has been told by Austen Wilks, in his *The Foundation Stone of St David's University College.*[2] That of the metaphorical foundation stone, the Royal Charter, has its place in this volume, as the original, collected from London by Burgess's successor at St Davids, John Banks Jenkinson, and the first principal, Dr Llewelyn Lewellin, is kept securely in the strongroom of the Roderic Bowen Library. It is truly a foundation stone, as all subsequent charters, and there have been quite a few, including those of 1852 which permitted the college to grant the degree of BD, and that of 1865 which authorized the granting of the degree of BA, build upon it, and/or refer back

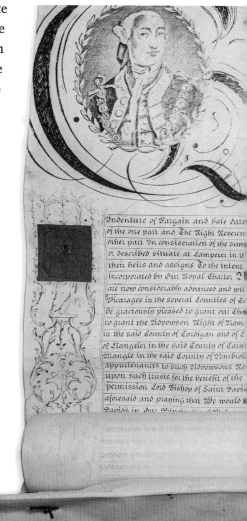

to it. The Lampeter Campus of University of Wales Trinity St David is the direct heir and descendant of St David's College, later St David's University College, and then University of Wales, Lampeter. With its foundation date of George IV's birthday in 1822 it can, and does, lay claim to pre-eminence over Durham and London universities. After Oxford and Cambridge, with whom it had a long and intimate relationship, it is the oldest degree-awarding institution in England and Wales.

The 1828 Charter is of considerable length. Even its modern printed form occupies fourteen pages.[3] At one level it breathes the air of the late eighteenth century and

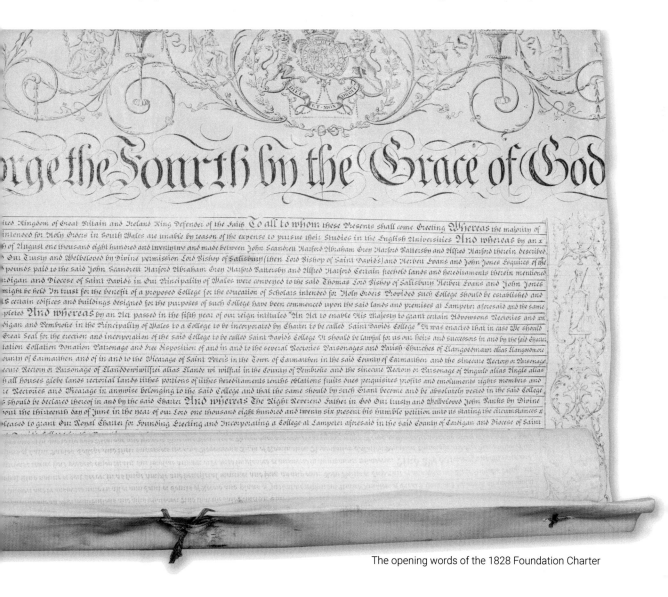

The opening words of the 1828 Foundation Charter

the Regency era, in which its founding fathers had been born and brought up. Bishop Burgess, disturbed by the poor educational standards of many of those who presented themselves for ordination in the Established Church in his diocese, had, soon after his consecration, resolved on the foundation of a college to provide them with that which, in most cases their financial situation prevented them from accessing, a university-level education. Lampeter, it was hoped and intended by the bishop and his supporters, would provide just such an education. Because the majority of its students in 1827 and for more than a century thereafter intended to take Holy Orders (and that is reflected in the 1828 Charter), it was long regarded as no more than a theological college. Yet that it has never been, for Burgess saw to it that no religious test be imposed on would-be students. As one historian of the college – and himself an alumnus – Professor William Gibson, wrote: 'Burgess had founded an institution from which those from Nonconformist churches and those intending to enter other professions were not excluded.'[4] Indeed, in all the clauses and paragraphs of the 1828 Charter there is no mention of a religious test. In this respect it is unique; at this date such a test remained for those matriculating at Oxbridge.

The initiative for gaining the Royal Charter in fact came primarily from John Scandrett Harford. This is well attested by entries in the diaries of the architect of the college, C. R. Cockerell. Harford obtained the services of the London lawyer, Edward Plumtree, to draw up its provisions. As another historian of the college, William Price, remarked: 'Mr Plumtree does not appear to have attempted to reconcile the charter with actual conditions in 1828.' Among other anomalies 'the names of the staff as given in the charter did not wholly correspond with reality' and the charter included what at that date were professorships which were, if not entirely fictional, then certainly a matter of hope or intention rather than reality – chairs in Natural Philosophy and Chemistry, and Mathematics.[5] These subjects indicate, however, that the founding fathers of St David's College had in mind from the outset, a broadly based curriculum. It is worth bearing in mind that John Scandrett Harford was a prominent Bristol banker, and John Jones the son of a London surgeon. Bishop Burgess himself was the son of a grocer, and his brother John carried on a widespread trade as such from premises in The Strand in London. These were not men of narrow experience or limited vision, and neither was King George himself, for all his notoriety in other respects. He was personally to be a generous benefactor to the fledgling college – it is his Royal Arms which adorn the tower of what is now known as the St David's Building. Although nowhere mentioned, it is not perhaps just a fancy that the founders hoped it might be 'The King's College of St David near Lampeter'.

It is, therefore, somewhat ironic that the 1828 Charter is headed not with a portrait of George IV but of his father, George III, who had died eight years before. Someone was evidently saving money, and using up 'blanks' from the previous reign!

John Morgan-Guy

The Arms of King George IV on the tower of the St David's Building.
Authenticated by Thomas Lloyd, Wales Herald Extraordinary

1 John Betjeman, Poet Laureate, in *The Spectator*, 11 November 1955.

2 Austen Wilks, *The Foundation Stone of Saint David's University College* (Llandysul: Gwasg Gomer, 1976).

3 Anon. *The Charters, Special Statutes, and Ordinary Statutes of St David's College in the County of Cardigan* (Lampeter: Welsh Church Press, 1913).

4 William Gibson, *In a Class by Itself. The Fight for Survival of St David's College, Lampeter* (Private printing, 2007), p. 4.

5 The chair in Science was endowed by Thomas Phillips, the college's generous benefactor, under the terms of his will, and first filed in 1853 by Joseph Matthews, who also taught Mathematics. See D. T. W. Price, *A History of St David's University College, Lampeter. Volume One: to 1898* (Cardiff: University of Wales Press, 1977), pp. 54–5.

'A Bird's-Eye View'

Charles Robert Cockerell – Architect of St David's College

Charles Robert Cockerell considered himself as 'half a Mediterranean'[1] and a born artist; a friend of Byron, Ingres and Canova, he may seem a surprising choice as the architect of a remote Welsh college.

Born in London on 27 April 1788 the third of eleven children, Cockerell was somewhat reluctant to follow in the footsteps of his father Samuel Pepys Cockerell. Samuel, the grandson of the diarist Samuel Pepys' nephew John Jackson, was a successful architect and surveyor. After a private education followed by enrolment at Westminster School, Charles worked for his father for five years. In 1809 he moved to the office of Robert Smirke who was rebuilding the New Convent Garden Theatre.

The following year Cockerell embarked on the Grand Tour which, although originally planned as a four-year journey, evolved into seven of the most significant and influential years of his life. The Napoleonic Wars had closed much of the Continent to tourism, so it was to Constantinople, travelling as a king's messenger with despatches for the fleets at Cadiz and Malta that Cockerell first departed. He continued on to Greece, arriving in Athens in June 1810, where he was embraced by the cosmopolitan society of scholars, artists and archaeologists. Despite the dangers and privations inherent in travelling, including vermin-infested accommodation, shipwrecks and privateers, Cockerell journeyed extensively, touring, drawing and excavating temples and ancient sites. In 1811 he visited the Temple of Jupiter Panhellenius on the island of Aegina and later toured the Peloponnese in southern Greece, stopping at Olympia and exploring the Temple of Apollo Epicurius at Bassae. His excavations and studies resulted in several important discoveries, including a 102-foot frieze and a previously unknown Ionic order in Bassae, as well as the use of polychromy at Aegina. In 1812, following a tour of the Hellenistic sites in Asia Minor, Cockerell spent three months in Sicily measuring and making drawings of the temple of Jupiter Olympius at Agrigento. These were later published in the supplementary volume of Stuart and Revett's *The Antiquities of Athens* (1830).

Napoleon's first abdication in April 1814 enabled Cockerell to travel to Rome, where his famous discoveries in Greece ensured that he was feted by the finest of Italian society. Intellectuals, ambassadors, envoys and artists flocked to see his drawings which he was preparing for publication. In 1816, whilst Cockerell was living in Florence, he was

TREASURES
The Special Collections of the
University of Wales Trinity Saint David

Charles Cockerell, College elevation and plan as envisaged c.1821–3

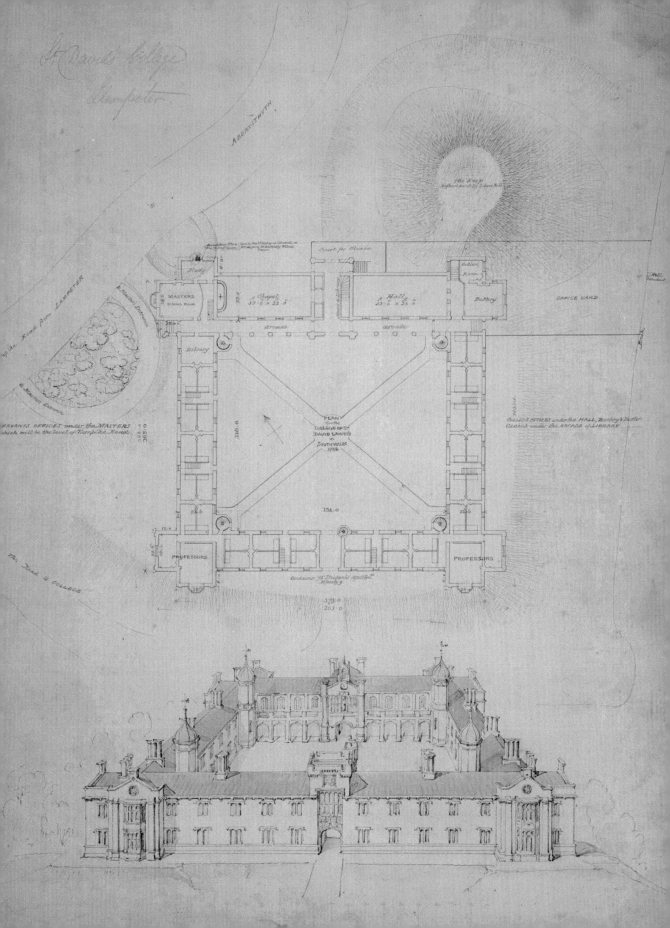

St David's College

Llampeter

ABERYSTWYTH

Road from LAMPETER

Chapel
33·0 × 22·0

A Hall
53·0 × 23·0

MASTERS
Dining Room

Buttery

Butler's Room

Court for Cloister

OFFICE YARD

Library

SERVANTS OFFICES under the MASTERS
which will be the level of Turnpike Road

COLLEGE OFFICES under the HALL, Buttery & Butler
CLOACA under the ARCADE of LIBRARY

PLAN
for the
COLLEGE OF St
DAVID LAMPER
in
SOUTH WALES
1822

The Road to COLLEGE

PROFESSORS

PROFESSORS

Contains 75 Students apartment
of each 9

379·0
203·0

persuaded by his father to undertake a design for a palace for the Duke of Wellington. His experiences over the last few years had made him an authority on classical architecture, but had done little to increase his practical expertise as an architect. So deflated was he by his failure to produce a satisfactory design, that he wrote to his father asking for permission to abandon architecture and to become an artist. This request was refused and in June 1817 Cockerell returned to London, yet his travels in Greece were to have an all-embracing influence over his future architectural career:

> I reflect on my travels in Greece which have opened my eyes [and] enlarged [and] elevated my ideas ... Greece has its merits which I feel now most powerfully. I see without prejudice. I am unconfined by the chains of school, I feel independent [and] free [and] have studied in a new [and] venerable field which has taught me the way to observe objects.[2]

His practice in Mayfair quickly received commissions. One of his early projects was the Literary and Philosophical Institution in Bristol, of which John Scandrett Harford of Blaise Castle was one of the leading lights. Harford, a scholar and collector, friend of Bishop Burgess and the owner of the Peterwell Estate in Lampeter, was influential in Cockerell's commission to design St David's College. The two later collaborated on a book on Michelangelo, *Illustrations Architectural and Pictorial of the Genius of Michael Angelo Buonarroti*, which included a twelve-page essay written by Cockerell, accompanying his illustrations reconstructing Michelangelo's designs for St Peter's Basilica in Rome.

Cockerell made the first of his many journeys to the remote town of Lampeter in December 1821, visiting the site on a further eight occasions between October 1823 and the consecration of the chapel in August 1827. Bishop Burgess had long been planning his scheme for a college and seemingly had approached other architects for designs, which, according to Cockerell, he rejected on the grounds that they had resembled prisons or stables rather than a college. The bishop was delighted with the architect's first bird's-eye view and plan, which initially included a cloister walk on all sides of the quadrangle, later limited to the north side only. Cockerell also designed a print of the college to encourage further donations to the building scheme. The work at Lampeter produced another local commission for Cockerell from John Jones (1780–1835), a member of the management committee of St David's College, who had recently inherited his father's house and estate at nearby Derry Ormond. He

George Perfect Harding, The college as envisaged by C. R. Cockerell, 1826.
Harding also reproduced the image for a snuff-box given to Bishop Burgess.

approached the architect to design a new country house, negotiating that the materials from the old house were to be re-sold for use at the college.

It was thus that a remote Welsh college was designed by a man who was later appointed architect to the Bank of England, made a member of the Royal Academy and Professor of Architecture, Chevalier of the Legion of Honour and Member of the Royal Academies of Bavaria, Belgium and Denmark; who became the first Royal Gold Medallist of the Royal Institute and was elected as the first professional President of the Royal Institute of British Architects.

Nicky Hammond

1 David Watkin, *The Life and Work of C. R. Cockerell* (London: A. Zwemmer Ltd, 1974), p. xxi.

2 Ibid. p. 18.

A Sketch from a Master

David Cox's drawing of St David's College

University of Wales Trinity St David's Special Collections is extremely fortunate to possess amongst its treasures a pencil-drawn view of St David's College from Lampeter bridge by David Cox Snr (1783–1859). Recognized as one of Britain's pre-eminent nineteenth-century watercolour landscape artists, he was born on 29 April 1783 in Deritend, Birmingham. Cox showed early artistic promise and was tutored by Joseph Barber, a member of the Birmingham School of landscape artists. At the age of fifteen he was apprenticed to a locket and miniature painter, before progressing to work as an assistant to the Italian scene-painter, De Maria, at the Birmingham Theatre.

In 1804 he moved to London, studying with John Varley and supporting himself by selling his drawings to London's print dealers, and within a few years he had exhibited his first painting at the Royal Academy. He supplemented his income by giving private lessons to members of the aristocracy, as well as publishing a number of successful teaching manuals. He became President of the Associated Artists in Watercolour in 1810 and following its demise two years later, was elected as an associate of the Society of Painters in Water Colours, becoming a full member in 1813.

In response to an advert in *The Times* for a drawing master, Cox moved to Hereford in 1814 where he combined his light teaching duties with sketching tours of Wales, Herefordshire and the Midlands. During these Hereford years his reputation grew and he began attracting influential patrons, including John Allnutt, a wine merchant and art collector, who was also a patron to John Constable.

Cox returned to London in 1827 and was to spend the next fourteen years there consolidating his reputation as a fine watercolourist. However, he had seemingly never lost his feeling for oil painting and an introduction to William James Müller rekindled this latent interest. Returning to Birmingham in 1841, he was to prove prolific in his new medium, producing in excess of 350 paintings over the next eighteen years, as well as continuing to regularly exhibit in watercolours.

Revolution and war had severely disrupted the Grand Tour itineraries of late eighteenth- and early nineteenth-century British aristocracy and the newly enriched middle classes. Forced to explore nearer to home, interest grew in the newly perceived romantic topography of the English Lake District, Scottish Highlands and Welsh mountains. An

TREASURES
The Special Collections of the
University of Wales Trinity Saint David

David Cox Snr, St David's
College from River Teifi bridge
c.1835–40 (detail)

Minster   River Kingston   N

accompanying demand grew for guidebooks to these districts, often illustrated with engravings after popular watercolourists of the day.

Prominent amongst these entrepreneurial travel writers was Thomas Roscoe, whose *Wanderings and Excursions in North Wales* (1836) and companion south Wales volume (1837) proved very successful. These contained a blend of Welsh history, folklore, customs, poetry and natural history, accompanied with a detailed route of the author's journeys, his observations on the villages and towns he passed through and the people he encountered. Cox, along with other artists including George Cattermole, Thomas Creswick and Copley Fielding, was commissioned to provide drawings for the accompanying engravings. Cox's style and interest in the picturesque was particularly suited to the more rugged landscape of north Wales. His contribution of over half of the drawings to that volume was acknowledged in the publisher's introduction to the south Wales volume:

> It may not be amiss here to mention the obligations which the proprietors of this work are under to that highly-esteemed artist and faithful delineator of scenery, Mr David Cox, whose pencil has enriched and enhanced the value not only of this volume, but also of that recently published on the Northern part of the Principality.[1]

It might possibly have been during his excursion to Wales in the late 1830s that Cox visited Lampeter. He seemingly knew the area to some extent, having first visited in 1819 and it was not too far distant when producing illustrations for Roscoe of Cardigan and Kidwelly [*sic*]. Furthermore, a sketch by him of *Llampeter Church* [*sic*] is also known to exist.[2]

In common with many other artists and writers Cox was inspired by the romantic beauty and grandeur of the Welsh landscape, first visiting north Wales in 1805 and 1806, whilst touring with Joseph Barber's son, Charles. Prior to 1844 Cox's sketching trips had been predominately to northern England and the border counties of Wales, yet in the summer of 1844 he made the first of what was to become an annual journey to the small Caernarfonshire village of Betws-y-Coed. He wrote enthusiastically to his son of its fine river scenery, rocks and mountains, claiming that 'In rocky-bedded scenery there is nothing I have seen can come up to them.'[3] Cox's visit coincided with the publication of the second edition of the north Wales volume, in which Roscoe had

David Cox Snr,
St David's College
from River Teifi
bridge, c.1835–40

extended what had been a brief paragraph on the village to a whole chapter describing its attributes. During his visits to Bettws, as it became known, Cox stayed at the Royal Oak Inn, drawing the village and its environs.

The resulting paintings were regularly exhibited at the Society of Painters in Water Colours. As a consequence of the reception they received, Cox's reputation and the influence of Roscoe's guidebooks, the first artistic colony in Britain developed at Betws-y-Coed. During the summer months the resident artists were joined by an influx of international professional and amateur artists, who spent their days sketching and painting in the open air and their evenings chatting in the Royal Oak's parlour. Cox, who from youth had enjoyed the company of other artists, was its presiding spirit and father figure, often with his cigar and pint of ale to hand. In later years as the village attracted greater numbers of artists, he moved from the inn to a small cottage owned by the innkeeper and, despite ill health, nonetheless continued to spend his summers at Betws-y-Coed until his final visit in September 1856.

Cox's son David (1809–85) followed his father in establishing himself as a successful landscape artist, always signing his works 'David Cox Junior'.

Nicky Hammond

1 S. Wildman, 'Hereford and London 1815–40', in S. Wildman, R. Lockett and J. Murdoch, *David Cox 1783–1859* (Birmingham: Birmingham Museums and Art Gallery, 1983), pp. 54–76.

2 Christie's London, 9 November 2019, sale no. 6209, lot 69.

3 N. Solly, *Memoir of the Life of David Cox* (London: Chapman and Hall, 1873), p. 162.

Monk's Blood or Red Wine?

Peter of Capua and *Distinctiones theologicae. Defectus to Surditas* (Lampeter MS 2)

Every manuscript has a story, but few capture the imagination of our student body as dramatically as Lampeter MS 2, more popularly known as 'The Monk's Blood Manuscript'. This mysterious codex was one of those donated by Thomas Phillips to St David's College in 1841. It is a partial copy of Peter of Capua's *Distinctiones theologicae*, a collection of short entries on biblical and theological matters, arranged in alphabetical order. The volume only contains entries from *Defectus* to *Surditas* (Weakness to Deafness); a full copy housed in Hereford Cathedral Archive (MS P.vi. 6) shows us that it would have once spanned *Alpha* to *Xristus* (*Christus*).

A cutting pasted to the inside of the front cover relates the first of the tales surrounding the manuscript, stating that the volume 'discovered' near Bangor was:

> supposed to have belonged to the Monks of that Monastery, who were murdered by the command of Ethelred the 2nd, and thought to be stained with their blood, having been discovered with a quantity of human bones.

But the legends abound: some say that following the Battle of Chester in *c.* 616, the victorious King Ethelfrid of Northumbria murdered the monks of Bangor-Is-Coed (Bangor-on-Dee) as punishment for them praying for God to intervene on the side of the Welsh army the king had just defeated. Indeed, the Venerable Bede records that 1,200 monks were massacred when their defender Brocmail abandoned them, and that only fifty escaped the slaughter; the manuscript was supposedly discovered among their bloody remains.[1] Yet another version of the story is that the monks were murdered during the Reformation when they resisted their property being seized. Unfortunately, none of these stories is likely to be true, and the blood-like splatters that stain the pages of the manuscript today are far more likely to be a spilled cup of claret.

Nonetheless, the manuscript is still an intriguing and significant one. The text's author Peter of Capua (d. 1214) was a man of some standing around the turn of the twelfth century. We know that he was born in Amalfi into a noble Italian family, and that he studied at the renowned University of Paris under the illustrious theologian Peter of Poitiers before becoming Master of Theology himself.[2] He must have distinguished himself as a teacher and thinker, as he was appointed by Pope Innocent III as a papal

TREASURES
The Special Collections of the
University of Wales Trinity Saint David

Spatter of discolouration,
Lampeter MS 2

legate, then cardinal; his missions included taking the cross and preaching the Fourth Crusade.[3]

It was during his time in Paris that it is thought he began work on the *Distinctiones theologicae*, which is essentially a handbook for preachers in the form of 'biblical distinctions', short explanations or interpretations of terms and concepts found in the Bible and other religious texts, designed to help with the composition of sermons. It was an increasingly important textual genre at the time, as the focus on preaching was increasing due to the threat of popular forms of heresy (such as the Cathars in southern France), though the information could be arranged in different ways depending on the organizational principle employed by the author. Peter of Capua's text, often found under the alternative title *Alphabetum in artem sermocinandi* in manuscript catalogues, was unusual for its time as the distinctions are arranged alphabetically. This rather prosaic – though practical – arrangement of the material was controversial, as it was deemed more appropriate for such information to be organized according to a higher, more spiritual or thematic schema.[4]

Aside from its supposed blood-stained pages, another intriguing feature of this particular codex is the odd format of the text. Measuring *c.* 300 × 285 mm, it is a highly unusual set of dimensions for a manuscript of any sort, which is usually determined by the size of the animal from which the skin was taken to make the parchment or vellum. Upon closer inspection, it would appear that the manuscript has been chopped off at the bottom, and that some four inches or so have been removed. The result is that entries found towards the bottom of a folio are cut off mid-sentence, or else are missing entirely. Who knows the reason for this mutilation? Presumably it was not hacked down at the same time as the unfortunate monks who were once its owners.

Harriett Webster

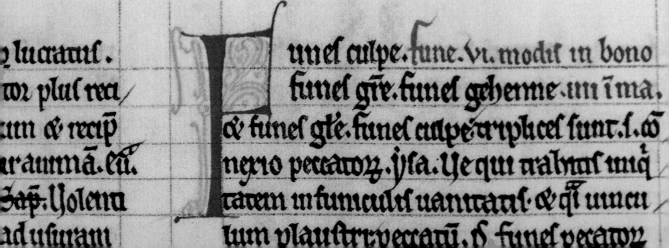

Ornamental capitals

1 Bede, *Bede's Ecclesiastical History of England: A Revised Translation*, A. M. Sellar (ed.) (London: G. Bell, 1907), p. 88.

2 Spencer E. Young, 'Parisian Masters of Theology: a Biographical Register', in *Scholarly Community at the Early University of Paris: Theologians, Education and Society* (Cambridge: Cambridge University Press, 2014), p. 215.

3 A contemporary chronicler and participant in the Fourth Crusade Geoffrey de Villehardouin records that Peter was sent to preach the crusade and papal indulgence offered by the pope after taking the cross himself: *Memoirs or Chronicle of The Fourth Crusade and The Conquest of Constantinople*, trans. Frank T. Marzials (London, 1908), p. 1.

4 For more on Peter of Capua, his *Distinctiones* and their historical context, see Marcia L. Coulish, 'Scholastic Theology at Paris around 1200' in S. E. Young (ed.), *Crossing Boundaries at Medieval Universities* (Leiden: Brill, 2011), pp. 29–50.

The Labour of a Lame Monk

The Lampeter Bible (Lampeter MS 1)

MS 1, known as the 'Lampeter Bible', was given to St David's College by Thomas Burgess.[1] Quite unusually, a colophon of twelve couplets on folio 427 tells that it was copied by a monk named G. of Fécamp, on the instruction of Abbot James of St-Pierre-sur-Dives, a Benedictine monastery in the Calvados area of Normandy, and that it was completed in the fourth year of writing, 1279. G. also tells us that he was lame – which may be why he was assigned the task of copying manuscripts as his daily manual labour, rather than something more physically challenging. How long the Bible remained at St-Pierre is not known, but it passed into Carthusian hands and by the fifteenth or sixteenth century it was in England.[2]

The Bible contains 427 folios. Its dimensions are 335 × 250 mm, and the writing space is 245 × 170 mm. The text is written in two columns, with running heads in red and blue. Historiated initials, that is, letters that carry a visual image of a person, episode or scene, mark the beginnings and ends of books of the Bible. The Bible opens (fol. 2r) with a prologue containing the letter of St Jerome who in the fourth century was responsible for the translation into Latin of what became known as the Vulgate (common) Bible. The first letter is a capital 'F' (*Frater*, 'brother') and in the bowl of the letter is depicted a seated ecclesiastic, wearing a mitre (depicting his status as a bishop or archbishop), who is engaged in writing. At first sight this might seem to be Jerome, but he would have been wearing his cardinal's hat rather than a mitre; the figure is probably Paulinus, bishop of Nola, a correspondent of Jerome, to whom Jerome addressed the letter that forms this prologue.[3] On this very first folio the evident humour of the illuminator can be seen in the images at the top of the 'F'. A variety of apes play musical instruments such as a trumpet, bagpipes and a portative organ. A boy with a bow and arrow shoots in the direction of birds. A dog chases a rabbit. In the descender more animals make music, and a donkey wearing a mitre reads from a book – possibly preaching. What may be shocking to a modern reader but is characteristic of the medieval ability to draw together the sacred and the profane, is the juxtaposition, at the base of the folio, of an image of the crucifixion of Christ and that of a child riding on the back of a bear which is led by a boy with a cudgel. Another child waits, with its mother, for its turn.

Another striking image is an extended initial 'I' (fol. 5r) of the seven days of creation. Here, and in the historiated initials throughout, the viewer is impressed by the

TREASURES
The Special Collections of the
University of Wales Trinity Saint David

Prologue to Genesis, probably
depicting Paulinus

Incipit epla iero

Frater ambrosius tua michi munuscula perferens detulit simul & sua suavissimas litteras que a principio amicicie fidem probate iam fidei et veteris amicicie notia preferebant. Vera enim illa necessitudo est et xpi glutino copulata quam non utilitas rei familiaris non presentia tantum corporum non subdola et palpans adulacio sed dei timor et divinarum scripturarum studia conciliant. Legimus in veteribus hystorys quosdam lustrasse provincias novos adiisse populos maria transisse ut eos quos ex libris noverant coram...

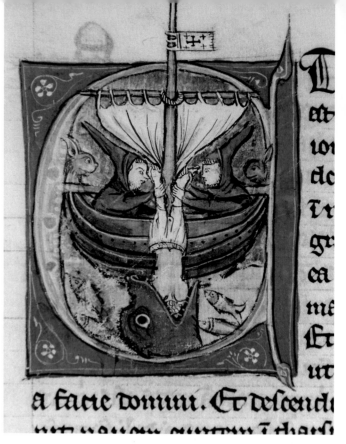

delicate artistry and fine brush-strokes. A favourite image among students who have delighted in the Bible is that of Jonah (fol. 325v). In a beautifully symmetric composition two men in pointed hats face each other in a small boat with its central mast and crossbar; animal heads form the stern and prow. Each of the men grasps Jonah by an ankle and they cast him down into the whale. His head, shoulders and arms have disappeared from view, and he appears to be about to slip out of his white undergarments.[4] This is an example of an image that matches the content of the biblical narrative. In other instances, the connection is typological. The opening of the book of Exodus shows a New Testament scene, Christ's entry into Jerusalem on Palm Sunday (fol. 22r). Here, the narrative of Exodus (the departure of the Israelites from Egypt, their passage across the Red Sea and the receiving of the covenant with God on Mount Sinai) prefigures Christ entering Jerusalem at the beginning of Passion week, which culminated in his death and resurrection. Some images seem out of place. It would be more usual to find the Ascension of Christ at the beginning of the Acts of the Apostles; here it opens the Epistle to Titus (fol. 410).[5] Several curly-haired and bearded disciples gaze up at the hem of Christ's garment and his feet as he disappears into Heaven.

Daniel in the lions' den

A further type of illustration – and another indication of the copyist's sense of humour – are the doodles that occasionally grow out of letters on the top line of a folio. Sometimes the letters extend upwards with added flourishes. On other occasions G. adds a face – are some of these a record of certain monks of St-Pierre? The mitred head on fol. 234 is surely that of Abbot James, who is also almost certainly the figure dressed in the black habit of a Benedictine monk with the mitre – a symbol of abbatial office – who in the opening initial 'O' of the *Canticum canticorum* (Song of Songs) kneels before the Virgin and Child (fol. 233v).

The Lampeter Bible is a treasure indeed, and a testament to the skill and devotion of the lame monk G. and the (nearly) four years that he spent in creating this sacred text.

Janet Burton and William Marx

1 For descriptions see N. Ker, *Medieval Manuscripts in British Libraries, vol. 3: Lampeter–Oxford* (Oxford: Oxford University Press, 1983), pp. 1–2; Robin Ryder, 'The Library of St David's College, Lampeter', *Trivium*, 1 (Lampeter: Trivium publications, 1966), pp. 36–9; See Alison Stones, *Gothic Manuscripts 1260–1320* (London: Harvey Miller Publishers, 2013), pp. 37, 53–60, for the relationship of the Lampeter Bible to other manuscripts from the duchy of Normandy and in particular the diocese of Rouen; Alison Stones, *https://uwtsd.ac.uk/library/special-collections/treasures-of-the-special-collections/*

2   Carthusian ownership is indicated by the way it was marked up for lections, or readings, and an English location by the appearance of English names in the margins.

3   Stones, *Gothic Manuscripts*, p. 54, identifies the figure here and in the Huth Bible (London: British Library, MS 38114–5) as Augustine.

4 Image: Stones. *https://uwtsd.ac.uk/library/special-collections/treasures-of-the-special-collections/*

5 Image: Stones. *https://uwtsd.ac.uk/library/special-collections/treasures-of-the-special-collections/*

A Medieval Bestseller

The Boddam Hours (Lampeter MS 7)

Lampeter MS 7, known as the 'Boddam Hours' after an eighteenth-century owner, was donated to St David's College in 1846 by Thomas Phillips of Brunswick Square, one of the major benefactors of the college library. It is a fine example of that medieval 'bestseller' known as the Book of Hours. Books of Hours were devotional works, designed to be used by the laity rather than for institutional use. They allowed lay men and women to follow a shortened form of the canonical hours, or offices, which were performed daily by monastic communities.[1] They were commonly known as 'Hours of the Blessed Virgin Mary'. These offices, or meditations, formed the core of a Book of Hours but were often supplemented by other texts such as the Penitential Psalms and the Office of the Dead, which encouraged people to ponder their sins and the need for repentance, as well as the prospect of the world to come. Some Books of Hours were sumptuous productions, with an extensive programme of illustration; others were more modest in their visual programme. This variation often reflected the wealth and social standing of the person who commissioned or owned the book. Some were very large; others reflect their daily use – they were small and easily portable, allowing users to pause at appropriate times in their daily schedule to take the book from a cupboard or lift it up from a chain around their waist in order to follow their devotions.

MS 7 is a modestly sized book containing the Hours of the Virgin, interspersed by the Hours of the Cross (devotions on the Crucifixion of Christ), the Seven Penitential Psalms, the Office of the Dead, and prayers to a number of saints.[2] As is to be expected, most of the text is in Latin, but some of the prayers are in French. The form of the liturgy follows that used in the diocese of Rouen, indicating a provenance for the manuscript. It has been dated to the fifteenth century and may well have been commissioned by the woman who appears on folio 68.[3]

Books of Hours often excite our interest for the images they contain. Those in the Hours of the Virgin follow a common pattern in illustrating various stages in her life: the Annunciation, Visitation, Nativity of Christ, Annunciation to the Shepherds, the visit of the Magi, the Presentation of Christ in the Temple, the Flight into Egypt and, finally, the non-biblical Coronation of the Virgin in Heaven. These images are conventionally used to mark the beginning of a particular office; thus, the Coronation of the Virgin generally prefaces Compline, the last office of the day. These illustrations might

Virgin Mary and Christ child, probably also depicting first owner of volume

Annunciation to the shepherds

act as an aid to devotion, allowing the user to ponder the significance of the lives of Mary and Christ. On another level, they might function as 'bookmarks', and allow a user quickly to find a particular office. Striking illustrations in the Boddam Hours are the Annunciation by the Angel Gabriel to the Blessed Virgin Mary, telling her that she was to bear the Son of God, which contains the legendary detail of a lily growing out of a winepot to symbolize Mary's purity (Matins); the Annunciation to the Shepherds, with the heavenly choir revealing the birth of Christ to a group of colourfully dressed men and women, clearly rather well-to-do shepherds; and a full-page illustration, at the beginning of the Penitential Psalms, of King David (author of the Book of Psalms), standing on the roof of his palace and catching sight of a statuesque Bathsheba in her bath in the garden. Within the text of a Sunday devotion, we find the pious woman in contemporary dress, mentioned above, who kneels in prayer beside a seated Virgin Mary teaching the Christ Child to read. He, however, appears more interested in the parrot he is holding. The medieval bestiary tells us that parrots symbolize education because they can be taught to speak which shows that what might be thought an incidental detail reinforces the meaning of the scene. All these images are contained within architectural frames.

Generations of Lampeter students have delighted in discovering and discussing the Boddam Hours, which shed such vivid light on the devotional and visual culture of the Middle Ages.

Janet Burton and William Marx

1 The literature on Books of Hours is vast. For an introduction see, for instance, Janet Backhouse, *Books of Hours* (London: British Library, 1985); Eamon Duffy, *Marking the Hours: English People and their Prayers 1240–1570* (London and New Haven: Yale University Press, 2006).

2 For descriptions see N. Ker, *Medieval Manuscripts in British Libraries, vol. 3: Lampeter–Oxford* (Oxford: Oxford University Press, 1983), pp. 10–12. For studies see C. V. Hewerdine, 'A Study of the Hours of Charles Boddam', unpublished MA thesis, University of Wales, 1981, and 'Symbolic decoration in a fifteenth-century book of hours', in *Literature and Fine Arts, Trivium*, 18 (Lampeter: Trivium publications, 1983), pp. 49–54.

3 Many Books of Hours have been identified as belonging to women. See, for instance, Charity Scott-Stokes, *Women's Books of Hours in Medieval England* (Cambridge: Boydell Press, 2006).

A Hugely Popular Manual

Giovanni Boccaccio and *Genealogia deorum gentilium* (Venice, 1492) (Lampeter INC 13/14)

Among the Roderic Bowen Library's early printed book collection is a beautiful volume, INC 13/14, the text of which is illustrated with full-page, hand-drawn genealogical trees of the Gods. This is a first edition print of Giovanni Boccaccio's *Genealogia deorum gentilium* produced in Venice in 1492. It was donated to the college in 1838 by Thomas Phillips 'of Brunswick Square, London'.

Boccaccio (1313–75) was an Italian writer and poet, most famous for authoring the *Decameron*, a collection of one hundred genre-defining short stories written in the Italian vernacular of his native Florence. These stories, set against the backdrop of the Black Death, went on to influence other eminent writers beyond Italy, such as Geoffrey Chaucer in England and Miguel de Cervantes in Spain. Within Italian culture he is considered one of the *Tre Corone*, the 'Three Crowns' of Italian literature, alongside Dante and Petrarch.[1]

As a Renaissance humanist, Boccaccio had a keen interest in the Classical world, and his most important work is often considered to be the *Genealogia deorum gentilium*, known in English as 'On the Genealogy of the Gods of the Gentiles'. It is a text written in Latin prose, commissioned by Hugh IV, King of Cyprus (and nominal King of Jerusalem) which Boccaccio began in around 1360, though it took many years to compile: indeed, he continued to tweak and amend the text right up until his death in 1375.[2]

Divided into fifteen books, the volume provides full genealogies and myths of classical Gods and associated figures from the Greek and Roman traditions and is a fine example of humanist scholarship, as it also explores the allegorical significance of the tales. It synthesizes the research undertaken by Boccaccio using both ancient and medieval sources: such works include the twelfth-century *Liber imaginum deorum* which is often attributed to the English scholar and theologian Alexander Neckham, as well as better-known classical texts such as Ovid's *Metamorphoses*.

The *Genealogia* amounts to a 'mythological manual' of sorts, recounting the stories of around 950 Greco-Roman mythological figures and their relationships to one another, relationships which are then beautifully illustrated by the family trees that accompany each chapter. These diagrams represent the earliest non-biblical use of this type of

TREASURES
The Special Collections of the
University of Wales Trinity Saint David

graphic, usually preserved for the depiction of Jesus' ancestors in the more common medieval artform known as the 'Tree of Jesse'.[3] In the volume held at the Roderic Bowen Archive, these hand-drawn illustrations use a mixture of red, green and iridescent gold ink to trace the lines of descent of the Gods, each mythological name is then written in a miniscule hand in either black or red ink into the leaves of the curling vines. The capitals at the start of each chapter and subsequent paragraphs are also rubricated by hand in alternating red and blue ink, after the style of a medieval manuscript.

Navigation of the dense text is made possible by a series of indices included in the volume, alphabetically arranged for ease of use, with references to the pertinent book and chapter number. The volume also contains an important treatise of sorts in Chapter 14, in which Boccaccio famously offers a defence of poetry (and therefore his own work). He suggests that far from being a 'nullity', poetry provides hidden meaning and allegorical truths, expressing ideas about the cultural and indeed moral value of studying and writing poetry which are also reflected in the works of other humanist contemporaries like Dante and Petrarch.[4]

The text was hugely popular amongst Renaissance humanist thinkers, despite its impressive length and unfinished nature, and by 1499 at least eight editions had been published, indicating that this was indeed a popular work among Renaissance humanists. Its wider significance lies in it becoming a model for future 'mythographies', and furthering Renaissance cultural and philological studies.

Harriett Webster

TREASURES
The Special Collections of the
University of Wales Trinity Saint David

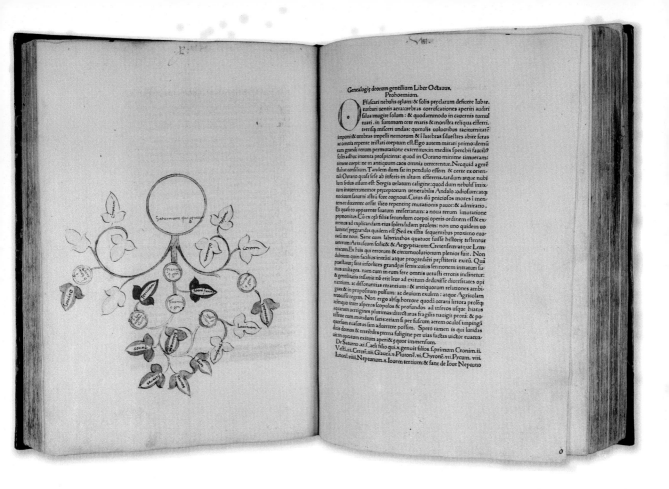

1 For further reading on the 'Three Crowns' of Italian literature see the recent study by Zygmunt G. Barański, *Dante, Petrarch, Boccaccio: Literature, Doctrine, Reality* (Cambridge: Legenda, 2020).

2 Elisabeth Woodbridge, 'Boccaccio's Defence of Poetry; As Contained in the Fourteenth Book of the "De Genealogia Deorum"', *Publications of the Modern Language Association*, 13 (1898), pp. 333–49.

3 For a full study of the nature and significance of these beautiful graphics, see Ernest Hatch Wilkins, *The Trees of the Genealogia Deorum of Boccaccio* (Chicago: The Caxton Club, 1923).

4 Woodbridge, 'Boccaccio's Defence of Poetry', p. 335.

A Vast Compendium

Jacobus a Voragine, *The Golden Legend (Legenda aurea)* (London: Printed by Wynkyn de Worde, 1498) (Lampeter INC 46)

The *Legenda aurea*, a vast compendium of saints' lives and readings for Christian festivals, was composed between 1250 and 1280, in Latin, by Jacobus a Voragine, a Dominican friar who became Archbishop of Genoa in 1291. It is arranged by the feasts of the Church's year, including saints' days, and the readings would have provided a fund of stories and *exempla* for sermons delivered both in a parish church and – given that Jacobus was himself a friar – by members of the mendicant orders in their mission of preaching. Its popularity is attested by the survival of a large number of manuscripts (in the region of 1,000) and by the fact that it was translated into many vernacular languages, including English. Like Books of Hours, the *Legenda aurea* was an early candidate for printing. The English translation was first printed in 1483 by William Caxton, a London merchant who in 1476 had established a printing press at the sign of the Red Pale in the grounds of Westminster Abbey.[1] Caxton was also the translator of the *Legenda* and the type of the 1483 printing was set by Wynkyn de Worde, a Dutchman whom Caxton employed from 1481.[2]

When Caxton died in 1491/2, de Worde took charge of the press. At first, he stayed in Westminster but moved to Fleet Street in 1500 or early 1501, marking the beginning of its association with printing. De Worde reproduced Caxton's 1483 edition of the *Golden Legend* many times. Lampeter is fortunate to possess a copy of his (extremely rare) 1498 printing of the *Golden Legend*. The book was donated to St David's College by its founder, Thomas Burgess.

The 1498 printing opens:

> Here begynneth the legende in latyn legenda aurea that is to saye in Englysshe the golden legend. For lyke as passeth golde in valewe other metallys so this legend excelleth all other bookes.

The volume begins with the life of Adam, then Noah, and other worthies of the Old Testament, and moves on to episodes in the life of Christ and the saints. A notable, though not unique, feature of the Lampeter *Golden Legend* is an example of cultural vandalism. A number of pages have been cut out from folio 60 onwards, between the feast of the Holy Innocents (28 December) and that of St Silvester (31 December).

Noah's Ark

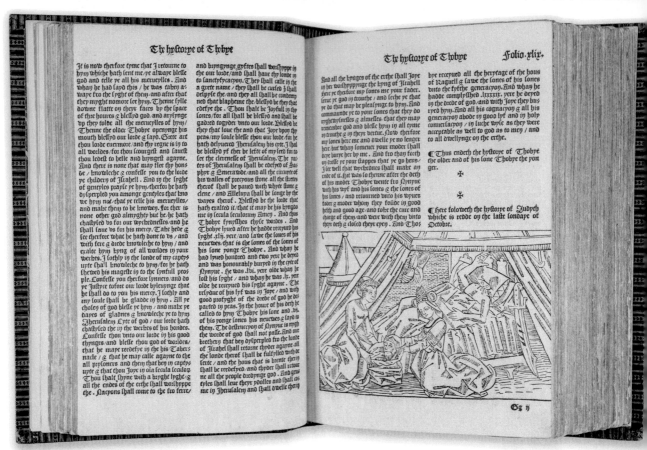

Tobit, followed by illustration of Judith and Holofernes

However, enough has been left of folio 59v and 63r – including a scored-through image – to allow us to identify the mostly excised passage as the life of Archbishop Thomas of Canterbury, better known as Thomas Becket. Thomas was murdered in his own cathedral church on 21 December 1170 by four knights allegedly acting on the orders of King Henry II. Thomas's road to canonization was rapid. He was declared a saint by the pope in 1173 and his tomb became one of the foremost pilgrim destinations in Europe. His feast day was on 29 December.

So, why the attempt, by one user of the Lampeter *Legenda*, to erase Thomas? Thomas's dispute with Henry II was an aspect of the problematic medieval relationship between Church and State, and, when pushed, Thomas insisted that his first duty was to the Church and the pope, not the king. Three hundred and fifty years later another king – Henry VIII – faced similar problems. As England broke with Rome, Thomas of Canterbury fell from favour. In 1538 his shrine was demolished and as part of a campaign

TREASURES
The Special Collections of the
University of Wales Trinity Saint David

King Solomon

Thomas Becket, showing scored-through illustration

to expunge his memory it was ordered that his name should be removed from service books and psalters, as well as readings of the saints, such as the *Legenda aurea*.[3] In common with other printings of the *Golden Legend* the Lampeter copy would seem to bear witness to the zealous application of Henry VIII's injunctions.

Janet Burton and William Marx

1 See Allan Barton, *https://medievalart.co.uk/2021/05/11/a-fifteenth-century-bestseller/*

2   A. W. Pollard and G. R. Redgrave, *A Short-Title Catalogue of Books Printed in England, Scotland, and Ireland, and of English Books Printed Abroad 1475–1640*, 2nd edition, revised and enlarged by W. A. Jackson, F. S. Ferguson and K. F. Panzer, 3 vols (London: The Bibliographical Society, 1976–91), II, 24876. For discussion see Barton, *www.medievalart. co.uk/2021/05/11/a-fifteenth-century-bestseller*

3   Similar damage has occurred in Cambridge, University Library Inc. 3.J.1.2 [3550]; see *https://exhibitions.lib.cam.ac.uk/incunabula/artifacts/legenda-aurea/*

A Much-travelled Prayer Book

Missale Vratislaviense (Mainz: Peter Schöffer, 1499) (Lampeter INC 10)

A missal is a book used by a priest at the celebration of the Mass and contains all the text, rubrics and music he needs at the altar. This large-folio missal was printed in 1499 and is according to the Use or Rite of Bratislava. An inscription in the front tells us that it was given in 1515 to the Collegiate Church of St Mary in Glogow, now in the Czech Republic, by a lawyer called Vincent Urganyk. How long it remained there, and what was its subsequent history, is unknown. What we do know is that it was given to St David's College, Lampeter, by Thomas Phillips in 1837.

Printer's Mark at the colophon

This particular missal is of great bibliographical significance and its story takes us to the very heart of the origins of printing in Europe. It was printed in 1499 in Mainz, the cradle of European printing, in the print shop of Peter Schöffer. Schöffer, a native of Gernsheim near Mainz, was born in 1425 and in his early years is believed to have worked as a manuscript copyist in Paris, probably in a workshop that produced books like the Boddam Hours, also featured in this volume. In 1451 he returned to Mainz and began to work for Johannes Gutenberg and Johannes Fust. Gutenberg was the first European to experiment with printing texts with moveable type, perfecting a process that was commercially viable. He and Fust opened a printing press to produce books using this process. Schöffer came to Mainz to manage the print shop and he was involved in the production of the landmark work of that press, the first printed Bible, the '42 line' or *Gutenberg Bible*. After the production of the Bible the partnership between

TREASURES
The Special Collections of the
University of Wales Trinity Saint David

D te leua
ui animã
meã deus
meus in te
cõfido nõ
erubescã
neqȝ irride
ant me in
imici mei

eterni uniuersi qui te expectãt nõ con
fundentur. ps Vias tuas dñe de
mõstra michi et semitas tuas edoce
me. Ab hoc die vsqȝ ad natiui
taté dñi Gl'a in excelsis nõ dr.

Excita qñs dñe põ- Coll.
tentiã tuã et veni: ut ab
imminêtibȝ peccatoȝ nroȝ peri
culis· te mereamur· ptegente eri
pi te liberante saluari. Qui.

Fratres: Scien Ad roma.
tes qȝ hoȝa est iã nos de
somno surgere. Nûc eni· pior
est salus nra qȝ cû credidimus
· Nox pcessit dies auté appropi
quabit. Abiicyamus ergo opa
tenebraȝ: et induamur arma
lucis: sic ut in die honeste am
bulem⁹· nõ in cõmessationibȝ
et ebrietatibȝ· nõ in cubilibus
et impudiciciis· nõ in cõtentio
ne et emulacõne: sed induimi
ni dñm ihesum christũ. Grad.

Uniuersi qui te expectãt nõ cõfun
dentur dñe. v̄ Vias tuas dñe no
tas fac michi et semitas tuas edoce
me. All'a v̄ Ostêde nob dñe mise
ricordiã tuã ɿ salutare tuũ da nobis

N illo tpe. Secũm Matheum.
Cû appropinquasset ihũs ihe
rosolimã et venisset bethfage
ad montê oliueti: tûc misit du
os discipulos suos dicens eis.
Ite in castellũ qd contra vos
est: ɿ statim inuenietis asinam
alligatã et pullũ cũ ea: soluite
et adducite michi. Et si qs vob
aliquid dixerit: dicite qȝ dûs
his opus habet: et cõfestim di
mittet eos. Hoc auté totũ factũ
est: ut adimpleretur qd dictum
est p ppheta dicentê. Dicite fi
lie syon: ecce rex tuus venit tibi
mãsuetus: sedens sup asinã et
pullũ filiũ subiugalis. Euntes
auté discipuli fecerũt sicut pre
pit illis ihesus. Et adduxerũt
asinã et pullũ: et imposuerunt
sup eos vestimenta sua ɿ eum
desupr sedere fecerũt. Plurima
auté turba strauerũt vestimê
ta sua in via: alii auté cedebant
ramos de arboribȝ ɿ sternebãt
in via. Turbe auté que precede
bant et que sequebãtur clama
bãt dicentes. Osanna filio da
uid benedictus qui venit in no
mine dñi. Offs Ad te dñe le
uaui animã meã deus me⁹ in te cõ
fido non erubescã neqȝ irrideant me
inimici mei etenĩ uniuersi qui te ex
pectant nõ cõfundentur. Secretũ

Hec sacra nos dñe potenti
virtute insidatos: ad suũ faci
ant purioȝes venire principiũ
Per. Prefatio quotidiana.

Gutenberg and Fust broke down, and Schöffer decided to work for Fust. He married Fust's daughter and on Fust's death in 1466 Schöffer took sole charge of the print shop they had established. This missal was printed in that print shop.

The missal was printed towards the end of Schöffer's life (d. 1503), but is typical of his output. Like many of the books produced in Mainz in this period for church use, the book is printed in a typeface called Textura or Gothic Book-hand, which Gutenberg and Schöffer had pioneered together. This clear typeface was designed to emulate the qualities of handwritten manuscripts of the fourteenth and fifteenth centuries.

In this period, it was typical to treat printed texts as though they were manuscripts and at key points gaps have been left by Schöffer in the printed text to allow for the inclusion of hand-illuminated initials. In this book these initials are richly executed with the application of gold leaf and decorative foliage flourishes.

Merchants had commonly used marks (trademarks) on their products throughout the Middle Ages and Fust and Schöffer were the first printers to incorporate a printer's mark in a book. It first appeared in a work of 1458 and this missal bears that same mark at the colophon at the back of the book, where the name of the printer and the date of the work are clearly printed in red type.

Allan B. Barton

The Crucifixion.
Hand-coloured image

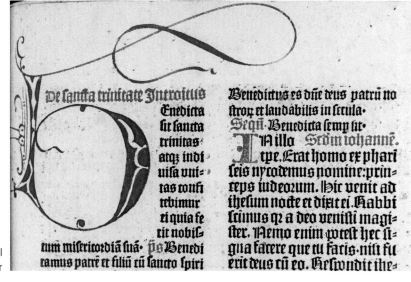

Hand-coloured ornamental
capital letter

A Liturgical Book – Economy Size

Missale ad consuetudinem insignis ecclesie Sarum (Paris: Opera Wolffgāgi Hopylij, 1511)

This missal was printed in 1511 in Paris by Wolfgang Hopyl (active 1489–1522/3). Hopyl, probably a native of Utrecht or The Hague, came to Paris in 1489, and settled there. This missal was printed there, almost certainly at his workshop in the Rue Saint-Jacques. Although printed in France the missal was produced for the English market and the liturgy it contains is according to the 'Use' of Sarum (Salisbury), the predominant liturgical variant of the Roman Rite in southern England and Wales in the fourteenth and fifteenth centuries. A 'Use' did not imply so much a difference in the Rite, as in, for example, the ceremonial actions of the sacred ministers, the bishop, priest or deacon, at the offering of the Liturgy. The Use of Sarum had been organized and codified early in the thirteenth century by Richard le Poer, Bishop of Salisbury (1217–28, and afterwards Bishop of Durham). He was responsible as well for the removal of his cathedral from the hill of Old Sarum and its re-establishment on its present site. Le Poer's 'Use' was subject to further minor revisions in the fourteenth century, mainly in respect of the Liturgical Calendar of Festivals and Feasts to be observed, and it is this 'New Use' that received widespread adoption thereafter.

Wolfgang Hopyl began printing missals and other liturgical books for export to England in 1494 when he entered into a partnership with Jean Himan, and they were sold through London booksellers – from 1494 through Nicolas Lecomte and after 1513 through Franz Birkmann. Birkmann (d. 1530) was certainly in London in 1504, but had settled in Cologne by 1511. With his brother Arnold he opened up a widespread book trade throughout north-western Europe, and the English market was served and supplied through their permanent branch at Antwerp. The great humanist scholar Erasmus named Birkmann as the principal book importer for the English market.

Hopyl's Missal is an example of that trade. It is significantly smaller than the Schöffer Missal which also features in this volume. The size of the book is worth noting: it made it economical to export to England in larger numbers, and much more saleable. These smaller missals, though not cheap, were within the means of the most modest parish community and their cost was a fraction of that of a manuscript equivalent. They were also made to last; to ensure this, and to further underline their value for money, the most heavily used part of the missal, the Canon of the Mass, is printed on durable vellum.

The Mass of St Gregory

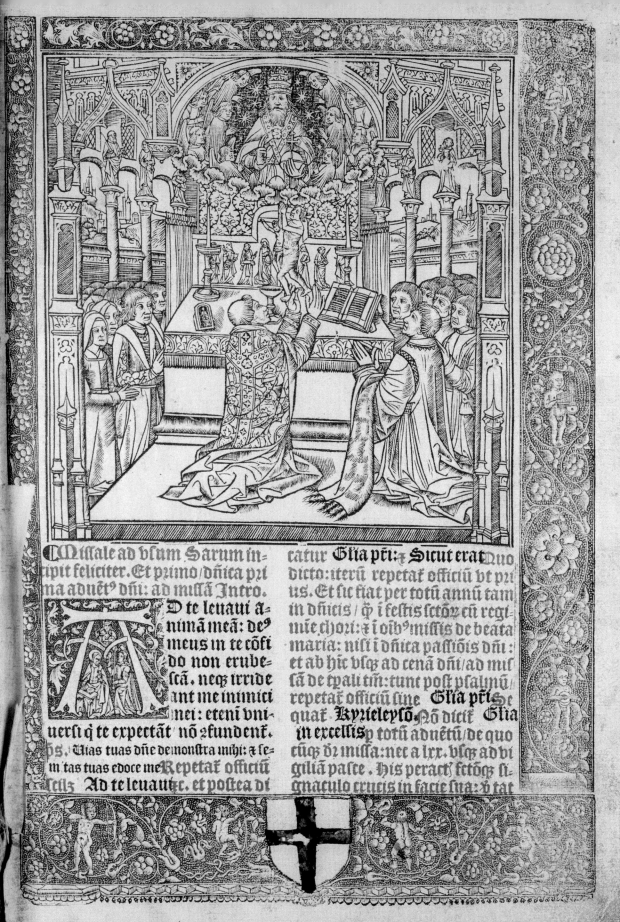

Missale ad vsum Sarum in=
cipit feliciter. Et primo / dominica pri=
ma aduentus domini: ad missam Intro.

A
D te leuaui a=
nimam meam: de=
us meus in te confi=
do non erube=
scam. neque irride=
ant me inimici
mei: etenim vni=
uersi qui te expectant non confundentur.
Ps. Vias tuas domine demonstra mihi: et se=
mitas tuas edoce me Repetatur officium
scilicet Ad te leuaui etc. et postea di=

catur Gloria patri: et Sicut erat Quo
dicto: iterum repetatur officium vt pri=
us. Et sic fiat per totum annum tam
in dominicis / quam in festis sanctorum cum regi=
mine chori: et in omnibus missis de beata
maria: nisi in dominica passionis domini:
et ab hinc vsque ad cenam domini / ad mis=
sam de temporali tantum: tunc post psalmum
repetatur officium sine Gloria patri se=
quatur Kyrieleyson. Non dicitur Gloria
in excelsis per totum aduentum / de quo=
cumque dicitur missa: nec a lxx. vsque ad vi=
giliam pasce. His peractis sanctorum si=
gnaculo crucis in facie sua: vt tat

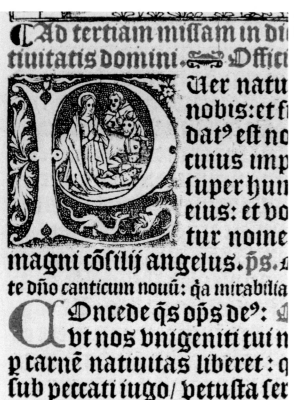

There was a ready market for such books and the sale of these cheap imported missals resulted in the Sarum 'Use', already firmly established, becoming ubiquitous in the years leading up to the Reformation. In the preface to the Church of England's *Book of Common Prayer*, 'Concerning the Service of the Church', it is stated that:

> Whereas heretofore there hath been great diversity in saying and singing in Churches within this Realm; some following Salisbury Use, some Hereford Use, and some the Use of Bangor, some of York, some of Lincoln; now from henceforth all the whole Realm shall have but one Use.[1]

That was the expressed intention of the compilers of the first *Book of Common Prayer* issued in 1549. More than 300 years of the 'Use' of Sarum came to an end in the upheavals of the English Reformation in the middle years of the sixteenth century.

Our copy of the Hopyl Missal was given to St David's College by Thomas Phillips in 1837. It had previously been in the library of Jean-François van de Valde, President of the Grand College of Louvain University, who died in 1823. Sometime thereafter it must have found its way onto the London book market. It is, despite its modest proportions, still a lavish work and is profusely illustrated with woodcuts. Very few of these have been cut specifically for the missal itself, and were reused from a range of earlier works. Indeed, some of the woodcuts continued to be used and reused in Parisian missals well into the 1550s.

Allan B. Barton

1 The fact that a particular 'Use' prevailed in a cathedral church did not necessarily imply that it was followed in the parish churches of the diocese. This may well explain why, for instance, although a 'Use' of Bangor is mentioned, no copy of such a 'Use' is known to exist.

cede quesum⁹
ulis celebranti
tiā delictoꝛum
us animis/eius
nt:ipso apud te
sociētur et me
iustus coꝛ suum
i solio. riij. Gꝛ.
sapientiam:et ligua
n. v⁹ Lex dei eius
supplantabunꝓ greſ
Tractus
nime ei⁹ tribuisti et
labioꝛum eius non
uoniā pꝛeueniſti eñ
 minis. v. Posuiſti su
i de lapide pꝛecioso.
o accēdit. In cō
siderium anime ei⁹ tri
ate labioꝛum eius non
ti in capite eius:coꝛ
o. Secreta.
ꝓ ob honoꝛē bea
ſſeſſoꝛis tui atꝗ
muerib⁹:et ipſi⁹
toꝛum nobis in
ue peccatoꝛum.
cōio. Beatus ſerꝰ
minus/inuenerit vi
vobis:super oīa bōa
Poſtcōio.
is dñe tui perti
nenti: interrede
o confeſſoꝛe tuo
conuerſationis
empla:et pertti
a. Per domini.
ardi vꝶ ſcti cuth
icti infra paſſiōe
et de eis vſꝗ ad
dē. ¶In annū
rie. Officium.

ſ Ave gracia plena dominꝰ

ROꝛate celi deſuper
et nubes pluāt iu
ſtū. aperiatur ter=
ra:et germinet ſal
uatoꝛē. In tempo
re paſcali alleluya
alleluya. ꝑs. Et iuſticia oꝛietur ſimul:
ego dominus creaui eum. Oꝛatio.

DEus ꝗ de beate marie vir=
ginis vtero verbū tuū an
gelo nūciante carnē ſuſcipere vo
luiſti:pſta ſupplicib⁹ tuis: vt qui
vere eā dei genitricē credim⁹ : ei⁹
apud te iterceſſiōtib⁹ adiuuemur.
Per eūdē. Lcō iſaie ꝓphete. vij.

IN diebus illis. Locut⁹ eſt
dñs ad achaz dicens. Pete
tibi ſignū a dño deo tuo in ꝑfun
dum inferni ſiue in excelſū ſupꝛa
Et dirit achaz. Nō petā: et nō tē
ptabo dñm. Et dirit. Audite er
go dom⁹ dauid. Nunꝗd parū vo
bis eſt moleſtos eſſe hoībus:quia
moleſti eſtis et deo meo. Propter

hoc dabit dñs ipſe vobis ſignum
Ecce virgo cōcipiet et pariet filiū:
ꝗ vocabiꝓ noīe ei⁹ emanuel. Bu
tyꝛū ꝗ mel comedet:vt ſciat repꝛo
bare malū et eligere bonum. Gꝛ
Tollite poꝛtas pꝛincipes veſtras:et eleua
mini poꝛte eternales/ꝗ introibit rex gloꝛie
v. Quis aſcendet in montem domini:aut
quis ſtabit in loco ſancto eius.innocēs ma
nibus/et mundo coꝛde . In tēpoꝛe pa
ſchali. Alleluya. v. Ave maria gra
tia plena dominus tecum: benedicta tu in
mulierib⁹. Secundū Alleluya erit
vnum de ſubſcriptis in officio ſe
quenti ſcilicet ſancti ricardi . Hac
die dicatur iſta ſequentia: licet in
quadꝛageſima ꝗtigerit. Seꝗntia

AVe mundi ſpes maria:
aue miꝮ/aue pia/aue ple
na gratia. Ave virgo ſingula
ris:que per rubū deſignaris / nō
paſſum incendia. Ave roſa ſpe
cioſa : aue ieſſe virgula. Cuius
fructus noſtri luctus : relaxabāt
vincula. Ave carens ſimili:inū
do diu flebili / reparaſti gaudiū.
Ave cuius viſcera:contra moꝛ
tis federa / ediderunt filiū. Ave
virginū lucerna:per quam fulſit
lux ſuperna/his quos vmbꝛa te
nuit. Ave virgo de qua naſci:ꝗ
de cuius lacte paſci/rex celoꝛū vo
luit. Ave gemma:celi lumina
rium. Ave ſancti ſpiritus ſacra
rium. O ꝗ mirabilis ꝗ ꝗ lauda
bilis/hec eſt virginitas. In qua
ꝑ ſpiritū facta paraclytū/fulſit fe
cūditas. O ꝗ ſctā ꝗ ſerena/ꝗ be
nigna ꝗ amena/eſſe virgo crediꝓ.
Per quā ſeruitus finiꝓ:poꝛta celi
aperitur:necnon libertas reddiꝓ.
O caſtitatis liliū: tuum pꝛecāre

Marine Inhabitants – Real and Imagined

Conrad Gessner, *Conradi Gesneri medici Tigurini Historia animalium. Liber I-IV* (Apud Christ. Froschouerum, 1551–8)

Conrad Gessner was the founder of modern descriptive zoology, as well as the father of bibliography.

Gessner (1516–65) was a native of Zurich. His father, Ursus Gessner, a furrier, was too poor to care for all his children. Conrad lived with his great-uncle, Johannes Frick, and after that, with his teacher, Johann Jakob Ammann. However, Gessner managed to get a good education. He learned Greek and Latin at the Großmünsterschule, and then moved on to Strasbourg to study Hebrew for five months. He studied and taught at several more universities, in France as well as Switzerland; his first academic post was as Professor of Greek in Lausanne. Alongside this, he qualified as a doctor of medicine in 1541. Living in Basel, he worked as Professor of Natural Science at the Collegium Carolinum as well as a physician. His last move was back to Zurich, where he taught natural philosophy at the Carolinum as well as continuing to practise medicine.

Gessner seems to have been under constant financial pressure; his need of money may have been a factor behind his huge output of scholarly publications. At this time Zurich was a trading centre and hub of routes across Europe, but certainly not a major centre for patronage. It was also a minor printing centre. Gessner, who lacked aristocratic backing, received unfailing encouragement and support from his publishers, including Christoph Froschauer and his own relatives Andreas and Jacob Gessner.

Gessner published at an average rate of more than two books a year, beginning with a Greek dictionary in 1537. His passion for cataloguing and classification made him something of a patron saint for librarians. In his first large-scale work, *Bibliotheca universalis* (1545), he attempted to list all the Latin, Greek and Hebrew works known up to that time. He made good use of contemporary publishers' catalogues and booksellers' lists. However, he was also anxious to include ancient authors whose works had been entirely lost. The first edition of *Bibliotheca universalis* detailed 3,000 authors and 10,000 titles.

TREASURES
The Special Collections of the
University of Wales Trinity Saint David

Sea monkey, sea lion and sea horse, from Conrad Gessner, *Fischbuch*, 1575

Von einer anderen gstalt eines scheützlichen Meerthiers.

Ises thier ist zu Meyland in eine hauffen steine fun den worden/vnd von dē hochgelertē herrē Hieronymo Cardano/an herr doctor Gäßner geschickt mit keiner weyteren beschreybung. Die gestalt aber deß schwantzes gibt zu daß es ein wasserthier sey/wiewol es sich mit dem kopff vnd den fingeren so es an den füssen erzeigt/etlicher massen den Affen vergleycht.

Von dem Meerlöuw.

Monstrum Leoninum.   Ein Meerwunder geleych einem Löuwen.

Von seiner gestalt.

Entzlich sol ein fisch sölicher gestalt gefangen worden seyn vor dē todt Papst Pauli deß dritten/in einer statt Centuncellis genañt/Dergleychē auch eins in dem jar 1284. welches geheület sol habē als ein mensch/vnd als ein wūder dem Papst Martino dem vierdten zūgefürt worden.

Von einem erdichten Meerpfärdt.

Equus

DE LEONE.

 E O rex quadrupedum, nomen Græcum, λέων, cuius etymon in Philologia dicam, non ſo-
lum apud Latinos, ſed pleraſcʒ etiam barbaras hodie in Europa gentes, ut infra patebit, ſer-
uat. Hebræi ueró plura diuerſáʒ huius feræ nomina habent. אֲרִי ari & אַרְיֵה arieh, Deute.
33. leo eſt, Chaldæus eo in loco habet אַרְיָוָן ariauan. Arabs אָסָד, aſad. Perſa שִׁיר, gehad.

Lion, from Conrad Gessner, *Historia animalium. Liber 1*, 1551

Over the course of twenty years, Gessner amassed a huge amount of material relating to the natural world. The four volumes of his magnum opus *Historia animalium* were published by Christoph Froschauer between 1551 and 1558. The total work, containing over 3,500 folio pages, was an encyclopaedia, intended for people to dip into rather than to read from cover to cover. Gessner aimed to include all that both modern and ancient authors had ever written about every animal species. His intention was always to accumulate as much information as he could, rather than establishing its reliability. For this reason, he included many creatures he had never directly observed, including the mythical and fictitious.

Following Aristotle's classification, the first volume described viviparous quadrupeds (mammals) and the second oviparous quadrupeds (reptiles and amphibians). The third volume dealt with birds and the fourth with aquatic animals. A final volume on

serpents was published in 1587, after Gessner's death. Within each volume, the various creatures are organized in alphabetical order by Latin name. *De camelo* (the camel) is followed by *de cane* (the dog). Gessner described each animal in a standard sequence of eight topics, starting with nomenclature, going through distribution, physiology and behaviour, and finishing with etymology and other cultural references. Carefully listing his sources, Gessner retained similar texts, as well as descriptions that appeared contradictory or false. He noted the information he had found in ancient and medieval sources, discussed it and then added what he

had been able to discover, either by his own observation or through his network of correspondents. He also included creatures whose existence was uncertain, writing of the unicorn, 'this image is as it is nowadays generally depicted by painters, of which I know nothing for sure.'[1] Ford comments that some of the creatures are hard to relate to reality![2] In the fourth volume, fictional sea monsters, including the monkfish and the sea lion, feature alongside real marine inhabitants. It was still believed that many monstrosities were in the sea, including counterparts of animals found on land. Much 'knowledge' was based on the work of the classical authors, who knew the Mediterranean but very little about the North Sea. Gessner wrote only thirteen sentences about what he called the Atlantic spotted dolphin, but thirty pages about the Mediterranean dolphin.

Each animal was represented with a woodcut illustration; the first volume contains ninety-six woodcuts. Ford points out that the drawings represent a unique cross-section of what was known at that time.[3] Gessner relied on his network of correspondents; these submitted twenty-five, or just over a quarter, of the images of mammals. However, he also used other sources, including broadsides, books and manuscripts. If an animal was uncommon, he was normally meticulous about noting the source of its picture. He copied some images, including sea monsters and the reindeer, from Olaus Magnus's map of the northern regions. The hyena came from an old manuscript by Oppian. In

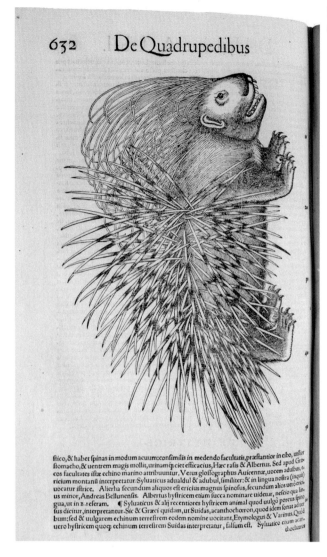

632 De Quadrupedibus

ftico, & habet fpinas in modum acuum: confimilis in medendo facultatis, præftantior in cibo, unfior ftomacho, & uentrem magis mollit, urinamép ciet efficacius, Hæc rafis & Albertus. Sed apud Græcos facultates iftæ echino marino attribuuntur. Vetus gloffographus Auicennæ, uocem adulbus, ericium montanū interpretatur: Syluaticus adualdul & adubul, fimiliter: & in lingua noftra (inqui) uocatur iftrice. Alierha fecundum aliquos eft ericius magnus fpinofus, fecundum alios uerò erich us minor, Andreas Bellunenfis. Albertus hyftricem etiam fucca nominare uidetur, nefcio qua lingua, ut in R. referam. ¶ Syluaticus & alij recentiores hyftricem animal quod uulgò porcus fpino fus dicitur, interpretantur. Sic & Græci quidam, ut Suidas, acanthochœron, quod idem fonat ad uer bum: fed & uulgarem echinum terreftrem eodem nomine uocitant, Etymologus & Varinus. Quòd uero hyftricem quoq echinum terreftrem Suidas interpretatur, falfum eft, Syluatico etiam acan thochœros

some cases, Gessner created a composite image, combining part of an animal with a description in a book. The walrus has a fairly accurate head, joined to a body with feet and claws. Gessner expressed his reservations, writing, 'I heard that the head was made after the skull of a real head, and the rest of the body was added from conjecture or from a report.' On the other hand, the porcupine depicts an animal shown round Zurich by a beggar. The images of fish were often based on a dried specimen.

Not surprisingly, the four volumes were expensive, costing 6fl. 17s. for the complete set – so just over twice the price of a Bible. Hoping to appeal to particularly wealthy people, Froschauer also produced hand-coloured copies after an exemplar. These coloured sets sold for nineteen florins – the equivalent of two coloured Bibles. Although the number of hand-coloured copies sold was likely to be small, Gessner appears to have planned the work with them in mind. The same woodcuts were used for species of weasels and martens, to indicate species that differed only by colour.

For Christoph Froschauer, there was more than one way of recouping his initial investment. *Historia animalium* was followed by a pictorial edition, *Icones* (1553, 1560); this kind of format would reach a different audience, as well as making good use of the costly woodcuts. Then two of Gessner's colleagues, Conrad Forer and Rudolf Heusslin, prepared an abridged German-language version. *Vogelbuch* was published in 1557, to be followed by *Thierbuch* and *Fischbuch* in 1563. More accessible than the original in language, size and price, they could reach a larger public. The Roderic Bowen Library holds a magnificent hand-coloured copy of *Fischbuch*, donated by

TREASURES
The Special Collections of the
University of Wales Trinity Saint David

Thomas Phillips in 1849. Bound with this is *Schlangenbuch*, the German version of the posthumous volume on snakes. Alongside this the library possesses volumes one to three of *Historia animalium*; these were given by Phillips in 1845.

Gessner died suddenly of plague on 13 December 1565.

Ruth Gooding

1 D. Margócsy, 'The camel's head: representing unseen animals in sixteenth-century Europe', *Nederlands Kunsthistorisch Jaarboek (NKJ)/Netherlands Yearbook for History of Art*, 61/1 (2011), pp. 62–85.

2 Brian J. Ford, *Images of Science: A History of Scientific Illustration* (London: British Library, 1992).

3 Ford, *Images of Science*.

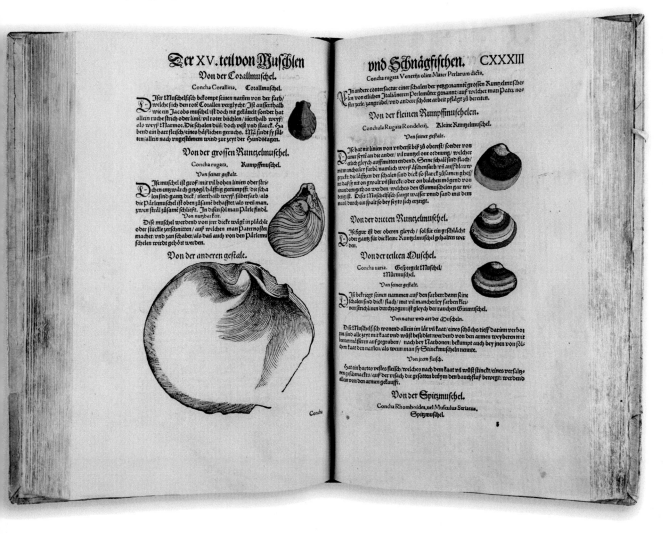

The Whole Wide World – Including Wales

Abraham Ortelius, *Theatrum orbis terrarum = The theatre of the whole world set forth by that excellent geographer Abraham Ortelius* (London: Printed by Iohn Norton, 1606)

Abraham Ortelius's *Theatrum orbis terrarum* was the earliest example of what we would recognize as a printed atlas.

'Mapbooks' had appeared before this. The Portuguese geographical discoveries of the fourteenth and fifteenth centuries were documented by manuscript charts bound together. Then many Italian atlases were issued to order, assembled to meet the needs of individual customers. Alongside this, during the fifteenth century, the works of Ptolemy (active second century AD) became available again. In contrast with medieval maps, which had often depicted a round world with the three known continents in a 'T' shape, Ptolemy's method of global projection showed north at the top. Medieval maps had been designed to illustrate knowledge; now accuracy became a central aim of cartographers.

Abraham Ortelius (1527–98) was a native of Antwerp and the son of a merchant, Leonard Ortels and his wife Anne Herwayers. Leonard died when Abraham was ten; by that time, however, he had already started to teach his son some Latin. Abraham must also have learned mathematics on his own.

Ortelius's original career was as an illuminator of maps; he was admitted to Antwerp's Guild of Saint Luke in 1547. In tandem with this, he soon started trading in books, maps, prints, antiques and coins. He attended the Frankfurt book fairs, where he met Gerhard Mercator in 1554. Business evidently went well. Ortelius was well enough off to be able to develop his own collections, probably inspired by the 'cabinets of curiosity' belonging to the learned people he met. He became one of the leading intellectuals of his day, an active figure in the early modern 'Republic of Letters'. Travelling extensively in western Europe, he developed a wide range of scholarly contacts. In Britain, his correspondents included William Camden, Richard Hakluyt, John Dee, Thomas Penny and Humphrey Llwyd.

TREASURES

The Special Collections of the
University of Wales Trinity Saint David

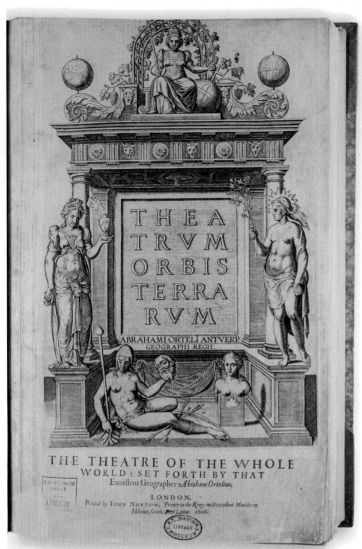

Ortelius published his first map, a wall map of the world, in 1564. Then, in 1570, he published his *Theatrum orbis terrarum*. This is considered the first true atlas, defined as 'a collection of uniform map sheets and sustaining text bound to form a book for which copper printing plates were specifically engraved'.[1] The first edition contained seventy maps on fifty-three sheets with accompanying text on the verso of each map. It was an encyclopaedic description of the world, like none so far produced. The maps were carefully organized to represent continents, groups of regions and nation-states, with one map of the world, four maps of the continents, fifty-six maps of Europe, six maps of Asia and three of Africa.

Ortelius was an editor rather than an original cartographer, obtaining maps and charts from the best sources. He listed eighty-seven map-makers whose work he had consulted; his most influential source for much of his work was his friend Gerhard Mercator's world map of 1569. Although the *Theatrum* was the most expensive book published in the second half of the sixteenth century, it was an instant success. The emerging wealthy Dutch middle class was interested in education and in science; the format of the atlas was far easier to use than sets of loose sheets. Ortelius regularly revised and expanded his atlas; twenty-one enlarged editions and thirteen supplements appeared during his lifetime, and thirteen enlarged editions after his death.

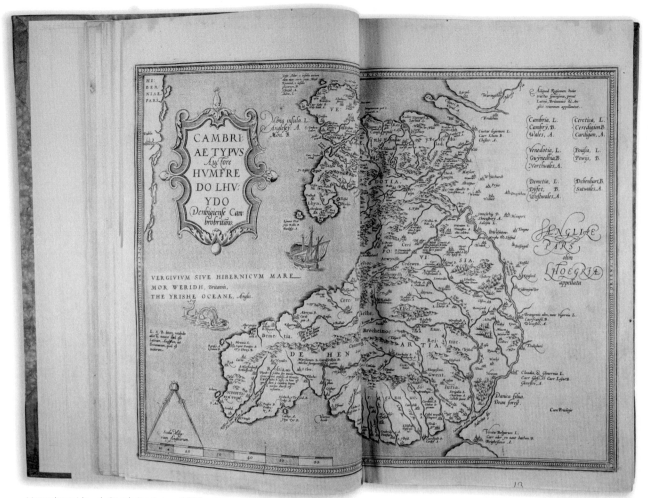

Humphrey Llwyd, *Cambriae typus*, 1606

In 1567, Ortelius met Humphrey Llwyd (1527–68), a Welsh antiquary, who had accompanied Henry Fitzalan, twelfth earl of Arundel, on a tour of Europe. Ortelius asked Llwyd's advice on a map of Britain. Llwyd supplied two maps included in *Additamentum*, the supplement to the 1573 edition of *Theatrum orbis terrarum*. One of these depicted England and Wales, the second only Wales. As this was the first published map to show Wales as a separate region, it is now probably Llwyd's greatest claim to fame. In a letter to Ortelius, Llwyd, by now seriously ill, described it as 'not beautifully set forth in all poynctes, yet truly depeinted, so be that certeyn notes be observed'.

Although it was a considerable improvement on earlier maps, the outline of the coast was still far from perfect. Llwyd omitted the Gower Peninsula. Milford Haven is shown facing south-west and the Llŷn Peninsula bends towards the south, making north Wales look disproportionately small. Llwyd showed the rivers in his native north Wales

TREASURES
The Special Collections of the
University of Wales Trinity Saint David

accurately, but, in west Wales, transposed the names of the Rheidol and the Ystwyth. He included the phrase '*Auctoris patria*' next to his own birthplace of Denbigh. Another inscription '*Tibius flu. L. Teifi B. hic fluvius solus in Britannia castors habet*' noted that the River Teifi, which flows through Lampeter and meets the coast at Cardigan, was the only British river where beavers could still be found.

Llwyd was a patriotic Welshman, determined to promote Wales's history and culture. He followed the legend of Brutus told in Geoffrey of Monmouth's *Historia Regum Britanniae* (*c.* 1136). In the eleventh century BC, Brutus, monarch of the island of Britain, is said to have divided his kingdom between his three sons. The second son, Cambus, received the area west of the Severn, therefore named Cambria. For Llwyd, Wales's boundaries extend to the Severn, so as far east as Worcester and Tewkesbury and including areas of Shropshire, Worcestershire, Herefordshire and Gloucestershire. Thus, Llwyd increased Wales's area by 2,100 square miles. He also showed Wales divided into its three traditional regions, Gwynedd, Deheubarth and Powys, although these had had no political status for several centuries. Where relevant, Llwyd recorded place names in Welsh, English and occasionally Latin. Some mistakes seem to have arisen because engravers were unfamiliar with the place names they had to copy. Llwyd appears to have used 'L.' as an abbreviation for llan; in the printed map Llanidloes has become L. Idlos and Llanrhystud Risthyd.

There are some decorative features, including a ship with three masts in Cardigan Bay and a sea monster near Fishguard. Llwyd also depicted mountains and forests pictorially. There are symbols for castles and churches, but little to show the relative importance of individual places. Llwyd's map proved popular; despite its deficiencies, it was reprinted nearly fifty times and continued to be published until 1741.

The Roderic Bowen Library holds a later edition of *Theatrum orbis terrarum,* printed in London by John Norton in 1606. It was donated by Thomas Phillips in 1834.

Ruth Gooding

1 Frans Koks, 'Ortelius atlas. Abraham Ortelius'. *https://www.loc.gov/collections/general-maps/ articles-and-essays/general-atlases/ortelius-atlas/*

A Monumental Venture

Walter Ralegh, *The History of the World* (London: Printed for Walter Burre, 1614)

Explorer, scientist, courtier and soldier, Sir Walter Ralegh (1554–1614) is often seen as the epitome of a Renaissance man. Having attracted the notice of Elizabeth I, he achieved great wealth and influence at court under her patronage. However, the accession of James I in 1603 proved disastrous for him. He was accused of plotting a coup and sentenced to death; he spent the next thirteen years imprisoned in the Tower of London.

Ralegh's conditions were relatively comfortable. He had two rooms in the Bloody Tower; he was allowed his library of over 500 volumes, a 'stilhows' or laboratory, and a garden for exercise. Most of the time, his wife was allowed to visit him without significant restriction. Ralegh was able to spend much of his time writing. He was also able to take up activities that might benefit both himself and the state. In particular, he made the acquaintance of James I's eldest son, Prince Henry.

Ralegh's major work during these years was his *The History of the World*, begun in 1607. He wrote with Henry in mind, producing a manual for him to educate himself through the grand, religious medium of the world's history. Ralegh commented in the preface: 'For it was for the service of that inestimable Prince Henry, the successive hope, and one of the greatest of the Christian world, that I undertooke this worke.' It was a monumental venture, running to about one million words.

Ralegh appears to have kept notebooks of his reading; his geographical notebook is held by the British Library. Every page is headed by a letter of the alphabet, with several pages for each. Ralegh would enter the name of a particular place, record its description and cite his authority in the margin. He then used his notes to write a systematic narrative, reflecting his own experience and understanding. As well as English, Ralegh drew on sources in Latin, French, Spanish, Italian and Greek. He was also able to consult his friends, some of them scholars. His original plan was to end the first volume with the Roman invasion of Britain, and then to produce two more volumes largely limited to English history.

Mark Nicholls defines the work as philosophical history;[1] Ralegh tried to reveal fundamental truths about the role and purpose of God and the lessons that could be

TREASURES
The Special Collections of the
University of Wales Trinity Saint David

Frontispiece

FAMA BONA

THE HISTORY OF THE

TESTIS TEMPORV
EXPERIENTIA

NVNCIA VETVSTATIS

MAGISTRA VITÆ

MORS OBLIVIO

LVX VERITATIS
VERITAS

VITA MEMORIÆ

At London Printed for WALTER BVRRE

1614

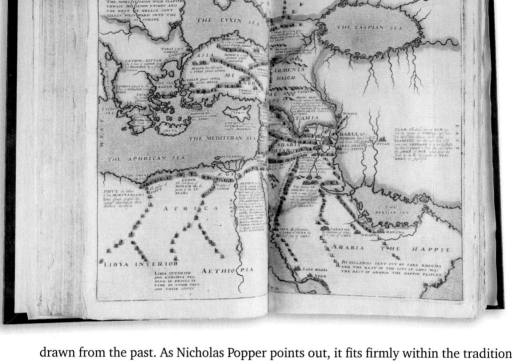

drawn from the past. As Nicholas Popper points out, it fits firmly within the tradition
of the universal history, a genre tracing the whole of humanity as a single, interrelated narration covering all known peoples and cultures.[2] The first two books (or
sections) mostly deal with the Old Testament, from the creation until the captivity in
Babylon. Alongside this, there are background events from other areas, particularly the
Egyptian, Assyrian and Babylonian empires. The last three books examine the Persian
and Greek empires, ending with the Roman conquest of Macedonia in 168 BC. Ralegh
focuses on military and political matters, with digressions on court behaviour and on
the mechanics of statecraft. His heroes tend to be soldiers and he is always ready to
demonstrate his own military experience.

The last part of the book to be written was the preface; in it Ralegh poses the controversial question, 'Why do kingdoms fall?'. He is also anxious to demonstrate his fitness
as a royal counsellor. Arguing that monarchs fail to learn the lessons of history, he
lists God's judgements upon kings. Writing of British sovereigns, he believes that
Henry I used 'force, craft, and cruelty' and that Richard III was 'the greatest Maister
in mischiefe of all that fore-went him'. Even worse, Ralegh writes of Henry VIII, 'if all
the pictures and Patternes of a mercilesse Prince were lost in the World, they might
all againe be painted to the life, out of the story of this King'. Although James I's
liberality and wisdom are contrasted with Henry's vices, James saw Ralegh's work as
a condemnation of kings by one of their subjects.

TREASURES

The Special Collections of the
University of Wales Trinity Saint David

Although the work was never finished, it was entered in the Stationers' Register on 15 April 1611 by Walter Burre, bookseller. It was published towards the end of 1614. However, on 22 December that year, James I ordered George Abbot, the Archbishop of Canterbury, to suppress it. John Chamberlain wrote that it 'is called in by the king's commaundment, for divers exceptions, but specially for beeing too sawcie in censuring princes'. Then, the king ordered that the volumes be passed to a John Ramsay 'to be disposed of at our pleasure'. As several copies survived, including that held by the Roderic Bowen Library, it seems that Ramsay may have sold them. Ralegh had been condemned for treason and was therefore 'civilly dead'. His book was published anonymously and without a title page, but with an elaborate allegorical frontispiece. The central figure is Clio, labelled *Magistra Vitae*, or the teacher of life; she holds a globe, carrying the known world. Anna Beer points out that particular features are marked on the map, including Caribbean islands, Cadiz, Dublin and a North Atlantic sea battle. These act as a key to Ralegh's biography.[3] The frontispiece is accompanied by a sonnet written by Ben Jonson.

A new edition of the book was published in 1617, the year before his long-delayed execution. This time, his name appeared on the title page. It became one of the most published and admired books of the turbulent seventeenth century, read by both Royalists and Parliamentarians. Oliver Cromwell recommended it to his son Richard, writing, 'Recreate yourself with Sir Walter Raughley's History: it's a body of history; and will add much more to your understanding than fragments of Story.'

The Roderic Bowen Library holds a copy of the first edition, with hand-coloured frontispiece and maps. It was one of twenty-five volumes given to the Foundation Collection from the library of St Edmund Hall, Oxford, in 1826, just before the opening of St David's College.

Ruth Gooding

1 Mark Nicholls and Penry Williams, *Sir Walter Raleigh: In Life and Legend* (London: Bloomsbury, 2011).

2 Nicholas Popper, *Walter Ralegh's History of the World and the Historical Culture of the Late Renaissance* (Chicago: University of Chicago Press, 2012).

3 Anna Beer, '"Left to the world without a Maister": Sir Walter Ralegh's *The History of the World* as a public text', *Studies in Philology*, 91/4 (1994), pp. 432–63.

A Richly Decorated Atlas

Gerhard Mercator, *Atlas or a geographicke description of the regions, countries and kingdomes of the world, through Europe, Asia, Africa, and America, represented by new & exact maps,* **translated by Henry Hexham (Amsterdam: chez Henry Hondius, 1636)**

Gerhard Mercator (1512–94) was the first person to use the term 'atlas' for a volume containing a collection of maps.

Mercator was born at Rupelmonde, now part of Belgium. His background was humble; his father was a cobbler. However, Gerhard was able to become a pupil at the University of Louvain, where he studied under Gemma Frisius – it was at this time that his original surname of Kremer was latinized to Mercator. He became a maker of mathematical and astronomical instruments, also learning to engrave. He founded his own studio in 1534. However, in 1552, he moved to Duisburg, at the confluence of the Rhine and the Ruhr. Duisburg was a tolerant town, an ideal home for a 'scholarly businessman, or rather a scholar forced to do business'.[1] Again, he opened a cartographic workshop.

In 1569, Mercator published a world map, entitled *Nova et aucta orbis terrae descriptio ad usum navigantium emendate accommodate* (New and more complete representation of the terrestrial globe properly adapted for use in navigation). Like all map-makers, he was faced with the challenge of representing the spherical earth on a flat surface. His system of projection was specifically designed to help sailors navigate following rhumb lines (or loxodromes). These always appeared on the map as parallel lines, with the curvature of the earth taken into account. Of course, this came at a cost, with massive distortion of the areas round the poles. Greenland looks roughly the same size as Africa! Mercator was also the earliest cartographer to divide the Americas into two named parts, (*Americae pars septentrionalis* and *Americae pars meridionalis*).

In 1569, Mercator announced his grand plan to publish a cosmography, a five-volume work covering the history of creation as well as astronomy, astrology and geography. However, even completing the atlas for this proved difficult. It was hard to obtain maps and accounts of travel. Engravers were in short supply and Mercator himself was obliged to take on other work in order to make a living. The first volume of the atlas was published in 1585, containing fifty-one maps of France, Switzerland, Germany and the Netherlands. For most maps, Mercator also included a piece of text, largely describing the political and ecclesiastical divisions of the area shown. The second

Title page

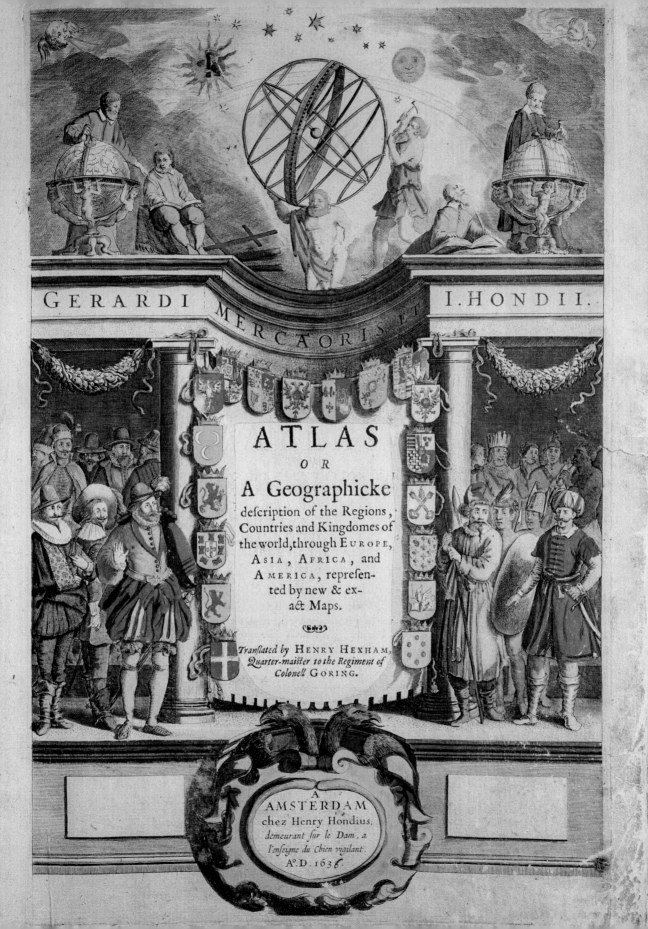

GERARDI MERCÆORIS ET I.HONDII.

ATLAS
OR
A Geographicke
description of the Regions,
Countries and Kingdomes of
the world, through EUROPE,
ASIA, AFRICA, and
AMERICA, represen-
ted by new & ex-
act Maps.

Translated by HENRY HEXHAM,
Quarter-maister to the Regiment of
Colonell GORING.

A
AMSTERDAM
chez Henry Hondius,
demeurant sur le Dam, a
l'enseigne du Chien vigilant.
Aº.D.1636.

volume of the atlas, issued in 1589, consisted of twenty-two maps of Italy, Greece and the Balkans. This was to be the last cartographic work Mercator published for himself. The next year he suffered a stroke; this left him partially paralyzed. He died in December 1594.

In 1595, Mercator's son, Rumold, published *Atlas sive cosmographicae meditationes de Fabrica Mundi et fabricati figura* (Atlas or cosmographic considerations on the creation of the world and a view on the created things). As well as the maps already issued, Rumold included twenty-nine maps his father had left unpublished, plus his own 1587 world map, his own small map of Europe and three maps of the other continents. Many of the new maps showed the British Isles; others represented Scandinavia, Iceland and Russia.

In the preface, Rumold explained that his father had chosen the name 'atlas' for the work. It is often said that atlases are named after Prometheus' brother Atlas, a Titan who was condemned to support the heavens on his shoulders. However, Keuning argues that Mercator had in mind a mythical king of Libya, who is said to have made the first celestial globe.[2] Mercator appears to have wanted to use the name of the first cosmographer in what he intended to be a cosmographical work. Indeed, in the first edition, Mercator's title page shows Atlas sitting on top of a mountain and studying globes!

Initially, Mercator's atlas was not particularly successful. It was not complete, lacking individual maps of the world outside Europe, and also of the Iberian Peninsula. It may not have helped that the various sections were really separate small atlases of individual countries. Furthermore, the volume had a formidable competitor in Ortelius's *Theatrum orbis terrarum*. Rumold Mercator died in 1600 and Mercator's grandchildren had little interest in cartography. In 1604, an entrepreneurial engraver, Jodocus Hondius, bought the copper plates at auction, thereby making his fortune. Having obtained additional maps, he brought out a new edition of the atlas in 1606. It was now a stately folio volume, containing 143 maps with descriptions. Hondius had added several maps of Spain, as well as of Africa, Asia and America. Hondius's brother-in-law, Petrus Montanus, wrote the text for the new maps, as well as enlarging Mercator's original descriptions. This time the atlas was successful; within a year, all the copies had been sold. Hondius followed it up with translations into French, Dutch and German, as well as a cheaper pocket-size edition, *Atlas Minor Gerardi Mercatoris à I. Hondio.*

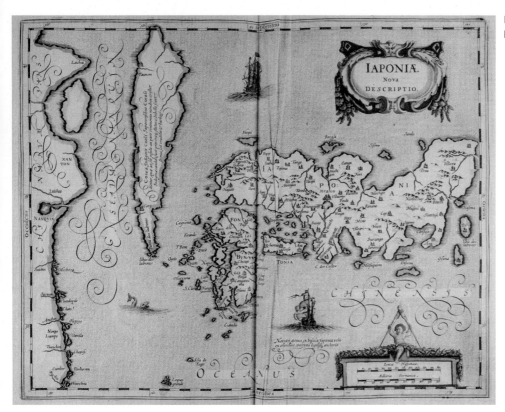

The Roderic Bowen Library holds a copy of the English translation, donated by Thomas Phillips in 1844. The two hand-coloured volumes were published in Amsterdam by Jodocus's son, Henry Hondius, in 1636, in competition with an English edition printed by T. Cotes for Michaell Sparke and Samuel Cartwright. Hondius's two volumes contain 195 maps. The translator was Henry Hexham, a British soldier and author who spent most of his life in the Netherlands. The first volume includes a magnificent double-page engraved portrait of Mercator and Hondius working side by side. The work was dedicated to the British monarch, Charles I. The maps are intricate and detailed, usually covering a double-page spread. They are also richly decorated; the map of Africa contains ships, a mermaid, a sea monster, elephants, lions and a crocodile. Sometimes, modern eyes notice an inaccuracy. For instance, Korea is shown as an island off the coast of China.

Ruth Gooding

1 M. A. Zuber, 'The armchair discovery of the unknown southern continent: Gerardus Mercator, philosophical pretensions and a competitive trade', *Early Science and Medicine*, 16/6 (2011), pp. 505–41.

2 J. Keuning, 'The history of an atlas: Mercator, Hondius', *Imago Mundi*, 4 (1947), pp. 37–62.

Overleaf: Gerhard Mercator and Jodocus Hondius working side by side

GERARDUS MERCATOR NAT
RUPELMUNDÆ III NON.MARTII AN
CIↃIↃXII: VIXIT ANN. LXXXII. M.VIII
XXVI:DENATUS IV NON.DECEMBR
ANNO CIↃIↃXCIV.

JODOCUS HONDIUS NATUS IN
o FLANDRIÆ DICTO WACKENE XVI
END. NOVEMBRIS ANNO CIƆIƆLXIII:
T ANN. XLVII. M. VII. D. XXIX : DENAT·
IV KAL. MARTII ANNO CIƆIƆCXII.

The Beginnings of Plant Anatomy

Nehemiah Grew, *The anatomy of plants. With an idea of a philosophical history of plants. And several other lectures, read before the Royal Society* ([London]: Printed by W. Rawlins, for the Author, 1682)

Nehemiah Grew was one of the founders of plant anatomy and a pioneer in the use of the microscope.

Nehemiah (bap. 1641, d. 1712) was the son of a Puritan clergyman, Obadiah Grew; he grew up in Coventry and then studied at Pembroke College, Cambridge. It is likely that he began to practise medicine after he graduated in 1662. He also started to explore botany, later writing, 'The first occasion of directing my thoughts this way, was in the year 1664, upon reading some, of the many and curious inventions of learned men, in the bodies of animals.' Inspired by the new research in animal anatomy, he hoped to make similar discoveries in plants.

In 1670, the Royal Society learned of Grew's researches; the next year he was elected a fellow, proposed by the curator of experiments, Robert Hooke. For a short time, Grew also worked as a kind of research fellow of the society, supported by its wealthier members. His first book *The Anatomy of Vegetables Begun: With a general account of vegetation founded thereon* was published in 1671. This was essentially a book of morphology, inspired by Grew's interest in the garden seeds he had accumulated. Around the same time, an Italian botanist, Marcello Malpighi, presented a paper on the same subject to the Royal Society. His work was to develop in parallel with Grew's.

Grew continued to research, supporting himself by deputizing for professors of physics and astronomy at Gresham College, and by lecturing for the Royal Society. He continued to write short quarto pamphlets on botany. *Idea of a Phytological History Propounded* was published in 1673, and then followed by publications on roots and trunks.

On 22 February 1682, the Council of the Royal Society recorded an order to gather Grew's work in one volume. His magnum opus *Anatomy of Plants* assembled all the research he had presented over the previous ten years. Published in a folio format, it combines the texts of his previously printed books, with his unpublished demonstrations on leaves, flowers, fruits and seeds. In addition, it includes six chemical discourses that Grew had read to the Royal Society between December 1674 and May 1677.

TREASURES

The Special Collections of the
University of Wales Trinity Saint David

Nehemiah Grew, *Sumach branch cut transversly*, 1682

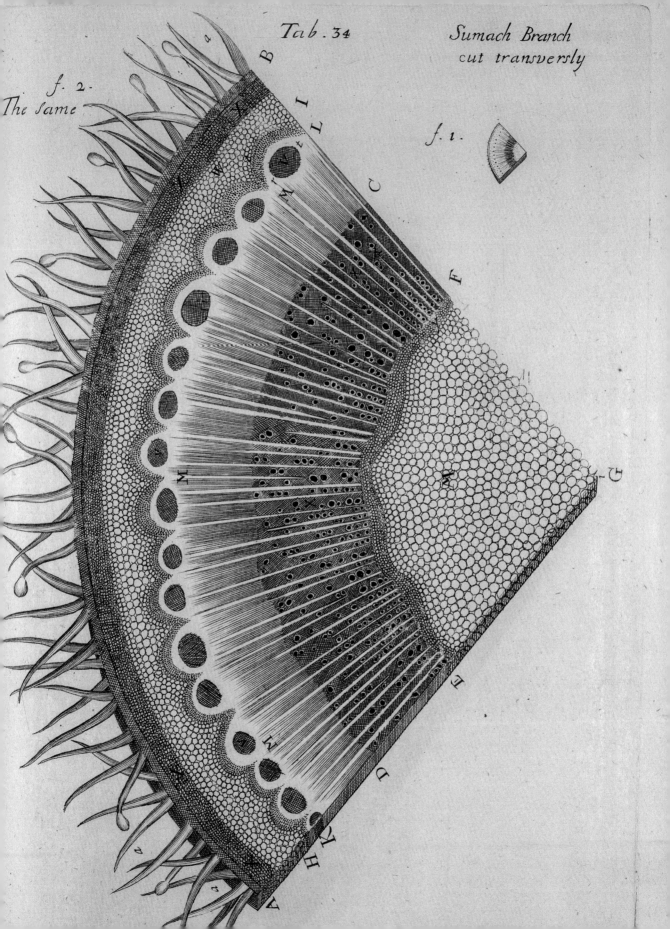

Tab. 34

Sumach Branch
cut transversly

f. 2.
The Same

f. 1.

At this time, botany hardly existed as a separate discipline; interest in plants had been largely confined to their medicinal value. Grew wrote in his dedication:

> There are Terræ Incognitæ in Philosophy, as well as Geography. And for so much, as lies here, it comes to pass, I know not how, even in this Inquisitive Age, That I am the first, who have given a Map of the Country.

What he had produced was a systematic and comprehensive investigation into the form and structure of plant organs. Most of his descriptions and observations were fresh. He used a number of botanical terms for the first time; these included 'radicle' for the part of a plant embryo that develops into the root system. It was also Grew who first drew attention to the sexual role of the stamen.

Grew was faced with the challenge of describing a plant in words. Alongside frequent medical analogies, he often used simple, domestic metaphors. For instance, he described the petals of the bud of the poppy 'as if Three or Four fine Cambrick Handkerchiefs were thrust into ones Pocket'. He wrote of fresh leaves clothed with hairs seeming to be 'vested with a Coat of Frize, or to be kept warm, like young and dainty Chickens, in Wool'.

The Anatomy of Plants contains eighty-three large-scale engravings, depicting the complex layers, fibres, vessels and sub-organs found in Grew's plant specimens. Unlike his colleague Robert Hooke, Grew distrusted the microscope and tried to limit his reliance on it as much as he could. In *Micrographia,* Hooke had dazzled his readers with striking images of secrets invisible to the naked eye. In direct contrast, Grew tried to display what could be seen accurately by those who looked carefully and deliberately.[1] In his preface, he described his aim of investigating 'How far it was possible for us to go, without the help of Glasses'. He went on to write, 'Having thus begun with the bare Eye; I next proceeded to the use of the Microscope.' Looking closely at a newly cut piece of wood, he realized that the gaps or knots in its fibres were full of a spongy pith. After examining this without the assistance of technology, he confirmed it using a low-power magnifying glass. Grew includes two plates of the sumach plant; the first of these portrays the plant exactly as it would appear to the naked eye. The second illustration is a large-scale drawing of its appearance under the microscope.

TREASURES
The Special Collections of the
University of Wales Trinity Saint David

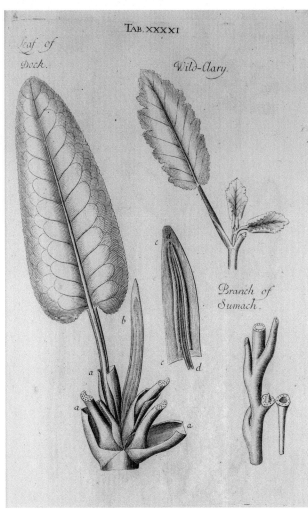

TAB. XXXXI

Leaf of Dock.

Wild-Clary.

Branch of Sumach.

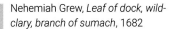

Nehemiah Grew, *Leaf of dock, wild-clary, branch of sumach*, 1682

Grew's volume was dedicated to Charles II, the patron of the Royal Society. Probably because of its lavish engravings, it was one of the first British scientific books to be published by subscription. This meant that Grew's research reached a far wider scientific audience than just members of the Royal Society. Each subscriber made a small contribution to allow an expensive work with relatively limited appeal to be issued. In this case, Grew himself organized and collected the contributions.

Grew appears to have decided to practise medicine more actively; in 1680, he became an Honorary Fellow of the College of Physicians. Although he continued to attend meetings of the Royal Society, his contributions to its research programme almost ceased. His last major publication was a theological work, *Cosmologia sacra, or, A Discourse of the Universe as it is the Creature and Kingdom of God*. Grew died on 25 March 1712.

Grew's work was not to be superseded for well over a century. The Roderic Bowen Library holds two copies of *The Anatomy of Plants*; one of these was donated as part of the Foundation Collections; the other was given by Thomas Phillips in 1849.

Ruth Gooding

1 A. Coppola, '"Without the Help of Glasses": The anthropocentric spectacle of Nehemiah Grew's Botany', *The Eighteenth Century*, 54/2 (2013), pp. 263–77.

The Preface that Never Was

George Hickes the Non-Juror and Lampeter MS T512a

As one historian pithily remarked, 'the term "Non-juror" has blurred edges'.[1] The Non-juring Movement, if such it may be called, was, to begin with, a schism within the Established Church of England but long lasting, enduring from the accession to the throne of William III and Mary II in 1689 until the closing years of the eighteenth century. It was occasioned by the refusal of the Archbishop of Canterbury, William Sancroft, and a number of his fellow bishops, along with at least several hundred of their clergy, to take an oath of allegiance to the new sovereigns, on the ground that they had already sworn one that they could not in conscience abjure to James II, who in their eyes – and not least in his own – was still the lawful and anointed king. These 'non-jurors' were at first suspended, and then deprived of their offices and benefices. Thus, the Established Church lost some of its most learned and, indeed, for example in Bishop Thomas Ken and the layman Robert Nelson, some of its most saintly, adherents. Unfortunately, but also characteristically, the schism proved to be fissiparous; as Gordon Rupp pointed out, it became increasingly introverted as the years passed, and 'a prey to personal quarrels in a communion where all the principal characters knew one another'.[2] Strong-minded individuals could – and did – hold tenaciously to their own view of what was right, and could be – and were – condemnatory of those whose views differed from their own.

Few among the early non-jurors were more forthright and unyielding in their views than the deprived Dean of Worcester, George Hickes (1642–1715). Hickes, said Rupp 'did not mince words or dodge the logic of his principles'.[3] Indeed, a historian of an earlier generation, C. J. Abbey, went so far as to pillory him as a man of 'blind zeal' possessing 'the true temper of a bigot'.[4] In some mitigation, Abbey conceded that Hickes was a scholar of immense erudition, as well as a formidable theological controversialist. He is perhaps best remembered as an Anglo-Saxon scholar, especially for his monumental *Linguarum Veterum Septentrionalium Thesaurus*, a comparative grammar of Old English and related Germanic tongues, published between 1703 and 1705, but it was he, perhaps more than any other of the leading non-jurors, who perpetuated the schism, obtaining the authority of the exiled James II to continue the non-juring episcopal succession, and his own consecration on 24 February 1693/4 as 'Bishop-Suffragan of Thetford'.

TREASURES
The Special Collections of the
University of Wales Trinity Saint David

Introductory Note, probably by
Thomas Bowdler II

This was designed for a Preface to a second Edition of
a Book Entituled A Vindication of some amongst ourselves,
which was written by D.r Hickes in answer to D.r Sherlocke,
This 2.d Edition had many Alterations & additions in it differ:
:ent from the former, but was seised at the Press, with M.r
Anderton, whome they put to death, none of that 2.d Impression
going abroad. —

One of Hickes's controversial pamphlets was his *Vindication of some among Our Selves against the False Principles of Dr Sherlock* of 1692. William Sherlock (1641–1707) had been Master of the Temple, but he had been deprived of his preferment as a non-juror. However, after the defeat of James II by William III at the Battle of the Boyne, he conformed, took the oaths, and was made Dean of St Paul's. This on its own would have earned him the contempt of Hickes, but in 1692/3 Sherlock published *A Vindication of the Doctrine of the holy and ever blessed Trinity*, which sparked a long and bitter controversy, a veritable pamphlet war, in which Robert South, Canon of Christ Church, Oxford, was Sherlock's most ardent opponent, effectively accusing him of Tri-theism. Hickes would have found such a controversy over the writing of one he would have regarded as a traitor to the cause, irresistible. His *Vindication* is among the extensive collection of Non-juring tracts and pamphlets housed in the Roderic Bowen Library and Archives at Lampeter (Class Mark T512). Described by its 1975 cataloguer, Brian Ll. James, as perhaps 'one of the best extant collections of Non-Juring literature' in the country,[5] it is part of a corpus of 11,395 pamphlets bound into 828 volumes, originally published between 1520 and 1843. No fewer than 9,000 of these constitute the Bowdler Collection and were donated to Bishop Thomas Burgess in response to his appeal for material for the library of his fledgling college at Lampeter by one resident of his diocese, Dr Thomas Bowdler IV (1754–1825). The collection had been assembled by three generations of his family (each named Thomas) during the seventeenth and eighteenth centuries, all of whom were themselves non-jurors. Thomas Bowdler II (1661–1738) had not only collected Non-juror literature, but had annotated many of those works, originally published anonymously, with the names and dates of the authors. He had also acquired the library of George Hickes, which is in all probability how T512A came to be included in the donation to Lampeter.

T512A is a handwritten manuscript, boxed in with, but separated out from, T512 when the volume was repaired in 1998 with funds from a Higher Education Funding Council for Wales conservation grant, and is, as stated by James David Smith, who studied the Lampeter Non-juring material:

a preface to an intended second edition of George Hickes's *Vindication* ... In a hand which former Founders' Library curator, the late Robin Rider, believed was by Thomas Bowdler II 'is an introductory note', stating that the new edition would have 'had many alterations & additions in it differ/ent from the former, but was seised [*sic*] at

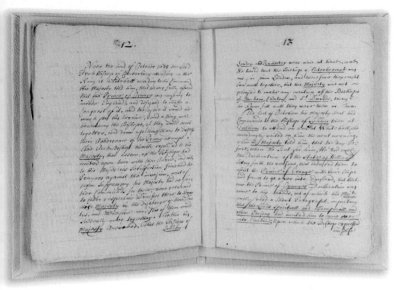

the Press, with Mr Anderton, whome they put to death,[6] none of that 2d Impression going abroad'.[7]

Smith notes that the preface comprises twenty-four pages:

on each of the first four leaves, the top left quarter has been cut away and another type of paper attached in its place. The missing text has been restored in a similar hand. It is not clear whether this is a repair of the damaged original or a revision.[8]

The pages, averaging 145 × 190 mm, are roughly cut. Throughout the text some words and phrases have been underlined in red ink, probably as an indication of what was to be emphasized in the printed version. It may well be that T512A is the only surviving copy of the preface to the intended second edition of the *Vindication* and thus an invaluable insight into Hickes's thinking after the appearance in print of the first.

John Morgan-Guy

1   Gordon Rupp, *Religion in England 1688–1791* (Oxford: Clarendon Press, 1986), p. 5.

2   Rupp, *Religion in England*, p. 5.

3   Rupp, *Religion in England*, p. 14.

4   C. J. Abbey and J. H. Overton, *The English Church in the Eighteenth Century* (London: Longmans, Green & Co., 1878), vol. 1, pp. 118–9.

5   Brian Ll. James, *A Catalogue of the Tract Collection of Saint David's University College Lampeter* (London: Mansell, 1975).

6   The arrest of William Anderton, a non-juring publisher, is detailed in another pamphlet in the Bowdler Collection, copies of which can be found in T197, 509, 652 and 660.

7   James David Smith, 'The Bowdler Collection as a Resource for the Study of the Nonjurors', in William Marx (ed.), *The Founders' Library University of Wales, Lampeter, Bibliographical and Contextual Studies. Essays in Memory of Robin Rider, Trivium, 29–30* (Lampeter: Trivium publications, 1997), pp. 155–67.

8   Smith, 'The Bowdler Collection', pp. 155–67.

Jonathan Swift's Hoax

Isaac Bickerstaff, *Predictions for the year 1708* (Sold by John Morphew, 1708)

The seventeenth century was a golden age for astrology in Britain. After official censorship collapsed in 1641, there was an explosion of new publications covering a vast range of subjects. However, after the Bible, the most popular type of literature was the almanac. Typically, an almanac was a combination of three components: a calendar, information on the year's astronomical phenomena and then astrological predictions. These forecasts nearly always included prognostications about the weather, crops and health, but also political and religious expectations. During the Civil War, the pamphlets and almanacs issued by astrologers played a significant and highly visible role. By the 1660s, around 400,000 almanacs a year were sold, roughly one for every three families.

John Partridge (1644–1715) was the most prominent almanac-maker of the early eighteenth century, and a national celebrity. He was born in East Sheen; his father, also John Partridge, was a waterman. The younger John Partridge started his working life as a cobbler; alongside this, he taught himself Latin, with some Greek and Hebrew, and studied medicine and astrology. Partridge's annual almanac, originally entitled *Mercurius Coelestis*, was first published in 1681. He was known for his pronounced views; he was a radical Whig, to the point of republicanism. He was also strongly anti-Catholic and anti-clerical.

By the beginning of the eighteenth century, educated people, influenced by the new scientific thinking, were beginning to reject astrology. In 1708, the Tory polemicist and satirist, Jonathan Swift, chose Partridge as the victim of an elaborate April Fool's Day hoax. As well as being a practical joke against superstition, it was also part of Swift's defence of established authority. An earlier satirical writer, Tom Brown, had parodied Partridge in 1690 with *Prophecies out of Merlin's Carmen,* and then in 1700 with *The Infallible Astrologer.* It is almost certain that Swift had read Brown's lampoons.

In Swift's pamphlet *Predictions for the Year 1708*, he assumed the fictional identity of Isaac Bickerstaff, a disgruntled but gentlemanly astrologer. In a supposed attempt to reform astrology, Bickerstaff alleged that he had spent much of his time correcting his previous astrological calculations. Ehrenpreis[1] points out that the 'fake writer'

TREASURES
The Special Collections of the
University of Wales Trinity Saint David

After Charles Jervas,
Jonathan Swift, 1751

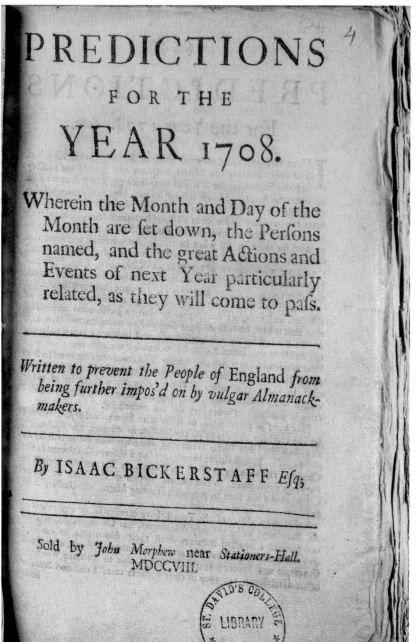

PREDICTIONS

FOR THE

YEAR 1708.

Wherein the Month and Day of the
Month are set down, the Persons
named, and the great Actions and
Events of next Year particularly
related, as they will come to pass.

---

*Written to prevent the People of England from
being further impos'd on by vulgar Almanack-
makers.*

By ISAAC BICKERSTAFF *Esq;*

Sold by *John Morphew* near *Stationers-Hall.*
MDCCVIII.

Title page

embodied several of Swift's real traits and tastes. He managed to keep up a judicious tone throughout, beginning with the words:

> I have long considered the gross abuse of astrology in this Kingdom, and upon debating the Matter with my self, I could not possibly lay the Fault upon the Art, but upon those gross Impostors who set up to be the Artists.

He went on to predict the deaths of several significant people, including the French Cardinal de Noailles. However, he described his first prediction as 'but a trifle':

> It relates to Partridge the Almanack-maker; I have consulted the Star of his Nativity by my own Rules, and find he will infallibly dye upon the 29th of March next, about Eleven at night, of a raging Feaver.

John Morphew issued the pamphlet, selling it for one penny a copy. It was successful beyond Swift's wildest dreams. Soon publishers were retailing pirated copies for half a penny each, as well as replies and imitations. Partridge himself ignored the publication.

Then, on 30 March, Swift issued another pamphlet, *The Accomplishment of the first of Mr Bickerstaff's Predictions, being an account of the death of Mr Partridge the almanack-maker upon the 29th instant*. Swift now adopted the persona of an anonymous author, this time a former revenue officer. He described visiting Partridge, to check the accuracy of Bickerstaff's predictions – Bickerstaff is described as having been four hours adrift in his forecast! Partridge, lying on his death bed, is described as confessing that he had always believed that 'all pretences of foretelling by astrology are deceits … and none but the poor ignorant vulgar give it any credit'. Ironically, he is portrayed admitting that astrology is false, but at the same time succumbing to its power.

The joke continued, growing into a fashionable craze. Imitations and sequels sprung up. The story spread to the continent and Swift's pamphlets were quickly translated into several European languages. One of the most entertaining follow-ups was *Squire Bickerstaff detected; or, the Astrological Imposter convicted*, said to have been written by Thomas Yalden. Partridge described his difficulties in combatting the popular belief in his death. After going to bed on the night of 28 March 1708, he heard the bell tolling to mark his decease. Then the undertaker arrived to drape his rooms for mourning

and the sexton attempted to arrange his funeral. After that, he could not leave his house for three months, without creditors asking him to settle his funeral expenses!

In the next edition of his almanac *Merlinus Liberatus*, Partridge indignantly insisted that he was still alive, and was also alive on 29 March 1708. He went on to attack the 'impudent lying fellow' who had foretold his demise. Swift's next contribution was *A vindication of Isaac Bickerstaff Esq; against what is objected to him by Mr Partridge, in his almanac for the present year 1709*. Swift argued that Partridge was dead because 'no man alive ever writ such damn'd stuff as this'. He went on to argue, 'So that Mr Partridge lies under a dilemma, either of disowning his Almanack, or allowing himself to be, *No man alive.*' There had been one other denial of Bickerstaff's predictions; it was insisted that Cardinal de Noailles was still alive. However, Swift declared that the word of a French Catholic was not to be believed, when set against that of a loyal English Protestant – for the fervently anti-Catholic Partridge, this must have been a crowning insult!

There was to be more bad fortune for Partridge. His almanacs did not appear for the next three years, seemingly due to an independent dispute with the Company of Stationers. He finally died, a relatively wealthy man with an estate worth over £2,000, in June 1715.

Swift had made the astrologer a laughing stock in educated circles. Such was his success that the pseudonym he had invented lived on. The next year, Sir Richard Steele issued his new periodical *The Tatler* under the supposed authorship of Isaac Bickerstaff, Esq.. Then, in the 1730s, Benjamin Franklin imitated the hoax, predicting and then announcing the death of an American astrologer, Titan Leeds.

Ruth Gooding

1 Irvin Ehrenpreis, *Swift: the Man, his Works, and the Age*. Vol. 2, *Dr Swift* (London: Methuen, 1967).

The Mystery of Number 81

The 'Missing' Issue of Daniel Defoe's *Review*

Daniel Defoe (1660–1731) may be best remembered as the author of *Robinson Crusoe* (1719) – the delight of generations of readers ever since – and of *Moll Flanders* (1722) and *Roxana* (1724), but he had been a tireless wielder of the pen for many years before they appeared in print. He was a prolific and versatile writer, with several hundred publications to his name. This career, as it may be called, he pursued (with various degrees of success) in conjunction with several others, including the ownership and management of a brick and pantile works. He was often chronically short of money, was declared bankrupt in 1692 and again in 1703, was familiar as an inmate of the Fleet Prison and of Newgate, fled into hiding from his creditors more than once, and finally died – once more in debt and in hiding – in April 1731. For all the ups and downs of his life, he was nonetheless a pioneering journalist and a widely read, if controversial, political pamphleteer.

Michael van der Gucht, *Daniel Defoe*, early nineteenth century, engraved by James Thomson (Wellcome Collection)

TREASURES
The Special Collections of the
University of Wales Trinity Saint David

Front page of the 'Missing'
No.81

REVIEW.

NOW, Gentlemen, the Peace being come to Town, and the Parliament approaching, I must let you alone to Scold and Rail at one another at what rate you please; to make good things bad, and bad things worse, that you may see what fruit you will have of those things whereof you are now ashamed: And in the mean time it is necessary to talk a little of the Consequences of this Peace, as they relate to my old subject of Trade; from which I have been only interrupted by what I thought necessary to speak about the Pretender, against whose Interest I hope I have sufficiently born my Testimony.

Nor shall I forget, *even all the way as I go*, to state the Circumstances of our Trade, as it may be expected to be, *in Case* of the Pretender's being set up; by which, if I do not embark all the Men of Trade against him, they must have lost their Trading Sences, and I must be very much mistaken in them.

I must begin with the State of our Trade, at the beginning of the Peace, which we have now, as they say, finithed —— Some proper Period must be plac'd to take our rise from, like the station of the Eye in Perspective, or no Proportion of things can be drawn; and I see no Period so proper as the present Peace.

I know I have two Extreams to shun; I have *Scylla* and *Charybdis* to steer between; and every Reader will expect I shall split upon one side or other; but I fear not passing clear of both: The Extremes are these; One Party says this Peace is *so prudently made, so securely fenc'd on every side; so calculated for the Encrease of our Commerce; for aggrandizing our Nation; for extending our Navigation; for giving Britain the Advantage every where;* That never were such flourishing Days of Trade known, as we shall infallibly have after this War, and the Peace will appear to be the only Cause of it.

I cannot give the Peace those fine Encomiums; nor do they that made it expect such Compliments from me I dare say; I cannot run such lengths in Panegyricking

our *encreasing Trade before hand; I see some capital Articles of our Trade which are in finking Circumstances, and all the Peace in the World can not restore them; nor do Peace and War influence those things one way or other.*

Others say, The Peace will ruin our Trade; the *French* are falling into our Manufactures; they will run away with the *Spanish* Trade, we shall be worm'd out of it entirely, by *France* and *Spain* being link'd together; we shall have no Wooll *from Spain,* but after the *French* are supply'd; we shall sell no Goods *in Spain,* but after the *French* Market is over; the Alliance between *France* and *Spain* will ruin our Trade.

I can not fall in with these Suggestions, any more than the other; nor do they appear rationally grounded; they are supported neither by Nature or Reason: the Fact is not true, or the Thing Practicable; allowing it to be in the Design, in short it is ridiculous.

These are the Rocks therefore which I must steer between: If Party Heats have run you up Gentlemen on both sides, to talk Nonsensically in Trade, *I am sorry for it:* But it must not follow, *I hope,* That if I state things on one side or other, *as they really are,* and not as they are suggested to be, *that therefore* my Discourse of Trade regards your Parties on either side, which as much as possible I would avoid.

I am none of those who applaud the Honour and punctual Dealing of the *French* King, with relation to executing the Stipulations of Treaties in their true Intent and Meaning: *Yet I cannot grant,* That either the *French* can be so subtle to *reserve,* the *Spaniards,* so horridly stupid, as to suffer; or *Britain* so blind, as not to see and resent it, when the *French* pretend to *reserve* any Footing, or possession of any Port or Place for Commerce, in the *Spanish West Indies,* after the Peace. It does not seem rational to entertain a Belief of any thing like it: This would be to make Tools of us all, to laugh at the Queen of *Great Britain,* and openly Contravene the new Treaty in the most essential Article of it; and in

short,

In 1704, Defoe engaged in his first exercise of what today might be called 'investigative journalism'. During the night of 26/7 November 1703, parts of southern and mid-England and Wales were ravaged by a storm of such severe hurricane strength that some 8,000 people lost their lives, thousands of houses were damaged, millions of trees uprooted and countless numbers of livestock lost. Defoe saw the devastation in London with his own eyes, and realized the potential for an 'eyewitness' account. Within days he published an appeal for information to 'all Gentlemen of the Clergy, or others, who have made observations of this calamity, that they would transmit as distinct an account as possible, of what they have observed' to his publisher. Cast in narrative form – and perhaps occasionally embellished – the result was *The Storm: or, a Collection of the most remarkable Casualties and Disasters which happened in the Late Dreadful Tempest both by Sea and Land* which appeared in July 1704. A book-length compilation, it followed on from Defoe's earlier (February 1704) *The Lay-Man's Sermon on the Late Storm,* a twenty-four-page pamphlet.

However, and beginning in the same year as these publications, what was arguably Defoe's most sustained journalistic work, *Review,* began its appearance. It was to run until June 1713, appearing some three times a week, and eventually amounting to well over 1,000 essays and 5,000 pages of text. It included comments on contemporary events at home and abroad, and, as Peter Miles observed, largely reflected the standpoint of Defoe's political master (who more than once had to bail him out financially), Robert Harley, Earl of Oxford.[1] Each issue of *Review* was numbered. The mystery was: what had happened to Number 81? It should have appeared early in April 1713, when *Review* was already in decline, and within weeks of its final demise. No copy had been traced, and as a result, as Miles pointed out, the question arose whether it had been published at all. Perhaps

> No. 81 was a chimera and what scholars were attempting to hunt down was merely an error of omission in the bookseller's notation … In addition, no contemporary reference to the publication survived.[2]

The question remained unresolved until L. J. Harris in 1973, in a short paper in *The Library* reported the existence of a copy of 'No. 81' in the tract collection of what is now the Roderic Bowen Library and Archives of University of Wales Trinity St David at Lampeter.[3] It had appeared on the same day as Parliament began to debate the terms of the Treaty of Utrecht, ending the conflict between England and France, and the

Treaty of Commerce, though evidently prepared for publication in advance of that. It has to be said that the text of 'Number 81' shows Defoe not to be overly enthusiastic about either, but particularly of the Treaty of Commerce. He was not to know, when composing 'No. 81', that the terms of that treaty would be rejected by the House of Commons only a few weeks later.

As an appendix to his essay, Peter Miles, then Lecturer in English at Lampeter, reproduced the complete text of 'No.81', thus for the first time making it available to scholars of Defoe, and to historians of the often-tortuous politics of the reign of Queen Anne.[4] Number 81 is one of an incomplete run of issues of *Review* from No. 16 to No. 82, that is, from 23 September 1712 onwards, bound together in T257 of the Roderic Bowen Library Tract Collection.[5] Each issue comprises a single essay, printed double-column on both sides of a sheet 180 × 220 mm, issued from the press of 'J Baker, at the Black Boy in Pater-Noster-Row', and priced at 'Three Half pence'. Other copies of the *Review* – but not of No. 81 – are bound into other volumes in the Tract Collection.

John Morgan-Guy

1   Peter Miles, 'The Text of Lampeter's Rare Issue of Defoe's "Review"' in William Marx (ed.), *The Founders' Library University of Wales, Lampeter, Bibliographical and Contextual Studies. Essays in Memory of Robin Rider, Trivium*, 29–30 (Lampeter: Trivium publications, 1997), pp. 143–54.

2   Miles, 'The Text of Lampeter's Rare Issue', pp. 146–7.

3   L. J. Harris, 'The Missing Number of Defoe's *Review*', *The Library,* 5th series, 28 (1973) pp. 329–32.

4   Miles, 'The Text of Lampeter's Rare Issue', pp. 150–4.

5   T257 was rebound in 1994. It includes Nos 16, 17, 22, 23, 29–34, 42–8, 50–2, 54–68, 70–2 and 74–82.

A Pioneering Ecologist

Maria Sibylla Merian, *Der Rupsen begin, voedzel, en wonderbaare verandering* **(Amsterdam: Gedrukt voor den Autheur. By Gerard Valk, 1714)**

Maria Sibylla Merian (1647–1717) was one of the world's first ecologists, as well as one of the earliest naturalists to make careful observations on insects, spiders and amphibians. She was also a talented botanical artist and one of the first female explorers.

Like almost all early modern women artists, Merian came from an artistic family. She was a native of the free imperial city of Frankfurt am Main. Her father, the engraver, publisher and topographical artist, Matthaeus Merian the Elder, died when she was only three. Her mother, Johanna Sibylla, quickly remarried Jacob Marrell, a successful flower painter. It was Marrell who taught the young Maria Sibylla to draw, to paint in watercolours and to engrave. Alongside this, she quickly became obsessed with the bugs that appeared in some of her stepfather's paintings. She was later to write, 'From my youth onward I have been concerned with the study of insects.'[1] Such was her curiosity that she began to collect insects and to rear them. She made detailed notes and drawings of their life-cycle, the plants they fed on and even their parasitoids. Initially, she reared silkworms, before going on to numerous other European insects, particularly butterflies and moths. Eventually her interests extended to frogs, lizards and snakes, all animals of a size she could capture herself. Her detailed observation was extraordinary, as she had developed all her skills herself.

Maria Sibylla married Johann Andreas Graff, one of her father's pupils, in 1665. She was eighteen; he was ten years her senior. The union was to produce two daughters, Johanna Helena and Dorothea Maria. After five years of marriage, the couple moved to Graff's hometown of Nuremberg. Maria Sibylla painted, embroidered and engraved, as well as teaching a group of female pupils flower-painting and embroidery. Her first book, *Neues Blumenbuch*, published in three parts between 1675 and 1680, was a collection of copperplate images of flowers. Intended as a selection of samples for copying, it contained no text.

Alongside this, Maria Sibylla continued collecting caterpillars, feeding them with appropriate leaves, recording their behaviour and drawing and painting them as they developed. Following Aristotle, it was still believed that insects arose through spontaneous generation, developing from putrid matter. Francesco Redi did not publish his theory that insects hatched from eggs until 1668; Marcello Malpighi issued his treatise

on the metamorphosis of silkworms in 1669. Maria Sibylla's journal indicates that she understood the various stages of insect metamorphosis almost ten years earlier. She also discovered the differences between butterflies and moths.

In 1679, Maria Sibylla published her first scientific book, *Der Raupen wunderbare Verwandelung und sonderbare Blumen-nahrung* (The wondrous transformation of caterpillars and their remarkable diet of flowers). This is popularly known as *The Caterpillar Book*. It contained fifty plates in quarto, all engraved by herself; a second volume, also containing fifty plates, followed in 1683. Each illustration showed one or more species of insect in their various stages: caterpillar; pupa with or without cocoon; moth, butterfly or fly. Many of the images also included the egg stage. Every picture featured a single plant, most often flowering. In this way, Maria Sibylla showed the caterpillar's preferred choice of diet, as well as the places where the female laid its eggs. She identified each plant by its German and Latin names. The images were accompanied by a text in which Maria Sibylla explained how her specimens had looked and behaved. Unlike some of her contemporaries, she seems to have used only a magnifying glass, rather than a microscope.

Towards the end of her life, Maria Sibylla worked on a third caterpillar book; her daughter published this posthumously in 1717. She also translated her first two caterpillar books into Dutch, entitled *Der rupsen begin* and published by Gerard Valk in Amsterdam. The Roderic Bowen Library holds a hand-coloured copy of the Dutch language second volume, presented by Thomas Phillips in 1847. It is bound in contemporary Dutch calf with roll-tool panelling and a central tooled lozenge.

Maria Sibylla's later life was eventful. In the mid-1680s, she and Johann Andreas split up. They eventually divorced and Maria Sibylla reverted to her maiden name of Merian. She seems to have undergone some kind of religious conversion. Together with her mother and her daughters, she entered a commune at Castle Walta in Wieuwerd, Friesland, run by a Pietist religious sect called the Labadists. (Jean de Labadie had emphasized the need for true believers to be separate from the evils of the world; he therefore founded his own community, where the elect could live as God intended.)

Notwithstanding the austerity of her surroundings, Maria Sibylla was still allowed to pursue her scientific interests. She dissected frogs and, in her journal for 1686, she described the development of frogs' eggs and the metamorphosis of tadpoles. She

and her daughters left Castle Walta in 1691 to move to Amsterdam, a flourishing commercial, banking and industrial city of 200,000 people. Once there, she again made her living as a painter and a teacher; her elder daughter, Johanna Helena, also began to sell flower pictures.

Maria Sibylla had seen beautiful butterflies and caterpillars that some of the Labadists had brought back from Dutch Guiana (now Suriname) in northern South America. However, no information about their development came with the specimens. Maria Sibylla took the daring decision to travel to South America herself, accompanied by her daughter Dorothea Maria. She commented, 'So I was moved to take a long and costly journey to Suriname.'[2] Valiant speculates that this may have been the first European voyage exclusively for scientific work.[3] Maria Sibylla reached Suriname in 1699, where she collected information and sketched specimens from her own garden and from the jungle. She remained there for almost two years before becoming seriously ill, probably with yellow fever. When she returned to Holland, she brought with her an extensive collection of natural history specimens. In 1705, she published the results of her expedition in a sumptuous folio volume, *Metamorphosis Insectorum Surinamensium*.

Maria Sibylla continued to work actively for as long as she could. Sadly, she suffered a stroke in 1715, dying at her home in Amsterdam on 13 January 1717. Very close to the day of her death, Tsar Peter the Great purchased two volumes of her pictures, containing 254 parchment leaves for 3,000 Dutch guilders. Her son-in-law George Gsell and her daughter Dorothea Maria moved to St Petersburg to become teachers at the newly formed Academy of Arts and advisers to the Tsar on art acquisitions.

Ruth Gooding

1 Natalie Zemon Davis, *Women on the Margins. Three Seventeenth-Century Lives* (Cambridge, Massachusetts: Harvard University Press, 1995).

2 Davis, *Women on the Margins*.

3 S. Valiant, 'Maria Sibylla Merian: recovering an eighteenth-century legend', *Eighteenth-Century Studies*, 26/3 (1993), pp. 467–79.

Producing a Laugh in the Coffee House

Satire and Humour in Bowdler T269

The name of Dr Thomas Bowdler (1754–1825) has entered the English language. In 1818, he published an expurgated version of the works of William Shakespeare in ten volumes; that is, he purged the text of whatever he deemed unsuitable for respectable and genteel readers. To 'bowdlerize' a text, removing whatever might raise a blush – or perhaps a behind-the-hand giggle – has remained the definition of such activity ever since.[1]

Not all the members of his family have been quite so prim. Take for instance T269 in the collection of tracts and pamphlets assembled by Dr Bowdler's predecessors, Thomas I, Thomas II and Thomas III, in the seventeenth and eighteenth centuries. Although the bulk of the collection is concentrated on political and religious affairs, that is not entirely true of what is between the covers of T269. The focus here is on satire and humour, and some examples of the latter are of what might be termed a distinctly earthy or scatological kind. Read aloud round a table in the coffee house or inn parlour, they would have been guaranteed to raise a laugh.

T269 contains thirty-one separate items, and has been rebound. The contents range from a single sheet, *The Exerceese of the Muckle Goon and Saundaleero's*,[2] through a sixty-seven-page pamphlet, *Academia, or the Humours of the University of Oxford in Burlesque Verse*, to the eighty-four-page *The Dispensary; a Poem* – no less than six cantos of rhyming couplets. Three pamphlets are in French (none with a date or place of publication), and one in Spanish. Most of the contents of T269 are anonymous, and, unlike his practice in, for example, the Non-juring tracts elsewhere, Thomas Bowdler II has made no effort to identify the authors. In a few cases an author *is* named: Mrs Alicia D'Anvers, Mr Cobb, H Crispe, for example.[3] In two cases, *The Dyet of Poland: A Satyr* 'printed at Dantzick in the year MDCCV by Anglipoloski of Lithuania' and *The Masquerade. A Poem* 'by Lemuel Gulliver, Poet Laureat to the King of Lilliput' penned 'from my Garret in Grub Street' (London, 1728, and sold for 6d a copy), the attribution is obviously fictitious. Jonathan Swift's ever-popular *Gulliver's Travels*, which propelled 'Lemuel Gulliver' to fame, and included his experiences in Lilliput, was published in 1726, so this pamphlet, whether or not it is by Swift, was capitalizing on its early success. There has been much speculation on the origin of the name 'Lemuel Gulliver'. Bernard Acworth in his 1947 study of Swift[4] claimed that the only previous use of the name Lemuel that he had traced was in the Old Testament Book

TREASURES

The Special Collections of the
University of Wales Trinity Saint David

Tract purporting to be by
Lemuel Gulliver

THE
MASQUERADE.

A
POEM.

INSCRIB'D TO

C⸺T H⸺D⸺G⸺R.

⸺*Velut ægri somnia, vanæ*
⸺*Species*⸺   Hor. Art. Poet.

By *LEMVEL GVLLIVER*, Poet Laureat to the
King of *LILLIPVT*.

LONDON,

Printed: and Sold by *J. Roberts* in *Warwick-Lane,* and
A. Dodd at the *Peacock* without *Temple-Bar.* 1728.

[Price Six Pence.]

of Proverbs, chapter 31, verses 1 and 4. The reference there to a 'King Lemuel' (from the Hebrew for 'Godward' or 'God is bright') is generally thought to be an allusion to Solomon, and thus to wisdom.[5] 'Gulliver' on the other hand may derive ultimately from the Old French *'goulafre'* meaning 'glutton', but Swift's coinage of the word is more likely to echo 'gullible'. Thus 'Lemuel Gulliver' is a contradiction in terms – one endowed with God-given wisdom who was at the same time easily deceived. It was the kind of contradiction that would have amused Swift, and probably his more discerning readers.[6]

This last leads naturally to the consideration of two of perhaps the most intriguing of the pamphlets in T269: *The Wonderfull Wonder of Wonders; Being an Accurate Description of the Birth, Education, Manner of Living, Religion, Politicks, Learning, Etc. of mine A-se* and *The Benefit of Farting Explaind: or, The FUNDAMENT-all Cause of the Distempers incident to the Fair Sex.* The former, it is claimed, is a third London edition of 1721, and printed from 'the original copy from Dublin'. It is ascribed to 'Dr Sw-ft', that is, of course, Jonathan Swift (1667–1745). Brian Ll. James, who catalogued the whole tract collection in 1975,[7] noted that this attribution is 'not certain'. Swift, Dean of St Patrick's, was certainly in Dublin at this time, and some of his later poetry, of which *The Lady's Dressing Room* (1730) and *Strephon and Chloe* (1731) are well-known and notorious examples, reveal that he was quite capable of writing in this vein. T269 contains two 'editions' of *The Benefit of Farting Explaind*, the 'seventh' and the 'ninth', both of 1722, and selling at 3d a copy. Are 'seventh' and 'ninth' truly the case, or merely a printer or bookseller's 'puff'? If taken as true, then this pamphlet was a runaway bestseller. (It certainly had sufficient notoriety to be referred to in Eric Partridge's 1937 *Dictionary of slang and unconventional English.*) Once again, though nowhere in the pamphlet itself, authorship has been ascribed to Swift; 'formerly' says Brian James.

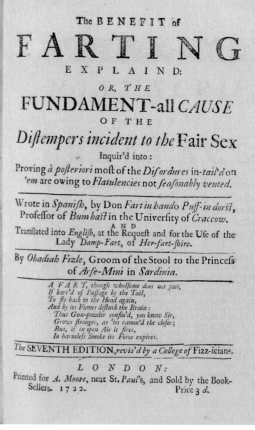

Scatalogical satire purporting to be by Dean Swift

TREASURES
The Special Collections of the
University of Wales Trinity Saint David

The fact that both of these works have been grouped together (numbers 28, 29, 30) in T269 may be a hint that Bowdler felt that they might well be by the same author, and possibly Swift. The ninth edition of *The Benefit of Farting Explaind* includes some marginalia, handwritten Latin quotations on pages 7 and 10, annotations which are rare in T269.

In his foreword to the Brian James catalogue of the Bowdler Tract Collection of seventeenth- and eighteenth-century works Julian Roberts said, 'Among the most obvious features of English literature of this period are that it is largely topical in content and that it is bibliographically ephemeral.'[8] The contents of T269 are perhaps more ephemeral than most, but nonetheless full of interest, amusement, and at least in some cases raising as yet unanswered questions.

John Morgan-Guy

1 The Roderic Bowen Library possesses a copy of the one-volume edition of Bowdler's *Family Shakespeare* published in 1863. It was given to the library in 2002 by the writer, novelist and columnist Sir Ferdinand Mount when he became an Honorary Fellow of the University.

2 Muckle-goon may derive from Scottish dialect: muckle = much, and goon = gown, to indicate, perhaps, a scholar. Saundaleero remains, so far, untraced.

3 Alicia D'Anvers (1668–1725) was a minor poet, who wrote in a satirical and sometimes earthy vein – not characteristic of women poets of her time. Her *Oxford-Act* is particularly bawdy. Mr Cobb is probably Samuel Cobb (1675–1713) critic and schoolmaster, who wrote light verse, sometimes patriotic and sometimes with an unrefined humour. H. Crispe remains to be identified.

4 Bernard Acworth, *Swift* (London: Eyre & Spottiswoode, 1947), p. 79.

5 Acworth has an interesting short discussion why Swift should have made use of the name Lemuel. Acworth, *Swift*, p. 79.

6 'Lilliput' may well be Swift's own invention. Some attempt has been made to find its origin in Lilliput, on the shores of Lough Ennell in Co. Westmeath in Ireland, but in Swift's lifetime that hamlet was named 'Nure'.

7 Brian Ll. James, *A Catalogue of the Tract Collection of St David's University College, Lampeter* (London: Mansell, 1975).

8 James, *A Catalogue of the Tract Collection*, p. viii.

Chinese Architecture at First-Hand

William Chambers, *Desseins des edifices, meubles, habits, machines, et ustenciles des chinois. Gravés sur les originaux dessinés à la Chine par Mr. Chambers, Architecte, membre de l'Académie Impériale des Arts à Florence. Auxquels est ajoutée une description de leurs temples, de leurs maisons, de leurs jardins, &c.* **(Londres: De l'imprimerie de J. Haberkorn . . .; se vend chez l'Auteur, 1757)**

William Chambers (1722–96) was the earliest European to study Chinese architecture first-hand.

Unusually, Chambers, the son of a Scottish merchant, was born in Göteborg, on the west coast of Sweden. He later wrote, 'I was born in Gothenburg, was educated in England, and returned to Sweden when I was 16 years old.' After leaving education, Chambers entered the Swedish East India Company, sailing to Bengal in 1740. Following this, he was part of two, potentially lucrative, voyages to Canton (Guangzhou), first on the *Riddarhuset* and then on the *Hoppet*. He commented that on these journeys: 'I studied modern languages, mathematics and the liberal arts, but chiefly civil architecture.' He also sent architectural memoranda, including drawings of Chinese houses, to Sweden's chief architect, Baron Harleman.

Chinoiserie, the style of European architecture and artefacts in the Chinese taste, first appeared in the seventeenth century. Inspired by fabulous accounts of the Far East as well as by the high quality of Chinese craft manufacture, it became an imaginative recreation of the East. This fashion for all things Chinese influenced a range of decorative arts in Britain in the mid-eighteenth century. Chinoiserie has been described as a mongrel style;[1] items were often made in a mixture of Chinese and Rococo tastes. Although Chinese building was thought to be relatively short-lived, the style was used for garden buildings and for areas within the house, for instance a dressing room or bedroom.

By the time Chambers returned to Europe from China, he was wealthy enough to be able to spend six years studying architecture in Paris and then Rome. In 1755, he left Italy to set up in architectural practice in London. Realizing he needed to promote himself through publication, he drew on his experience of Chinese buildings. His second book, *Designs of Chinese Buildings, Furniture, Dresses, Machines and Utensils*, came out in May 1757. 'Several lovers' of chinoiserie appear to have persuaded

TREASURES
The Special Collections of the
University of Wales Trinity Saint David

William Chambers [Chinese costume], 1757, engraved by C. Grignion

XX

1

2

3

4

5

6

C. Grignion sculp.

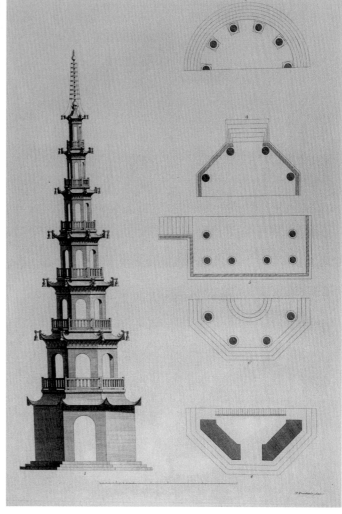

him to publish it; Eileen Harris suggests that the most significant of these may have been Augusta, the Dowager Princess of Wales.[2] This was the first time Chinese architecture was treated as a subject worthy of the kind of serious study given to western antiquities. In the preface, Chambers wrote that he intended 'only to give an idea of Chinese architecture', therefore putting 'a stop to the extravagancies that daily appear under the name of Chinese'. He saw Chinese styles as 'so much inferior to the antique' and 'so very unfit for our climate'. However, he pointed to the novelty and variety associated with them, commenting that 'an architect should by no means be ignorant of so singular a stile of building'. Architects might introduce Chinese elements in 'extensive parks and gardens, where a great variety of scenes are required', or in the inferior parts of 'immense palaces, containing a numerous series of apartments'. Chambers also believed that the British could learn from Chinese models of garden design. The part of his book that attracted most interest was his essay, 'The art of laying out gardens among the Chinese'.

The volume was one of the most handsome architectural books of its day. Dedicated to George, Prince of Wales (later George III), the 164 subscribers included aristocrats Chambers had met on the Grand Tour as well as craftsmen, architects and future patrons. Nineteen pages of text were followed by twenty-one plates produced by the best engravers, including Paul Fourdrinier, Edward Rooker and Charles Grignion. The range of subjects depicted is similar to that found in pattern books; they include buildings, gardens, furniture, domestic objects and clothes. All the illustrations are

TREASURES
The Special Collections of the
University of Wales Trinity Saint David

based on the area around Canton that Chambers had visited. Like most European travellers, he wrongly thought that Chinese styles were almost uniform throughout the country. As he would have had limited access to household interiors, some of his drawings were based on 'export' pictures by Cantonese artists.

Despite the magnificence of the volume, its influence in Britain was limited. By this time, the fashion for chinoiserie was already waning. Only three English buildings, including Chambers's temple at Ansley, are known to have been inspired by his designs.[3] Initially, most of the volume's influence came on the continent, where the fashion for chinoiserie flourished in the 1770s and 1780s. For instance, Carl von Gontard built a dragon house for Frederick II of Prussia, based on Chambers's Ta-ho pagoda. In Sweden, the Chinese pavilion at Drottningholm Palace was inspired by Chambers's drawings. Ironically, Chambers's book was more influential in Britain after his death. In 1790, the future George IV added a Chinese drawing room to his London home, Carlton House. Many of the details were based on Chambers's designs.

Only a few months after *Designs of Chinese Buildings* was published, Chambers was appointed architect to the Princess Augusta at Kew and architectural tutor to the Prince of Wales, (later George III). A lifetime of royal patronage followed. He eventually became comptroller and surveyor general of the Office of Works, as well as one of the founders of the Royal Academy of Arts. Leaving chinoiserie behind, the majority of his work combined English Palladianism and French Neoclassicism. His most famous building is probably Somerset House, built to house a variety of public offices and learned societies.

The Roderic Bowen Library holds a French translation of *Designs of Chinese Buildings*, issued simultaneously with the English edition. This was donated as part of the Foundation Collections.

Ruth Gooding

1 John Harris, 'Chambers, Sir William (1722–1796)', in *Oxford Dictionary of National Biography* (Oxford: Oxford University Press, 2004).

2 Eileen Harris, 'Designs of Chinese buildings and the dissertation on Oriental gardening', in J. Harris (ed.), *Sir William Chambers: Knight of the Polar Star* (London: A. Zwemmer, 1970), pp. 144–8.

3 Ibid.

A View from the Quarterdeck

A Log Book from HMS *Elizabeth* 1759–61 (Lampeter MS 11)[1]

A log book is the biography of a ship. In it is to be found a record of the day-to-day activities that make up the lives of those who serve aboard her, from the captain and the commissioned officers down through the ranks to the youngest and smallest of her ship's boys and powder-monkeys. Many of those activities are regular, to the point of being monotonously humdrum, but these may be interspersed with incidents that are far from ordinary. There is the daily record of the weather conditions encountered on the voyage, the ship's position, as calculated by her officers, the state of the vessel herself, and of her stores, the health of her crew, the imposition of punishments for a variety of misdemeanours and the tally of deaths through sickness or accident. Such a record is the bread and butter of any biography. And, as with the life of an individual, there can be more than one essay in biography, so it is with the life of a ship; there is more than one log book. The initial responsibility of the keeping of the log rested at the date of that held in the Roderic Bowen Library with the ship's master, initially in the form of a rough log, which could be a hastily scribbled preliminary draft, which he later transcribed into what became the official log. This was the definitive biography, which could not – or should not – be subsequently altered or changed, unless such changes were clearly indicated, and at least initialled by the person responsible for the alterations. Upon this official log a number of others depended. The captain of the ship kept his own log, compiled from the master's, but with his own personal additions and observations included. Then there were the lieutenants' logs, compiled in a similar way, and usually kept meticulously, as promotion could depend upon it, such logs having to be presented for scrutiny at an examining board.

It is far from clear into which category Lampeter MS 11 falls, as it is anonymous. It covers the period 1759 to 1761, and came to the college as part of one of the munificent donations, this one dating from 1847, of Thomas Phillips, who, as a long-time servant and surgeon with the East India Company, himself had more than a passing familiarity with the waters of the Indian Ocean and China Seas where the *Elizabeth* was stationed during those years. It can be stated with some certainty that it is not the log of the *Elizabeth*'s captain, Richard Tiddeman, as his papers and journals, including those for the years covered by Lampeter MS 11, are deposited at the National Maritime Museum in Greenwich (NMM MS TID/8 and 9). HMS *Elizabeth* was an old ship; she had been laid down as far back as 1706, but rebuilt in 1737. From the mid-1750s the two-decker '74' became the dominant ship-of-the-line warship,

TREASURES
The Special Collections of the
University of Wales Trinity Saint David

'Butcher's Bill' of the British Squadron
9–10 September, 1759

The State & Condition of the Company of his Majestys Ship Elizabeth the Day of Action.

Killd in Action	Died since of their Wounds	Wounded	Sick on Shore	Sick on board	Number on board att this Time
22 1 Died of same Night	26	54 of which Number 23 are Dangerous	6	31	440

The Form of the English Line of Battle on the 10 of September 1759. The Elizabeth to lead the Van on the Starb'd Tacks and the Weymouth on the Larboard Tacks

Frigates	Ships Names	Commanders Names	Number of Men	Number of Guns	Number Kill'd	Number Wound'd
	Elizabeth	Cap'tn Rich'd Tiddeman	400	64	23	54
Royal George	Newcastle	Cap't Collin Mackey	350	50	35	70
	Tyger	Cap't W'm Brinton	420	60	27	135
Revenge		Rear Adm'l Stevens				
Queenborough to repeat Sig'ls	Grafton	Cap't Rich'd Kempleflett	535	60	10	70
	Yarmouth	Vice Adm'l Pocock / Cap't Jn'o Harrison	540	66	0	30
Protector Fire Ship	Cumberland	Cap't Rich'd Somerset	520	50	0	30
	Salisbury	Cap'tn Digby Dent	350	50	10	20
	Sunderland	Hon'ble Jam's Colvill	420	60	2	"
	Weymouth	Sir Will'm Baird	420	60	"	"
		Total	3935	536	131	425

Officers Killd & Wounded in ye Squadron

The Master of ye Yarmouth Killd, the 2'd Lieuten't of ye Grafton wound'd the Cap't of ye Cumberland wound'd, the Boatsw'd & Deputy Purser of the Elizabeth Killd, the Cap'tn and 1st Lieuten't of the Tyger wound'd, the Captain and Cap'tn of Marines of the Newcastle Killd, and three of the Lieuten't wound'd The 1st Lieutenant of the Salisbury Wounded

but vessels like the *Elizabeth*, mounting 64 guns, were, nonetheless, very suitable for service in such far-flung corners of the globe as the Indian Ocean. Her captain, Richard Tiddeman, was an experienced sea officer; in 1759 he had thirty years' service with the Royal Navy behind him, including periods in command of the *Harwich* and the *Grafton*, though admittedly the years 1750–8 had been spent ashore on half-pay, until the outbreak of the Seven Years' War with France had brought him back to active service.

From the point of view of the historian, the most interesting entries in Lampeter MS 11 are those concerning the clash between the British squadron under the command of George Pocock, and the French, under the Comte d'Aché on 9/10 September 1759. The two had met twice before, in April 1758, and the second time four months later. Neither encounter had been decisive, though the former had led indirectly to the capture and dismantling by the French of the East India Company's Fort St David. The details of the third – and final – engagement between the two forces are recounted in Lampeter MS 11, as they are in Tiddeman's log at Greenwich. Taken together, they provide a vivid, and what might be called a 'broadside-by-broadside' account of the battle, in which the *Elizabeth*, leading the van, took a hazardously prominent role. Ultimately d'Aché broke off the action, and, after effecting temporary repairs to his ships at Pondicherry, withdrew to the French naval base at Mauritius. He did return to Indian waters. This timid behaviour, leaving the French land forces in India unsupported, was in due course to spell the end of French ambitions in the sub-continent.

Richard Tiddeman was never to return home to England. In October 1762, still in command of the *Elizabeth*, but now with the rank of commodore, he was engaged in the successful attack upon, and surrender of, the Spanish settlement at Manila, but on the seventh of that month was drowned when, in rough water and driving rain, his barge overturned. He was, as his senior in that expedition, Sir Samuel Cornish, said of him, a man of 'natural gallantry' and held in 'general esteem' – someone, in fact, who upheld the highest traditions of the Royal Navy.

There are several puzzling features about MS 11. At present it comprises 75 pages (*recto verso*, 250 × 400 mm) but ends abruptly. It may, therefore, be incomplete, as the current binding would seem to be too insubstantial to have been sufficient protection of the contents at sea. Then there are the 'paste-ins' to that cover. Inside the front is a map depicting 'The Seat of War on the Coast of Coromandel' by Thomas

Jefferys 'Geographer to His Majesty'. Jefferys (1719–71) was the leading map supplier of his day, engraving and printing many maps for governmental and commercial agencies. Pasted into the back cover is a plan of Fort St George, headquarters of the British forces in this part of India, also by Jefferys, and 'A View of the Attack on the Fort of Geriah by Admiral Watson 13th Feb 1756' engraved by 'P Canot'. Both of the latter have been, rather crudely, cut from other publications. Geriah Fort had been the stronghold of the Maratha pirate Tulagee Angria, who preyed on East India Company ships off the Malabar Coast. Watson's successful attack, though Tulagee himself escaped, was to destroy that particular threat to EIC trade. The action was depicted in an oil painting, now at the National Maritime Museum (Macpherson Collection, BHCo. 377) by Dominic Serres (1722–93), the French-born former ship's captain who settled in England, specialized in maritime painting – he became Marine Painter to George III – and in 1768 was one of the founders of the Royal Academy. It is this painting, engraved by Pierre-Charles Canot (1710–77), which is the paste-in to MS 11. Serres's work is dated 1771, so Canot's engraving must have been made between then and his death six years later – some ten or fifteen years after the last entry in MS 11. In whose possession was this particular copy of the log, or who was responsible for the binding and paste-ins, remains a mystery.

John Morgan-Guy

1 For a more detailed account, particularly of the action of 9/10 September, see John Morgan-Guy, 'Close action off the Coromandel coast: a Founders' Library manuscript and the British fight for India', in W. Marx and J. Burton (eds), *Readers, Printers, Churchmen, and Travellers: Essays in Honour of David Selwyn, Trivium*, 35 (Lampeter: Trivium publications, 2004), pp. 97–120.

A Scholar of Passion

Thomas Pennant, *The British zoology. Class I. Quadrupeds. II. Birds Published under the inspection of the Cymmrodorion Society* (London: Printed by J. and J. March . . . for the Society, 1766)

Thomas Pennant (1726–98) was a naturalist, antiquarian and pioneer travel writer.

Pennant came from a long-established Welsh gentry family. He was born to David and Arabella Pennant at Downing Hall, in Whitford, near Holywell, Flintshire. Thomas's lifelong interest in natural history seems to have been sparked when he was about twelve. A relative, John Salisbury, gave him a copy of Francis Willughby's *Ornithology* (1678). He later wrote that this 'first gave me a taste for that study, and incidentally a love for that of natural history in general, which I have since pursued with my constitutional ardor'.[1]

Pennant became an undergraduate at Oxford University in 1744, studying at Queen's College and then Oriel College. In 1746 or 1747, while he was still an under-graduate, he toured Cornwall; he commented that this 'gave me a strong passion for minerals and fossils'.[2] He also noted the encouragement given him by the naturalist and historian, Revd Dr William Borlase. Pennant continued his passion for geology through the 1750s, going on fossil-hunting tours of Wales and Ireland, and actively collecting specimens. He also published several articles in the Royal Society's *Philosophical Transactions*; the subjects ranged from earthquakes experienced in Wales to penguins, tortoises and fossil corals. Alongside this, he corresponded regularly with some of the leading naturalists of the time; these included Benjamin Stillingfleet, John Ellis, Emanuel Mendes Da Costa and even more notably, Carl Linnæus. He exchanged specimens with foreign collectors, including Prince Ignazio Biscari of Sicily, Baron Charles de Geer of Stockholm and Erich Pontoppidan, the Bishop of Bergen.

Eventually Pennant's attention transferred to other branches of natural history, particularly zoology and especially ornithology. Borlase wrote to him in 1761, 'You have exhausted the fossil kingdom, and you do well now to direct your studies to the Animal, which, I think, must also submit to you in time.' Then, in June 1762, Pennant wrote to Da Costa, 'I formed the great Design of a British Natural History.' Although he actively collected material for *British Zoology* from 1761, it was not published for another five years. Partly this was due to difficult family circumstances: Pennant's

TREASURES
The Special Collections of the
University of Wales Trinity Saint David

Peter Paillou, *The squirrel, the dormouse*, 1766, engraved by P. Mazell

The Squirrel

The Dormouse

P. Paillou pinx.   P. Mazell sculp.

father died in 1763; then, tragically, his wife Elizabeth died in June 1764, leaving him with two small children. In a bid to deal with his resulting depression, Pennant spent six months in 1765 touring the continent. This gave him the opportunity to meet some of Europe's leading naturalists and to examine their collections.

As it was expensive, *British Zoology* was to be issued in four separate parts, each costing two guineas; the subscribers would pay for the parts separately. When the complete volume finally came out, *British Zoology* was a handsome elephant folio volume, containing ninety-eight coloured plates of birds and nine of mammals. It was published anonymously, but with the name of the Cymmrodorion Society of London on the title page. Any profits were intended for the Welsh School, near Gray's Inn Lane, London.

In *British Zoology*, Pennant had produced the first handbook on British birds since Francis Willughby's *Ornithology*, by now ninety years old. Pennant's book was also one of the earliest works of natural history to use coloured plates on a large scale. He combined each description of a mammal or bird with a relevant illustration. He named each creature according to John Ray's classification system, giving first its genus and then its species. Rather than describing its anatomy, Pennant then described the main external features and characteristics. He combined this with anecdotal material associated with sightings in the wild. Peter Cotgreave has described the book as a model modern editors would do well to emulate, containing an ecological and evolutionary commentary far better than in some modern guides.[3] Pennant was reluctant to take information from secondary sources. Where possible, he relied on his own observation; if necessary, he used a description given him by one of his network of correspondents. These correspondents provided him with a system of academic advice and criticism, showering him with a constant supply of observation and information.

The quality of the coloured plates is superb; eighty-four of these were taken from original watercolours by Peter Paillou, a specialist bird artist. Pennant described him as

> an excellent artist, but too fond of giving gaudy colours to his subjects. He painted, for my hall, at *Downing*, several pictures of birds and animals, attended with suitable landscapes. … All have their merits, but occasion me to lament his conviviality, which affected his circumstances and abridged his days.[4]

Peter Paillou, [Finches], 1766,
engraved by P. Mazell

The names of two other artists involved in *British Zoology* are recorded: Peter Brown and George Edwards. The engraver was Peter Mazell, who went on to engrave the plates in nearly all Pennant's later publications. Pennant commented of him, 'and of whose skill and integrity I had always occasion to speak well'.

Despite all this, the lavish first edition of Pennant's book was a commercial failure. Aimed at the libraries of wealthy gentlemen-scholars, it was unaffordable for many field workers. Also, Pennant had failed to consider the practicality of using such a sizeable volume out in the field. His correspondent Benjamin Stillingfleet felt, 'The large edition can never be generally usefull, few people can purchase it and those few cannot make the use of it they would wish, not being portable.' Pennant himself realized, 'I was, at the time of undertaking this work, unexperienced in these affairs, and was ill-advised to publish on such large paper.'

In 1768, the publisher Benjamin White re-issued *British Zoology* in two octavo volumes, illustrated with seventeen plates. This time round its reception was encouraging. The next year, Pennant completed a third volume dealing with reptiles and fish; he issued a fourth volume, concerned with crustaceous marine insects, vermes and shells, in 1777. Such was the popularity of *British Zoology* that five editions were published between 1766 and 1812. It soon became recognized as a standard reference work. The Roderic Bowen Library's copy was donated by Thomas Phillips in 1846.

Pennant went on to be a prolific writer, known for his accounts of his tours of England, Scotland and north Wales, as well as for more volumes on natural history. He was also a correspondent of the Hampshire clergyman Gilbert White; forty-four of the letters in White's *Natural history of Selborne* were addressed to Pennant.

Ruth Gooding

1 Thomas Pennant, *The Literary Life of the Late Thomas Pennant, Esq. by himself* (London: Sold by Benjamin and John White, 1793).

2 Pennant, *The Literary Life*.

3 P. Cotgreave, 'The historian and the dodo', *History Today*, 47/1 (1997), pp. 7–8.

4 Pennant, *The Literary Life*.

TREASURES
The Special Collections of the
University of Wales Trinity Saint David

George Edwards, *The long legged plover*, 1766, engraved by P. Mazell

The Indefatigable Hydrographer

The Charts, Plans and Views of Alexander Dalrymple

The Hon. Alexander Dalrymple (1737–1808), seventh son of Sir James, 2nd Baronet of Hailes, Co. Haddington, has been called 'the originator of official British hydrography'.[1] Joining the East India Company in 1752, as a 'Writer' at the tender age of fifteen, he spent more than a decade based in Madras, including time exploring widely – the Philippines, Borneo, the Indian Ocean and the China Seas. From the early 1770s he was more or less permanently resident in London, where he remained, a clubbable bachelor, until the end of his life. But he was never by any means idle; his ever-growing library was the seat of his industry. From its resources and his researches in the archives of East India House and elsewhere there flowed a seemingly never-ending stream of printed charts, plans, views, journals and memoirs which only ended with his death. From 1779 he was the official publisher of such material for the East India Company, all of it of considerable interest and in very many cases of inestimable value to those who commanded the company's ships on their widespread trading voyages. From 1795 he added to this responsibility that of being the Hydrographer to the Royal Navy, an office he pioneered and the work of its department he organized, vital during the French Revolutionary and Napoleonic Wars. His output was nothing short of astounding. Andrew Cook, who has catalogued his work, has identified no fewer than 1,116 separate printed items.

Nowhere, says Cook, is there a single, complete, comprehensive collection. In 1841 Thomas Phillips, in one of his generous donations to the Library of St David's College, Lampeter, gave a significant number, which are now housed in the Roderic Bowen Library. Phillips, who had himself served as a young man – in Dalrymple's lifetime – as a Royal Naval surgeon, and subsequently in India with the East India Company's armed forces, as well as voyaging in the China Seas, the Indian Ocean and to Australia, would have had a personal interest in much of Dalrymple's output, and indeed the Lampeter collection may therefore have come from his personal library. The collection includes five 'volumes' encompassing altogether forty-six separate items: plans, journals, memoirs and observations. Each of these is numbered, and soft-bound in sturdy marbled covers. Here are, for example, the *Journal of the Jane from a manuscript at East India House* and dated 1781, *Remarks made at Mauritius, 1755, by Charles Frederick Noble*,[2] and, much further afield, *Memoir of a Map of Lands around the North Pole*, 1789, and *Memoir concerning the geography of the Countries*

Andrew Werner, *Plan and view of Gingerah commonly called Donda Rajapore on the Malabar coast*, 1774, engraved by P. Begbie

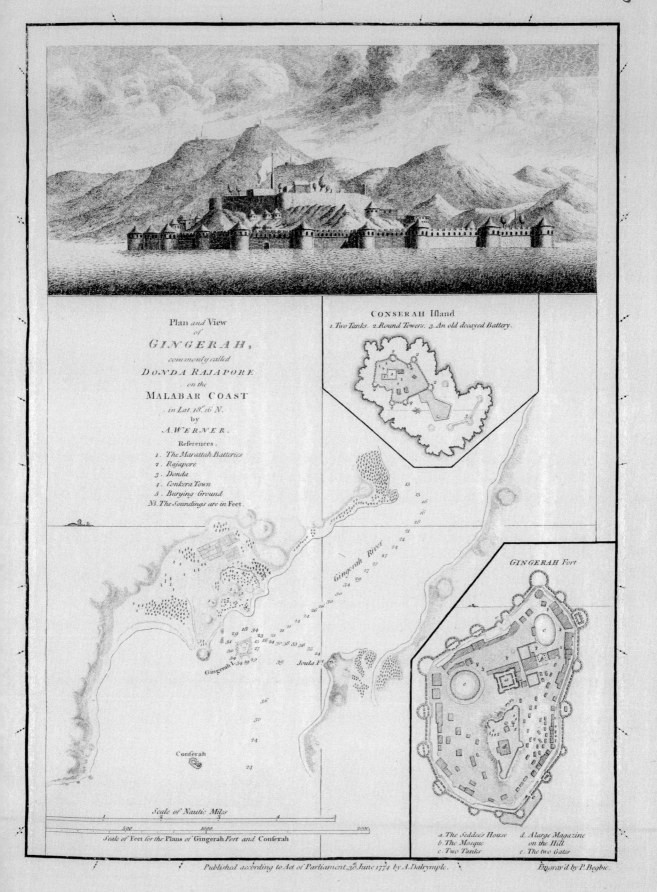

Plan *and* View
of
GINGERAH,
commonly called
DONDA RAJAPORE
on the
MALABAR COAST
in Lat. 18.° 16' N.
by
A. WERNER.

References.
1. *The Marattah Batteries*
2. *Rajapore*
3. *Donda*
4. *Conkera Town*
5. *Burying Ground*
N3. *The Soundings are in Feet.*

CONSERAH Island
1. *Two Tanks.* 2. *Round Towers.* 3. *An old decayed Battery.*

Gingerah River

GINGERAH Fort

Gingerah

Joula Pt

Conserah

Scale of Nautic Miles

Scale of Feet for the Plans of Gingerah Fort and Conserah

a. *The Seddee's House*
b. *The Mosque*
c. *Two Tanks*
d. *A large Magazine on the Hill*
e. *The two Gates*

Published according to Act of Parliament 30 June 1774 by A. Dalrymple. Engrav'd by P. Begbie.

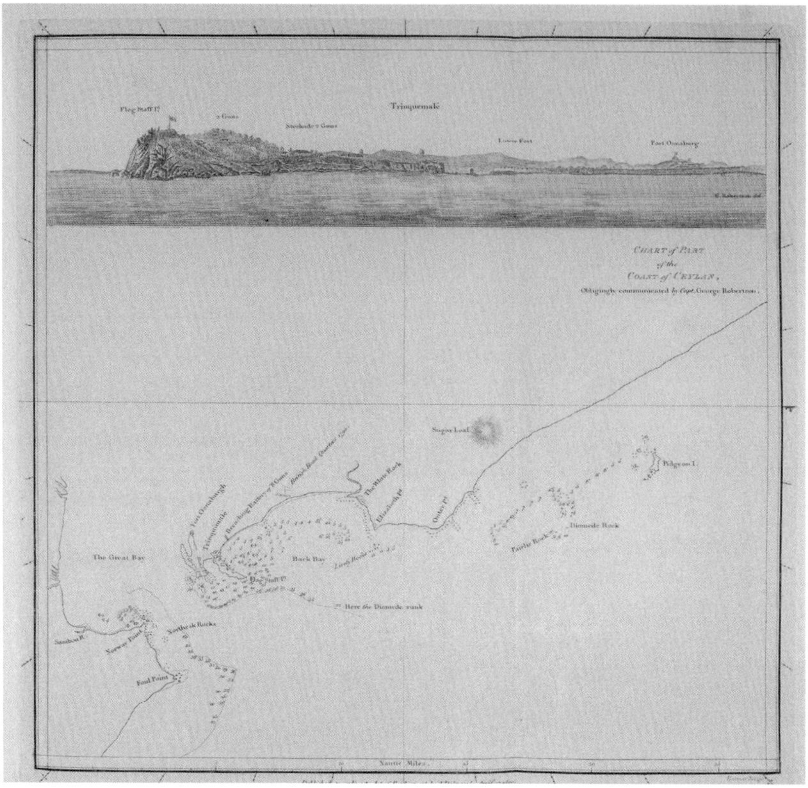

George Robertson,
*Chart of part of the
coast of Ceylan*,
writing by T. Harmar

situated on Rio de la Plata and rivers falling into it, 1807. The five 'volumes' are, in fact, wooden boxes, leather bound and embossed to look like folio volumes, which could be shelved as such in a library. The forty-six items contained therein all date from after 1779, when the cost of their production was borne by the East India Company. Most, but not all, are 'first editions'. Number 14 of 'volume 2' is of particular interest; it is the third edition, dated 1787, of a memoir of passages to and from China in June 1782, and contains the note 'only few copies originally printed, given by the Secret Committee of the East India Company for information of their China ships during the latter part of the war'. (The reference here is to the first Anglo-Maratha War of 1775–82, a conflict in India between the forces of the East India Company and the Maratha Empire.)

Space forbids a detailed examination of the collection at this point; in the 'volumes' of the accompanying plans and charts are views of coastlines, which would aid an officer on the quarterdeck of a Company ship to identify his landfall. Here are, for example, a view of the Fort at Gingerah on the Malabar Coast, a plan of the Vaubanesque citadel at Saigon from a French manuscript, and a 'View of the Harbour where the Swedish East India Company Ship *Calmar* wintered in 1745/6', with the vessel herself prominently depicted centre-stage.

Of especial interest in the Lampeter collection are the three volumes of *An Historical Collection of the Several Voyages and Discoveries in the South Pacific Ocean* which Dalrymple printed, it seems at his own expense, in 1770. On the flyleaf of volume one is a handwritten note to the effect that volume three contains accounts of voyages in the South <u>Atlantic</u> Ocean [original underlining] 'which is scarce'. This volume three contains a *Journal of Winds and Weather at the Falkland Islands 19 February 1766 – 19 January 1767*. Volume two is well illustrated with fascinating engravings, and is the subject of a separate discussion in this publication.

Very many of the memoirs and descriptions in this Phillips benefaction richly repay reading, and are of historical importance. There are, almost to pick at random, for example, *Directions for the Mouth of Rio de la Plata by the Hon Duncombe Playbell Bouverie, Captain of H.M.S. Medusa*,[3] and *Astronomical Observations of Captain Beaufort of H.M.S. Woolwich … in 1805*, and issued in 1808.[4] *Medusa* was a relatively new ship, a 32-gun frigate, launched in 1801, and suitable for this kind of survey, this one a valuable preparation for Sir Home Popham's (1762–1820) quixotic invasion of 1806–7, in support of the revolt against Spanish rule, and with a vaguely defined hope of expanding British trade and influence here. *Woolwich*, by contrast, was an elderly 5th-rate of 44 guns, effectively superannuated (she was finally wrecked in the West Indies in 1813) and realistically only suitable for the kind of 'observations' that Beaufort, of 'Beaufort scale' fame, was carrying out.[5] The Lampeter Dalrymple collection touches on British naval, colonial and mercantile history at many points.

John Morgan-Guy

1 Andrew S. Cook, *Alexander Dalrymple (1737–1808), Hydrographer to the East India Company and to the Admiralty as Publisher* (unpublished PhD thesis, University of St Andrews, 1993), vol. 1, p. 7.

2 Noble was the author of several works on exploration and navigation.

3 Bouverie (1780–1850) was the second son of the Earl of Radnor. A young man at the time of his survey, he ultimately rose to Flag rank.

4 Francis Beaufort (1774–1857) became ultimately, like Dalrymple, Hydrographer to the Navy. Dalrymple himself commended his work on the River Plate.

5 The Beaufort scale – a way of measuring wind force and speed – is still used in marine forecasts.

Sailing Round Cape Horn

Alexander Dalrymple, *An historical collection of the several voyages and discoveries in the South Pacific Ocean. Volume II, Containing the Dutch voyages* (London: Printed for the author; and sold by J. Nourse, T. Payne and P. Elmsly, 1771)

Among the volumes of charts, plans and memoirs assembled and published by Alexander Dalrymple which are now housed in the Roderic Bowen Library is one entitled *An Historical Collection of the Several Voyages and Discoveries in the South Pacific Ocean*. It is volume two of a series of three with that overall name, and, as its subtitle indicates, *Containing the Dutch Voyages*. It was printed for Dalrymple in 1771, and consists of 140 numbered pages, plus 'A Chronological Table of the Discoveries in the Southern Hemisphere and Pacific Ocean', 'Vocabulary of Languages in some of the islands visited by Le Maire and Schouten', and an index to the whole, in which the pages are unnumbered. The first sixty-four pages are taken up with 'The Voyage of James Le Mair and William Schouten, 1616' and the following fifty-five with 'The Voyage of Abel Jansan Tasman, 1642'. Both had been published before, an English translation of the former as early as 1619.

All three explorers and navigators named in this volume are men of considerable interest. 'James Le Mair' was, more accurately, Jacob Le Maire (*c.* 1585–1616), a Belgian mariner. He sailed in company with Willem Schouten (*c.* 1567–1625), a Dutch navigator, in 1615 and 1616, seeking a passage into the Pacific Ocean by a western route. This they accomplished by rounding Cape Horn at the southern tip of South America. It was Le Maire who named the cape – 'Hoorn' after his companion's birthplace in Holland. The entire voyage of exploration, visiting many of the south Pacific islands, was ultimately a circumnavigation of the globe, though only Schouten completed it, Le Maire dying on the return voyage.

The account in this volume is accompanied by three engraved illustrations. The first represents the 'inhabitants of Horne Island. Two kings meeting each other'; (Horn Island lies in the Torres Straits Islands archipelago). The second shows 'Horn Island Road. Vessel at Anchor in the river mouth, Union Bay'; and the third is a chart showing the relationship between what was then named Amsterdam Island and Rotterdam Island and the coast of New Zealand. The two former are bound together between pages 58 and 59, and the latter between pages 64 and 65. The two illustrations of Horn Island and its people are full of interest. They are 'narratives', in that they depict

TREASURES
The Special Collections of the
University of Wales Trinity Saint David

Representation of the inhabitants &c. of Horne Island

a number of activities being carried out simultaneously, thus bringing to life for the reader what Le Maire and Schouten saw and experienced during their stay.

The 1642 *Voyage of Abel Jansan Tasman* is similarly illustrated. Tasman (1603–59) was a Dutch merchant and seafarer. His 1642 voyage – and another of 1644 – were carried out under the auspices of the Dutch East India Company, and had as their underlying motive explorations for possible new sources of trade. Tasman is credited as being the first explorer to reach New Zealand (which would indicate that the chart associated with the Le Maire and Schouten voyage depicts a later stage of discovery than that they themselves made), and also Fiji and Van Dieman's Land (now known as Tasmania). In respect of the prospects for new avenues for trade the voyages were

The continent south of the rocky point; Staten Landt or the States Land south of the Rocky Point, engraved by J. Collyer

rather disappointing, but in expanding knowledge and understanding of the south Pacific they can be counted a success.

Dalrymple's 1771 edition contains six engraved illustrations. There are views from ships making landfall, of, for example, Three Kings' Island in 40 fathoms on the north-west side (opposite page 74), and The Island Amsterdam bearing east-north-east distant three miles (opposite page 75). Two of the illustrations are similar to those in the Le Maire and Schouten *Voyage*, being narrative depictions. The first of these is at Amsterdam Island, showing ships at anchor, native proas, fishing, local landscape and, prominently in the foreground, groups of male and female figures, intended to record appearance and clothing (between pages 80 and 81). The second, at Rotterdam Island, repeats the theme (between pages 82 and 83). Three of the six engravings are signed 'J. Collyer, sculpt.'. This is Joseph Collyer, ARA (1748–1827), a prominent and popular London engraver, perhaps best known for his engravings of portraits. Collyer's dates would suggest that the illustrations in this particular volume were commissioned by Dalrymple to accompany his reprinting of these Dutch voyages. They are, nonetheless, fascinating works of art, and certainly enhance the contents of this volume.

John Morgan-Guy

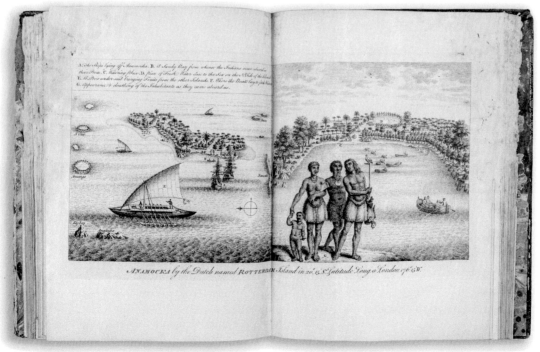

Anamocka by the Dutch named Rotterdam Island

An Artist of Prodigious Energy

Sydney Parkinson, *A journal of a voyage to the South Seas, in His Majesty's ship, the Endeavour. Faithfully transcribed from the papers of the late Sydney Parkinson, draughtsman to Joseph Banks, Esq. on his late expedition, with Dr. Solander, round the world. Embellished with views and designs, delineated by the author, and engraved by capital artists* (London: Printed by Stanfield Parkinson, the editor, 1773)

Sydney Parkinson was the artist for James Cook's first expedition, visiting Tahiti and then New Zealand and Australia.

Eighteenth-century astronomers realized it might be possible to calculate the distance between the earth and the sun through observing the transit of Venus – the passage of Venus across the disk of the sun. These transits occur in pairs every 120 years; they were predicted for June 1761 and June 1769. Hampered by the war between Britain and France, attempts to observe the first of these were unsuccessful. However, 1769 saw a major international scientific enterprise; 151 observers saw the transit from seventy-seven locations. Britain's contribution included mounting an expedition to the recently discovered South Pacific island of Tahiti, thought to be a key site for observation.

Sponsored by the Royal Society and the Admiralty, the party set sail on 25 August 1768. Its leader was Lieutenant James Cook (1728–79). The son of an agricultural labourer, Cook had worked on coal ships in the North Sea before joining the navy. He had spent time in North American waters and gained practical experience in surveying, astronomy and mathematics. His ship, the *Endeavour*, was a 336-ton Whitby collier, selected for its strength, shallow draught and storage capacity. The members of the crew included the astronomer Charles Green and the botanist Joseph Banks, with his assistants Daniel Carl Solander and Herman Diedrich Spöring, plus two artists Alexander Buchan and Sydney Parkinson.

Sydney Parkinson (d. 1771) was born in Edinburgh; the year of his birth is uncertain. His father Joel Parkinson was a Quaker brewer; Sydney was apprenticed to a woollen draper. However, he early on showed a talent as an artist of natural history subjects. It is possible he studied under William de la Cour, who had opened Britain's first publicly funded art school in Edinburgh. After the family moved to London, the Free Society of Artists exhibited some flower paintings by Parkinson in 1765/6. He also received

Sydney Parkinson, *The head of a chief of New Zealand*, 1773, engraved by T. Chambers

Plate XVI

The Head of a Chief of New-Zealand, the face curiously tataow'd, or mark'd, according to their Manner.

some commissions from Joseph Banks, who then recruited him to join the *Endeavour* as one of his private entourage. Parkinson was to be responsible for natural history drawings, Alexander Buchan for topography and for portraits. However, Buchan, an epileptic, died four days after the ship reached Tahiti. Parkinson's responsibilities were increased therefore, although he was helped by Herman Spöring, a competent amateur draughtsman.

The expedition reached Tahiti in mid-April 1769. There, at Matavai Bay, they built a fortified encampment, Fort Venus, 'to secure us against the natives'. However, they were able to establish good relations with leading islanders, including Tuteha, the chief of the area round the landing site, and Purea, a leading woman. As well as circumnavigating the coast of Tahiti, Cook mapped seventy-five other islands in the group, naming them the Society Islands.

The Admiralty had also commissioned Cook with a second set of orders. After he left Tahiti, he was to sail south, to the 40th parallel, and search for land. At that time, it was believed that there must be a major continent, 'Terra Australis Incognita', in the southern hemisphere; this was thought necessary to balance the landmasses in the north. However, Cook reached 40° south without sighting land; he therefore turned west to New Zealand. He sighted land on 7 October. Over the next five months, he surveyed the coast of both main islands of New Zealand, proving they were not part of any continent. He landed at six places on the North Island and two on the South Island, spending around seven weeks on shore.

Leaving New Zealand, the *Endeavour* sailed westwards, reaching the coast of eastern Australia in April 1770. Cook then sailed north in search of a harbour where he could take on supplies. Towards the end of the month, he landed at a place he named Botany Bay, after the great quantity of plants Banks and Solander collected. He then sailed north again; Cook took possession of the whole eastern coast for Britain, eventually naming it New South Wales. However, the *Endeavour* ran aground on the Great Barrier Reef, at a point Cook named Cape Tribulation.

Sydney Parkinson's activity was prodigious; often he stayed up all night drawing or writing in his journal. He made at least 1,300 drawings or sketches, often in rough seas and in cramped conditions. His output included 276 finished and 676 unfinished drawings of plants, 83 finished and 212 unfinished drawings of animals

TREASURES
The Special Collections of the
University of Wales Trinity Saint David

Sydney Parkinson, *Two of the natives of New Holland*, 1773, engraved by T. Chambers

Plate XXVII

Two of the Natives of New Holland, Advancing to Combat.

and possibly 100 or so drawings of people, scenery and boats. In May 1770, Banks noted in his diary, 'In 14 days just, one draughtsman has made 94 sketch drawings, so quick a hand has he acquir'd by use.'[1] Parkinson was the first European artist to visit Australasia, and therefore also the earliest to depict an authentic Australian landscape. He was one of the first to depict a kangaroo, an animal 'as large as a greyhound, of a mouse colour and very swift'. For New Zealand, his two heads of Maoris have become the visual archetypes of the Maori warrior.

Eventually Cook sailed for home, on his way stopping off in Batavia (the modern Jakarta) for repairs to the *Endeavour*. Sadly, Batavia was known as an unhealthy city; the canals built by the Dutch colonists acted as natural reservoirs of disease. The crew of the *Endeavour* was struck down by malaria and then dysentery. Those who perished included Parkinson; he died on 26 January 1771.

Parkinson's belongings, including his journal, were given to Banks to care for. As Banks had been Parkinson's employer, he believed it was his right to publish the papers. However, he lent a copy of the diary to Parkinson's mentally unstable brother, Stanfield, on condition that the family would not copy or publish anything. Stanfield, however, seeing the papers and drawings as his inheritance, decided to publish his brother's journal. John Hawkesworth, the editor of the official account, was forced to take out an injunction to delay this. In a compromise, Banks retained Parkinson's official papers but paid his executors £500 for the balance of his salary.

Stanfield published an edition of his brother's journal in 1773. It included a ghost-written preface scurrilously misrepresenting Banks. Banks's conduct was said to argue

> a high degree of insolence or avarice: possessed, as he was, of so large a collection of curiosities, as well as of my brother's drawings and designs, was it not covetous in him to desire also the little store bequeathed to me.

Horrified, a family friend, John Fothergill, bought up some 400 copies of the imprint.

TREASURES

The Special Collections of the
University of Wales Trinity Saint David

Sydney Parkinson, *View of an arched rock on the coast of New Zealand*, 1773, engraved by J. Newton

It is not clear whether Parkinson ever intended to publish his writings. His journal is a handsome piece of work nevertheless, containing twenty-seven engraved plates of Parkinson's drawings as well as a frontispiece portrait of him. Moreover, his prose is good enough to stand on its own merits, and he included much colourful detail omitted by others. He recorded a more extensive set of Tahitian and Maori customs and languages than any other writer of his time. His vocabularies of Tahitian, Maori, Malay and other languages occupy just over a quarter of the volume. Under the language of New Holland (Australia), he defines 'kangooroo' as 'the leaping quadruped'.

Having obtained the rights to the journal, Fothergill published a second edition in 1784, including a reply to the earlier preface. The Roderic Bowen Library holds a copy of the first edition, given by Thomas Phillips in 1844.

Ruth Gooding

1 Joseph Banks, *The Endeavour Journal of Joseph Banks* (Sydney: MS held in the Mitchell Library, State Library of New South Wales, *c.* 1771).

The Tradition of "Living" Anatomy

Jean-Nicolas Jadelot, *Cours complet d'anatomie* (Nancy: Jean-Baptiste-Hyacinthe LeClerc, 1773)

Cours complet d'anatomie, peint et gravé en couleurs naturelles by Arnauld Éloi Gautier D'Agoty, and explicated by Jean-Nicolas Jadelot (1738–93), was printed in folio at Nancy by Jean-Baptiste-Hyacinthe Leclerc, in 1773.[1] Nothing is known of the copy's custodial history before it was presented to the college in 1846 by Thomas Phillips (1760–1851), who was himself a surgeon and member of the London (later the Royal) College of Surgeons, having served an apprenticeship at Hay before becoming a pupil of anatomist and surgeon John Hunter.[2] Although there is no conclusive evidence that any of the books which Phillips sent to Lampeter had been in any sense in his personal possession, the subject matter of this one certainly resonates with his endowment of a chair of Natural Science in 1852.[3] The copy was professionally rebound in the twentieth century.

Despite the work's title, the presentation of anatomy is fundamentally myology, the study of the structure, arrangement and action of the muscles, with connecting tendons, ligaments and bones. Its author, Jean-Nicolas Jadelot, was Professor of Anatomy and Physiology at the University of Nancy. The French text consists of a 'Myology Tree' with descriptions of the muscles (sig. A^r–G^v, pp. 1–14). This is followed by thirteen numbered plates ('tables') III to XV (the two missing plates are those representing external anatomy in the figures of Apollo and Venus). The plates are keyed to explanations in French and Latin (sig. H^r–N^r, pp. 15–25). These striking illustrations are coloured mezzotint copperplate engravings on full-page tables, typically of a male subject. Mezzotint was the first tonal method to be used in printmaking, allowing shade to be produced in engravings composed of black to white tones without using line or dot-based techniques. The inventor of printing in colours from mezzotint plates was Jakob Christoph Le Blon (1667–1741). The plates in *Cours complet d'anatomie* were designed and engraved by Arnauld Éloi Gautier D'Agoty (1741–80?). Each plate is signed, in manuscript, 'A. E Gautier Dagoty. Pinxit. et. Sculp. Cum Priv. Regis', or similar, although Plan IX is signed 'A. E. Gautier Dagoty pinxit Cum Priv.' and 'L. Gautier Dagoty Sculp', which may indicate that the engraver of this plate was Louis Charles, a brother, who flourished about 1770.[4]

TREASURES

The Special Collections of the
University of Wales Trinity Saint David

Arnauld Éloi Gautier D'Agoty,
[Human body], 1773

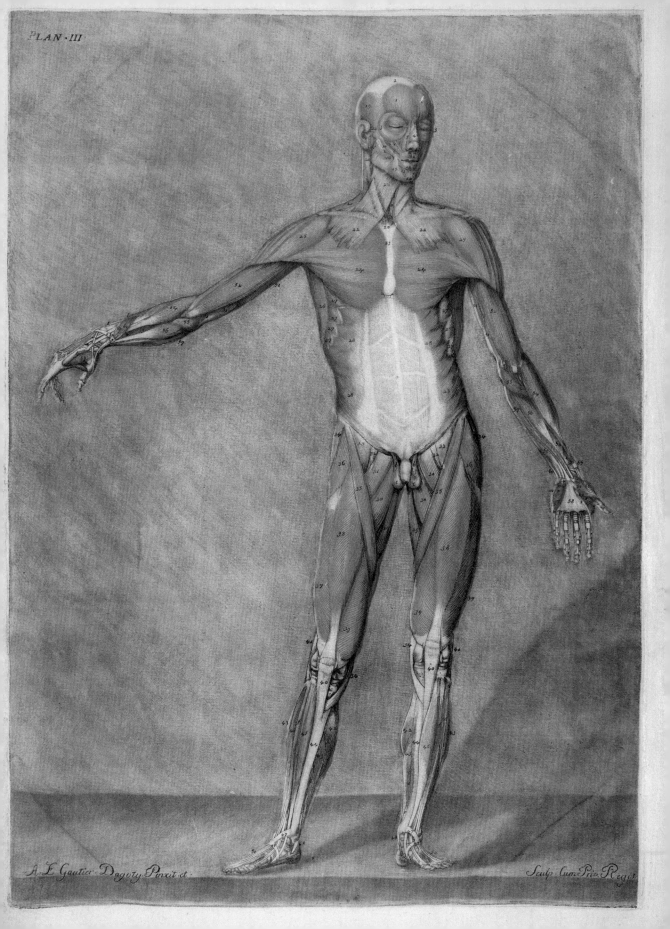

A. E. Gautier Dagoty Pinxit et.

Sculp. Cum Priu. Regis.

The artist's father was the famous artisan-entrepreneur Jacques-Fabien Gautier D'Agoty (1710?–81), who not only engraved but performed his own dissections,[5] though he also worked with specimens prepared by noted anatomist Jacques-François-Marie Duverney (1661–1748).[6] Around 1738, Jacques-Fabien Gautier D'Agoty joined the colour-printing workshop of Le Blon, though he soon quit, dissatisfied, clearly regarding himself as more than an assistant.[7] The process he learned was based on Newton's theory in *Opticks* (1704) that the whole gamut of tonic values is composed of the cardinal colours blue, yellow and red,[8] a theory, however, he would later attack.[9] The declared aim of the process is truth to the natural tones of colour, hence the '*en couleurs naturelles*' in the title of *Cours complet d'anatomie*. It involves engraving on a separate plate each part of the work which is to be printed in a separate cardinal colour, which by superimposition of impression should combine to give the composite result.[10] Since the time taken to engrave the plates, each printed separately in turn, allowing the sheets to dry between the processes, followed sometimes by a coat of varnish, was considerable, the plates were costly to produce and publish.[11] Le Blon secured a patent in England and the coveted *privilège exclusive du roi* for his method in Paris.[12] After his death, Jacques-Fabien Gautier D'Agoty acquired his privilege and claimed to have developed his process somewhat independently,[13] and to have added a fourth black plate to expedite the process, contrary to the underlying Newtonian theory, but in accord with his own theory that black and white are the primitive colours and that red, yellow and blue are secondaries. It seems that Le Blon himself may have introduced a black plate, but in a way that convinced Gautier D'Agoty that Le Blon did not understand the truth of the relationships between the colours.[14]

The need for a relatively inexpensive technique to create multiple copies of anatomical illustrations for medical students was recognized throughout Europe. The Gautier D'Agoty family workshop turned to developing this market, the addition of colour offering a method to distinguish muscles, veins and other parts.[15] Arnauld Éloi Gautier D'Agoty's *privilège du roi* appears in *Cours complet d'anatomie* (sig. *ᵛ). The style of his engravings is distinctively naturalistic, presenting anatomy as it might have appeared on a single dissection.[16] However, 'the kind of display used in naturalistic illustration relies heavily upon knowing how to read a series of conventions'.[17] Plan XI presents the anterior view of the head in four stages of dissection (figures 1, 2, 7 and 8). A shadow is cast on the background by each of the figures, and two (7 and 8) are wrapped in the cloths used during dissection to absorb blood. Counterbalancing realism, the écorchéd (flayed) full-body figures, like Plan III, are represented as in the living body. The

TREASURES

The Special Collections of the
University of Wales Trinity Saint David

Arnauld Éloi Gautier D'Agoty,
[Skulls], 1773

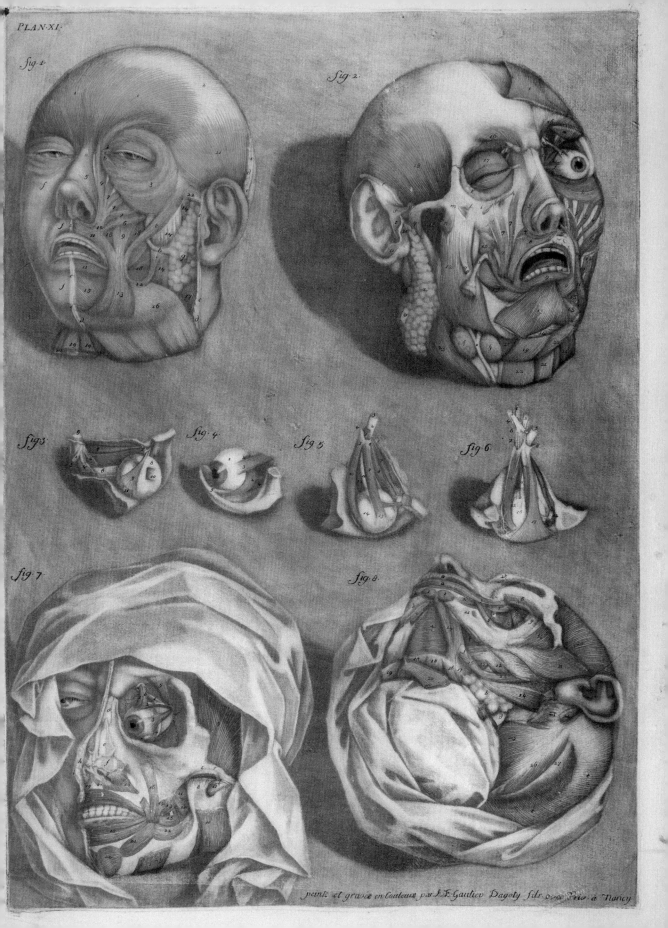

fig.1

fig.2

fig.3

fig.4

fig.5

fig.6

fig.7

fig.8

peinte et gravée en Couleurs par J.F. Gautier Dagoty fils avec Prio à Nancy

convention of 'living anatomy' began in the early sixteenth century when the description of structure was not separated from the description of function, and the anatomical order and purpose of the body derived from the soul which animated it.

Despite its rich potential, it is questionable whether coloured mezzotint engraving was ever satisfactory in practice.[18] Mezzotint is capable of a rich range of tone, but it may not be the art for imitative realism in colour.[19] Le Blon's *privilège* specifically noted the colour method's suitability for anatomical illustration,[20] but although colour can be used effectively for anatomical-teaching purposes, there is little natural variation in the colours of post-mortem tissues.[21] The technique moreover did not lend itself easily to the expression of fine detail, and according to Mimi Cazort et al., 'none of the Gautiers ever mastered the scraping and burnishing techniques necessary to bring out the sharp edges and details, techniques then reaching a state of perfection in England'.[22] So coloured engravings of this kind did not become popular for medical illustrations.

Peter Mitchell

1 A bibliographical description may be found in D. J. Culpin, *Catalogue des Ouvrages du Fonds Français, 1601–1850: conservés dans la 'Founders' Library', Université du Pays de Galles, Lampeter*, Introduction, notices et index rédigés par D. J. Culpin, avec la collaboration de Philippe Parker, avec un répertoire des incunables et des éditions du seizième siècle rédigé par Trevor Peach (Cardiff: University of Wales Press, 1996), p. 375.

2 D. T. W. Price, 'Thomas Phillips of Brunswick Square', in William Marx (ed.), *The Founders' Library, University of Wales, Lampeter, Bibliographical and Contextual Studies: Essays in Memory of Robin Rider, Trivium*, 29–30 (Lampeter: Trivium publications, 1997), p. 170.

3 D. T. W. Price, *A History of St David's University College, Lampeter. Volume One: to 1898* (Cardiff: University of Wales Press, 1977), pp. 88, 182.

4 Arthur M. Hind, *A History of Engraving & Etching from the 15th Century to the Year 1914: Being the Third and Fully Revised Edition of 'A Short History of Engraving and Etching'* (Boston, Massachusetts: Houghton Mifflin, 1923; reproduced New York: Dover, 1963), pp. 309 n. 3, 442.

5 *Bryan's Dictionary of Painters and Engravers*, new edition revised and enlarged under the supervision of George C. Williamson, 5 vols (Port Washington, New York: Kennikat Press,

TREASURES
The Special Collections of the
University of Wales Trinity Saint David

1964), II, p. 220; Sarah Lowengard, *The Creation of Color in 18th-Century Europe* (New York: Columbia University Press, 2007), Ch. 12; Deanna Petherbridge (ed.), *The Quick and the Dead: Artists and Anatomy* (London: The South Bank Centre, 1997), p. 88.

6   Mimi Cazort, Monique Kornell and Bruce Hugh Russell, 'Catalogue of Works', in M. Cazort, M. Kornell and K. B. Roberts, *The Ingenious Machine of Nature: Four Centuries of Art and Anatomy* (Ottawa: National Gallery of Canada, 1996), p. 228. The anatomist is incorrectly identified as Guichard Joseph Duverney, who died in 1730, in Petherbridge (ed.), *The Quick and the Dead*, p. 88, and in Philip Oldfield and Richard Landon, *Ars Medica: Medical Illustration Through the Ages* (Toronto: University of Toronto Press, 2006), p. 52.

7   Lowengard, *The Creation of Color in 18th-Century Europe*, Ch. 12.

8   Hind, *A History of Engraving & Etching from the 15th Century to the Year 1914*, p. 307.

9   Royal College of Surgeons, 'Jacques-Fabien Gautier D'Agoty – *Exposition anatomique des organs des sens*, 1775' *https://www.rcseng.ac.uk/library-and-publications/library/blog/jacques-fabien-gautier-dagoty-exposition/*

10   Hind, *A History of Engraving & Etching from the 15th Century to the Year 1914*, pp. 307, 310.

11   John L. Thornton and Carole Reeves, *Medical Book Illustration: A Short History* (Cambridge: The Oleander Press, 1983), p. 78.

12   S. T. Prideaux, *Aquatint Engraving: A Chapter in the History of Book Illustration* (London: W. and G. Foyle, 1968), p. 36.

13   Hind, *A History of Engraving & Etching from the 15th Century to the Year 1914*, p. 309.

14   Prideaux, *Aquatint Engraving*, p. 36; Thornton and Reeves, *Medical Book Illustration*, p. 78; Hind, *A History of Engraving & Etching from the 15th Century to the Year 1914*, p. 308; Lowengard, *The Creation of Color in 18th-Century Europe*, Ch. 12.

15   Lowengard, *The Creation of Color in 18th-Century Europe*, Ch. 12.

16   Carol Déry, 'Reading the Body: Materia Medica in the Founders' Library', in P. Mitchell (ed.), *The Nature and Culture of the Human Body: Lampeter Multidisciplinary Essays, Trivium*, 37 (Lampeter: Trivium publications, 2007), p. 106.

17   Martin Kemp, '"The mark of truth": Looking and Learning in Some Anatomical Illustrations from the Renaissance and Eighteenth Century', in W. F. Bynum and R. Porter (eds), *Medicine and the Five Senses* (Cambridge: Cambridge University Press, 1993), p. 87.

18   Prideaux, *Aquatint Engraving*, p. 37.

19   Hind, *A History of Engraving & Etching from the 15th Century to the Year 1914*, p. 310; Martin Kemp and Marina Wallace, *Spectacular Bodies: The Art and Science of the Human Body from Leonardo to Now* (Berkeley, California: University of California Press, 2000), p. 52.

20   Cazort, Kornell and Russell, 'Catalogue of Works', p. 226.

21   Thornton and Reeves, *Medical Book Illustration*, p. 78.

22   Cazort, Kornell and Russell, 'Catalogue of Works', p. 226.

A Jaunt to Dalmatia

Robert Adam, *Ruins of the Palace of the Emperor Diocletian at Spalatro in Dalmatia* **(s.l.: printed for the author, 1774)**

The architect and designer Robert Adam (1728–92) was a leading exponent of the Neoclassical style, taking inspiration from the 'classical' art and culture of ancient Greece and Rome.

Adam came from a family of Scottish architects; his father William and his brothers John and James were all members of that profession. Robert studied at Edinburgh University, before joining his father's office in 1746. Eight years later, in 1754, he set out on the Grand Tour, planning to educate himself in the art and architecture of the classical world. At this time, most architects were seen as on a par with builders and other tradesmen. In direct contrast, Adam hoped to be able to talk to his aristocratic patrons as a well-travelled, intellectual equal.

After spending some time in France, Adam reached Florence on 30 January 1755 and Rome on 24 February 1755. He remained conscious of his relatively low social standing, writing home, 'If I am known in Rome to be an Architect, if I am seen drawing or with a pencil in my hand, I cannot enter into genteel company.' Although he set himself to look and learn determinedly, his training was that of the talented dilettante rather than the professional artist. In Florence, he made the acquaintance of a French architect, Charles-Louis Clérisseau. Clérisseau acted as Adam's cicerone, serving as a combination of antiquarian guide and teacher of watercolour and draughtsmanship. Alongside this, Adam studied landscape design with Jean-Baptiste Lallemand and architectural composition with Laurent-Baptiste Dewez. He also became a close friend of the noted architect-engraver, Giambattista Piranesi. On 21 June 1755, Adam wrote:

> Piranesi who is I think the most extraordinary fellow I ever saw is become immensely intimate with me … and says that I have more genius for the true noble architecture than any Englishman ever was in Italy.

Adam also gathered a team of young draughtsmen to work on a number of grand antiquarian projects. He knew that archaeology was the way in which he could be noticed as an architect; if he could publish a handsomely presented antiquarian work, it would be 'a great puff, conducive to raising all at once one's name and character'. Lacking the time and money to visit Greece or the Middle East, Adam decided on a

TREASURES
The Special Collections of the
University of Wales Trinity Saint David

Charles-Louis Clérisseau,
View of the inside of the Temple of Jupiter, 1764, engraved by D. Cunego

'jaunt to Dalmatia' and to the Emperor Diocletian's palace at Spalatro (now Split). At this time, the site was undocumented and little known.

Diocletian had built his huge palace for his retirement from public life; it appears to have been completed around 305 CE. Originally, it formed a large rectangle with corner towers and high walls. In the centre was an arcaded courtyard or peristyle; the octagonal Temple of Jupiter, later to become Diocletian's own mausoleum, was situated to one side of this. However, such was the size of the palace (nine and a half acres) that the later town was built within it. Forced to flee from the Avars, the inhabitants of the town of Salona occupied the palace and made it into a fortified town. The original buildings were adapted and reused; the courtyards became a network of streets and the Temple of Jupiter a cathedral.

Accompanied by two draughtsmen, Adam and Clérisseau managed to make a reasonable survey in just five weeks in July and August 1757. The work was clearly done to a tight timescale. Furthermore, Adam was hindered by the Venetian authorities' suspicion that he was a spy, engaged in surveying the fortifications. Still, Clérisseau produced picturesque views, perspectives and topographical drawings of the townscape and main buildings. Presumably, the two draughtsmen made the measured drawings, which were to be a significant part of Adam's eventual publication. Sketches made on site would be worked up into finished drawings.

Adam returned to Britain in January 1758. However, it was to be seven years before his book was published. In Venice, Clérisseau supervised the engraving of the plates together with Adam's younger brother, James. (Bryant comments that the finished volume might well be credited to Clérisseau, rather than to Adam![1]) At this stage, many of the original compositions were edited; often this was adding groups of figures to give atmospheric effect. Then, proofs of the engravings had to be checked against either the original drawings or Adam's memory in London or that of Clérisseau in Venice. Eventually the copperplates were transported from Venice to the printers in London, where titles and key letters were added to them. Adam's cousin, the historian William Robertson, contributed the introduction in exchange for ten cases of claret. Adam himself wrote a commentary on the various plates.

Adam's main aim in publishing his volume appears to have been to enhance his reputation. He intended to impress potential clients with his scholarship, taste and ability to apply the lessons of the past. As an author of an archaeological book,

he was expected to produce a compromise, combining a scholarly work with a pictorial folio. In his publication, perspective scenes alternate with measured drawings of cornice mouldings and the bases of columns. Other plates give a sense of fallen majesty; local peasants are pictured cooking amongst the ruins or sprawling on broken columns. Sometimes, a feature or detail has been moved for effect. Alongside this, Adam attempted to reconstruct how the palace originally looked, as well as portraying what he saw.

The finished work contained sixty-one plates, forty-seven portraying views and fourteen plans, elevations and sections. Most plates are signed by their engravers, but not by Clérisseau. It appears that Adam wanted to imply but not state explicitly that he was responsible for the illustrations. Adam appears to have used a hierarchy of binding colours: royal owners received copies bound with red goatskin, blue leather was used for Knights of the Garter and Green for Knights of the Thistle. Copies for the ordinarily wealthy were bound in brown.

The volume was dedicated to George III. Maybe Adam thought (wrongly) that praising the king's architectural knowledge and taste would help to secure him a commission to design a new royal palace. The list of more than 500 subscribers was headed by Frederick the Great, King of Prussia (to whom Adam sent a copy).

By the time, *Ruins of the Palace of the Emperor Diocletian* was published, Adam was established at the head of his profession. He went on to create an instantly recognizable style, known by his own name.

The Roderic Bowen Library's copy of *Ruins of the Palace of the Emperor Diocletian* was donated by Thomas Phillips in 1845.

Ruth Gooding

1 Julius Bryant, *Robert Adam 1728–92: Architect of Genius* (London: English Heritage, 1992).

A Small Book with a Famous Owner

Arnaud Berquin, *L'ami de l'adolescence*, (Paris: Au Bureau de l'Ami des Enfants, 1784–5)

The Roderic Bowen Library holds three small volumes of French children's periodicals, one signed by Jane Austen and two by her sister Cassandra.

The author of the volumes was Arnaud Berquin (1747–91), an author of moral tales and one of the best-known children's writers of his day, in Britain as well as France. The son of a merchant, Berquin was born in Bordeaux and educated at the Jesuit college there. He moved to Paris around 1770. Although he never married, he related well to children.

Berquin launched his publication *L'Ami des enfans* in December 1782. Aimed at children under eleven, it was sold by subscription and published in twenty-four monthly instalments. He followed this with *L'Ami de l'adolescence* aimed at slightly older children; this ran from September 1784 to July 1785.

Berquin's writings were meant to be read by whole families as a shared experience; his playlets were to be performed by parents and children together as 'domestic festivals'. He mostly wrote short plays and stories in simple language, and with a concern for realism. The background is that of the prosperous middle classes. Leaving out references to mythology, legends and fairy tales, Berquin explained, 'they will here see only what occurs or may occur within the limits of their families.'[1] He also commented that his 'little dramas' were intended to bring children of both sexes together 'in order to produce that union and intimacy which we are so pleased to see subsist between brothers and sisters'.[2] He wrote about child characters and described relatively minor everyday events, the sort of things his young readers might already have encountered. He sought to encourage generosity, kindness to servants and to animals,

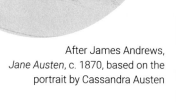

After James Andrews,
Jane Austen, c. 1870, based on the
portrait by Cassandra Austen

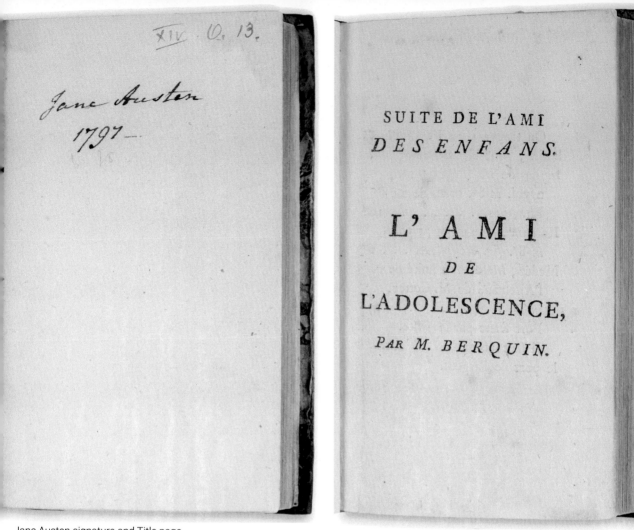

Jane Austen signature and Title page

charity to the poor and hard work. His characters' flaws are exposed and corrected; often they learn from experience. Influenced by Rousseau, his moral outlook was optimistic. He saw children as infinitely malleable as well as basically good; even the most difficult children could be changed. As they knew the difference between right and wrong once it was pointed out to them, there was no need to lecture them. This meant Berquin's formula pleased both parents and children. His works were also seen as providing a wholesome alternative to the crude, ribald and sometimes unorthodox material found in the chapbooks accessible to children and often read by semi-literate servants.

Berquin's work was quickly translated into English; *The Children's Friend* appeared from November 1783 onwards, with two numbers a month. Alongside this, a

French-language edition was published in London in 1783 and 1784, aiming to help British children learn French. The four volumes of the French language version sold for 10s., the English translation for 8s.. *The Friend of Youth,* the English translation of *L'ami de l'adolescence,* quickly followed. Maria Edgeworth commented that '*The Children's Friend* is to be found in every house where there are any children'.[3]

Jane Austen (1775–1817) could read French easily, although she never learned to speak it with any fluency. She is known to have owned several French-language numbers of Berquin's series. Her copies of *L'ami des enfans* seem to have been an eleventh birthday present from her aunt Philadelphia Hancock and Hancock's daughter Eliza. (Her marriage to a French aristocrat meant that Eliza was now Comtesse Eliza de Feuillide. Austen was to maintain her friendship until Eliza's death in 1813.) Eliza enjoyed private theatricals and may have been particularly interested in this aspect of Berquin. However, Austen too wrote playlets; Paula Byrne even suggests that Austen parodied Berquin's writings in her juvenile playlet *The Visit.*[4] Berquin's *Little Fiddler* portrays a social visit in which a young man is expelled from his family circle, owing to his rudeness to his sisters and her visitors. In contrast, in *The Visit,* Austen satirizes dining-room etiquette; her characters make pompous formal introductions to each other, but then discover there are not enough chairs to go round.

The Roderic Bowen Library holds three volumes of *L'ami de l'adolescence,* containing fourteen fortnightly parts, and previously owned by Jane Austen and her sister Cassandra. The third of these, containing the issues for 1785, is neatly signed 'Jane Austen 1797–' on the front free endpaper. It seems likely that Austen acquired this later therefore, when she was in her early twenties. We also hold two more volumes, composed of the issues for 1784. Cassandra has signed these Cass Elizth Austen. Jane Austen's bibliographer, David Gilson, suggested that they might also have belonged to Jane and that Cassandra signed them after her sister's early death.[5] Printed in small volumes to suit small hands, the three books measure only 130 × 90 mm. Each is bound in contemporary half calf with marbled boards.

These items come from the collection of David Salmon (1852–1944), the principal of Swansea Training College from 1892 to 1932. A bibliophile as well as an education-alist, Salmon collected books throughout his life.

Ruth Gooding

1 Richard De Ritter, 'From wild fictions to accurate observations: domesticating wonder in children's literature of the late eighteenth century', in A. O'Malley (ed.), *Literary Cultures and Eighteenth Century Childhoods* (London: Palgrave Macmillan, 2018).

2 Paula Byrne, *Jane Austen and the Theatre* (London: Hambledon Continuum, 2002).

3 Joyce Hemlow, 'Fanny Burney and the courtesy books', *PMLA*, 65/5 (1950), 732–61.

4 Byrne, *Jane Austen and the Theatre*.

5 David Gilson, *A Bibliography of Jane Austen* (Winchester: St. Paul's Bibliographies, 1977).

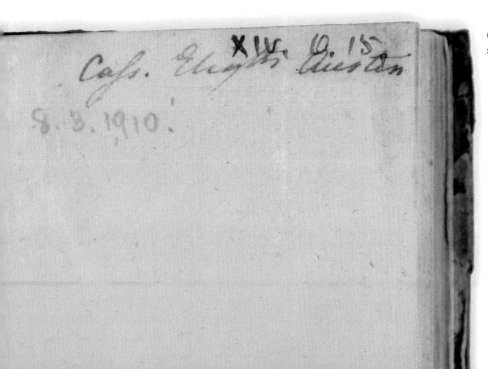

Cassandra Austen signature

Journal of a "First Fleet" Surgeon

John White, *Journal of a voyage to New South Wales with sixty-five plates of non descript animals, birds, lizards, serpents, curious cones of trees and other natural productions* **(London: Printed for J. Debrett, 1790)**

John White (1756?–1832) was chief surgeon of the expedition that established a convict settlement at Botany Bay.

White appears to have been born in County Fermanagh in central Ireland. He entered the navy on 26 June 1778, becoming third surgeon's mate on HMS *Wasp*. He received his diploma of the Company of Surgeons three years later. His naval service took him to India and the West Indies, before he became surgeon of the *Irresistible* in June 1786. Soon afterwards, he was selected as chief surgeon of the First Fleet expedition to establish a convict settlement in Botany Bay.

On 13 May 1787, eleven ships, under the command of Captain Arthur Phillip, set sail for the eastern coast of Australia. Almost 1,500 people were on board, just over half of them convicts. Many of these were in poor health due to their imprisonment and the resulting poor diet of salted goods. White arranged for fresh meat and vegetables to be issued for some time before sailing. On the ship, he ensured that attention was paid to sanitation and to the taking of regular exercise. In the event, only forty-eight people died on the eight-month voyage out. The ships sailed to Tenerife, then across the Atlantic to Rio de Janeiro and then back to Cape Town. They eventually crossed the Indian Ocean to reach New South Wales. They landed at Port Jackson in Botany Bay in January 1788, the middle of the southern summer. Governor Phillip erected a flagstaff at Sydney Cove on 26 January 1788 – the origins of Australia Day.

Once the fleet landed, White, as surgeon, built sick tents which were 'soon filled with patients afflicted with the true camp dysentery and the scurvy'. There was a shortage of medical supplies and an inadequate diet. White and one of his assistant surgeons, Denis Considen, were amateur naturalists and spent time searching the bush for edible plants. At the same time, they collected animal and plant specimens for study by British scientists. White was also able to accompany Phillip on explorations further inland.

Life in the new colony was harsh. The convicts, controlled by four companies of marines, were expected to become a self-sufficient community of peasant proprietors.

TREASURES
The Special Collections of the
University of Wales Trinity Saint David

Sarah Stone,
The white fulica, 1789

The White Fulica.

The First Fleet had carried with it livestock, seeds and seedlings, agricultural implements and enough food for two years. By April 1790 the weekly distribution was made up of only a kilogram of crumbling salt pork, a kilogram of rice alive with weevil and a kilogram of old flour. White described the country as being 'so forbidden and so hateful, as only to merit execrations and curses'. He was among those who offered to fish on alternate nights to supplement the rations. The Second Fleet arrived in 1790, bringing supplies with it; however, around 500 convicts who landed were either dying or seriously ill. White and his assistants were able to nurse more than half of them back to health. The Third Fleet landed in mid-1791. However, the situation started to ease. By the end of 1792, there were 600 hectares under crop, and thriving fruit and vegetable gardens.

White had started to write a journal when he left London in March 1787; he carried this on to 11 October 1788. Ford has described it as 'the vivid observations of a doctor whose work takes him among all sections of the community, and an enthusiastic naturalist dropped into a new world'.[1] During his voyage out, White commented on anything relating to public health. He reported the demise of several convicts, along with the causes of death: dropsy, 'lowness of spirits and debility', 'melancholy and long confinement' and so on. He described his treatment of those shipmates who were suffering scurvy, and commented on water rationing, 'People subject to long voyages should never be put to a short allowance of water.'

When he reached New South Wales, he described the local natural history, alongside writing about the new settlement. His observations included comments on the medicinal properties of local plants and trees. He discovered that gum from the eucalyptus trees was 'very serviceable' in treating dysentery and that native currants could cure scurvy. White also observed the lifestyle of the indigenous peoples. Ten months, after the First Fleet had landed, he sent his manuscript to Thomas Wilson, who prepared it for publication. His *Journal of a Voyage to New South Wales* was issued as a handsome quarto volume early in 1790. The title page contains a vignette of a scene from Port Jackson, taken from one of White's drawings. The book was lavishly illustrated with sixty-five copper engravings, mostly of the distinctive Australian flora and fauna. These illustrations were drawn in Britain from specimens White had sent home. There is a long appendix, describing zoological and botanical specimens, including the kangaroo. The descriptions were written by English specialists, including John Hunter. The book finishes with 'A diary of the winds, weather, temperature of the air,

A Kangaroo.

& c' on the voyage out. The volume was successful and later translated into French, Swedish and German.

White struggled with life in the newly established colony. In December 1792, he applied for leave to return to Britain. Eventually, his request was granted; he sailed home in the *Daedalus,* leaving New South Wales in December 1794. By this time, the colony was far healthier than it had been. However, White was reluctant to return to Australia; he resigned his appointment in August 1796. He spent three years serving in various ships and then became surgeon at Sheerness Navy Yard from 1799 until 1803 and at Chatham Yard from 1803 until 1820. He died at Worthing on 20 February 1832.

The Roderic Bowen Library's copy was given by Thomas Phillips in 1841. Phillips also worked in New South Wales, only a couple of years after White. He landed in Botany Bay in May 1796 to undertake a tour of duty as Inspector of Hospitals.

Ruth Gooding

1 E. Ford, 'Some early Australian medical publications', *Medical History,* 16/3 (1972), pp. 205–25.

William Blake and 'Night Thoughts'

Edward Young, *The complaint, and the consolation; or, Night thoughts,* illustrated by William Blake (London: Printed by R. Noble for R. Edwards, 1797)

The illustration of *The Complaint, and the Consolation; or, Night Thoughts* was the largest commercial project of William Blake's career.

Blake (1757–1827) had served an apprenticeship as an engraver, working under James Basire. Basire was engraver to the Royal Society and the Society of Antiquaries, so the young Blake was introduced to the intellectual life of London. He became a journeyman copy engraver, but alongside this began training as an original artist, enrolling as a student in the Royal Academy of Arts. He also adopted and adapted the technique of relief etching, meaning he could create words and images in a single process. He produced his first illuminated book, *Songs of Innocence*, in 1789. These illuminated books supplemented his work as an engraver. His main employer, Joseph Johnson, seems to have introduced him to some of England's leading liberal writers and artists.

In 1795, the publisher Richard Edwards engaged Blake to execute designs for a new four-volume, *de luxe*, large paper edition of Edward Young's *Night Thoughts*. This religious, meditative poem was comprised of almost 10,000 lines of blank verse divided into nine books or 'nights'. Ward has described it as an 'immensely popular and long-drawn-out rumination on life, death, and immortality'.[1] Written in reaction to personal loss, the speaker laments the loss of Lucia, Narcissa and Philander. These were loosely based on Young's dead wife, stepdaughter and son-in-law. The nocturnal speaker finds Christian consolation; increasingly the theme turns to theodicy (the study of why God permits evil), Christian apologetics and conversion. He frequently addresses Lorenzo, an apostate adversary. The poem includes the famous line, 'Procrastination is the thief of time'. In its day, it was enormously popular. It was originally published from 1742 to 1746.

Richard Edwards had in his possession Young's own copy of *Night Thoughts*, corrected by the author himself. Blake, a known radical, was an unlikely associate of the conservative Edwards. However, Bentley speculates that the two men may have known each other through one or more of Edwards's brother James, Blake's main commercial patron Joseph Johnson, and the painter Henry Fuseli.[2]

TREASURES
The Special Collections of the
University of Wales Trinity Saint David

24.

To man's false opticks, from his folly false,
* Time, in advance, behind him hides his wings,
And seems to creep decrepit with his age :
Behold him, when past by ; what then is seen,
But his broad pinions swifter than the winds ?
And all mankind, in contradiction strong,
Rueful—aghast—cry out on his career.

Leave to thy foes these errors, and these ills ;
To nature just, their cause and cure explore.
Not short Heaven's bounty, boundless our expence ;
No niggard nature ; men are prodigals :
We waste, not use our time ; we breathe, not live :
Time wasted is existence, used is life :
And bare existence, man, to live ordain'd,
Wrings and oppresses with enormous weight :
And why ? since time was given for use, not waste,
Enjoin'd to fly ; with tempest, tide, and stars
To keep his speed, nor ever wait for man :
Time's use was doom'd a pleasure ; waste, a pain ;
That man might feel his error, if unseen ;
And, feeling, fly to labour for his cure ;
Not, blund'ring, split on idleness for ease.
Life's cares are comforts, such by Heaven design'd ;
He that has none, must make them, or be wretched :
Cares are employments ; and without employ
The soul is on the rack ; the rack of rest,
To souls most adverse ; action all their joy.

Here, then, the riddle mark'd above, unfolds ;
Then time turns torment, when man turns a fool :
We rave, we wrestle with great nature's plan ;

At this time, there was a considerable market for lavish illustrated editions, with full-page illustrations and text on facing pages. Blake's work here was very different. Edwards provided him with pages of Whatman paper, approximately 420 × 325 mm. A window, slightly off-centre, had been cut from this; into this window, pages of the printed text of Young's poem were glued. Blake's images surround the printed text; text and design compete for the reader's eye far more obviously here than in other illustrated works. Often his designs dominate the page; his figures frequently take up an entire margin from top to bottom. Most of the preparatory work was done on the page itself, although Blake made a few preliminary sketches. When he had completed the figures, he applied watercolours and firmer outlines. The speed with which he worked, producing about five illustrations a week, meant he often translated Young's words in a highly literal way. Themes such as time and death were pictured as monstrous human figures. Blake seems already to have possessed a coherent system of artistic signs. He also tended to produce symmetrical pairs of illustrations; on a double-page spread they will be seen in combination or confrontation with each other. Ackroyd points out that the appearance of each page resembles that of Blake's previous illuminated books.[3] He worked for over two years on the project, creating 537 large watercolours. These were bound in two large volumes, each with a frontispiece. They were intended to serve as a basis for the selection of subjects to be engraved by Blake. Blake asked for a payment of 100 guineas for the watercolours. In the event, the fee was just 20gns or 9d for each design, although with the expectation of future payment for later engravings. Nevertheless, this was still a 'despicably low price!'.[4]

After this, the watercolours were examined to see which would be engraved. The text box was not quite central, so Blake needed to know whether a particular design would be on a recto or verso page. The text had to be carefully estimated to see where each page would end. In some cases, this 'casting off' failed; a few illustrations refer to lines on previous pages. The plates were outline engravings only, rather than the highly finished engravings used in some similar works. It would have been impossible for Blake to produce such engravings within the time available. The outline engravings would have been suitable for hand-colouring and Blake did indeed colour a number of copies.

Bindman comments that this work was Blake's first attempt to 'make illustrations act as a commentary that "corrects" the text'.[5] In some cases, Blake's designs depart

significantly from Young's ideas and attitudes. His views can be seen in the caricature picture of the 'author' and in occasional references to apocalypse. Several designs show the death of tyrants. Often the illustrations include the beginnings of ideas, seen afterwards in Blake's other works.

The publication was not a success and only the first of the four planned volumes was ever published. This comprised the first four nights of the poem and contained forty-three plates. (Blake had expected to make 107 more engravings for the later volumes.) Bindman[6] attributes the failure to the changed economic circumstances caused by the French War. The war had triggered inflation and a general calling in of credit, as well as cutting off the export trade in illustrated books. Edwards closed his business shortly afterwards, to become Head Registrar of (the Vice Admiralty Court of) Minorca. Blake's watercolours remained in the Edwards family for eighty years, before they were eventually transferred to the British Museum.

The Roderic Bowen Library's copy was given by Thomas Phillips in 1846.

Ruth Gooding

1 A. Ward, 'William Blake and his circle', in M. Eaves (ed.), *Cambridge Companion to William Blake* (Cambridge: Cambridge University Press, 2003), pp. 19–36.

2 G. E. Bentley, 'Richard Edwards, publisher of church-and-king pamphlets and of William Blake', *Studies in Bibliography*, 41 (1988), pp. 283–315.

3 Peter Ackroyd, *Blake* (London: Sinclair Stevenson, 1995).

4 Bentley, 'Richard Edwards', pp. 283–315.

5 D. Bindman, 'Blake as a painter', in M. Eaves (ed.), *Cambridge Companion to William Blake* (Cambridge: Cambridge University Press, 2003), pp. 85–109.

6 Bindman, 'Blake as a painter', pp. 85–109.

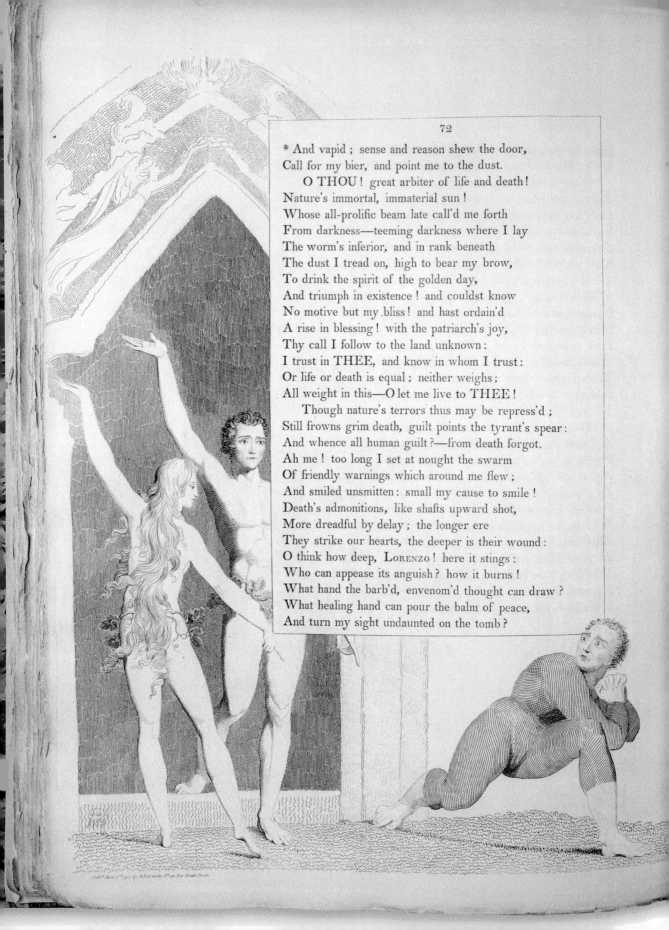

* And vapid ; sense and reason shew the door,
Call for my bier, and point me to the dust.
  O THOU ! great arbiter of life and death !
Nature's immortal, immaterial sun !
Whose all-prolific beam late call'd me forth
From darkness—teeming darkness where I lay
The worm's inferior, and in rank beneath
The dust I tread on, high to bear my brow,
To drink the spirit of the golden day,
And triumph in existence ! and couldst know
No motive but my bliss ! and hast ordain'd
A rise in blessing ! with the patriarch's joy,
Thy call I follow to the land unknown :
I trust in THEE, and know in whom I trust :
Or life or death is equal ; neither weighs ;
All weight in this—O let me live to THEE !
  Though nature's terrors thus may be repress'd ;
Still frowns grim death, guilt points the tyrant's spear :
And whence all human guilt ?—from death forgot.
Ah me ! too long I set at nought the swarm
Of friendly warnings which around me flew ;
And smiled unsmitten : small my cause to smile !
Death's admonitions, like shafts upward shot,
More dreadful by delay ; the longer ere
They strike our hearts, the deeper is their wound :
O think how deep, LORENZO ! here it stings :
Who can appease its anguish ? how it burns !
What hand the barb'd, envenom'd thought can draw ?
What healing hand can pour the balm of peace,
And turn my sight undaunted on the tomb ?

With joy—with grief, that healing hand I see;
Ah! too conspicuous! it is fix'd on high!
On high?—what means my phrensy? I blaspheme;
Alas! how low! how far beneath the skies—
The skies it form'd! and now it bleeds for me:
But bleeds the balm I want?—yet still it bleeds.
* Draw the dire steel?—ah no!—the dreadful blessing
What heart or can sustain, or dares forego?
There hangs all human hope!!! that nail supports
The falling universe!!! that gone, we drop!
Horror receives us, and the dismal wish
Creation had been smother'd in her birth:
Darkness his curtain! and his bed the dust!
When stars and sun are dust beneath his throne:
In heaven itself can such indulgence dwell?
O what a groan was there! a groan not his,
HE seized our dreadful right; the load sustain'd;
And heaved the mountain from a guilty world:
A thousand worlds so bought were bought too dear.
Sensations new, in angels bosoms rise;
Suspend their song, and make a pause in bliss.
 O for their song to reach my lofty theme!
Inspire me, night! with all thy tuneful spheres inspire,
Whilst I with seraphs share seraphic themes,
And shew to men the dignity of man;
Lest I blaspheme my subject with my song.
Shall pagan pages glow celestial flame,
And christian languish? on our hearts, not heads,
Falls the foul infamy: my heart! awake;
What can awake thee, unawaked by this?—

An Ambitious Plan Disappointed

Robert John Thornton, *A new illustration of the sexual system of Linnæus*, volumes 1–3 (London: Printed for the author by T. Bensley, 1799)

In *A New Illustration of the Sexual System of Linnæus*, Robert John Thornton hoped to produce a British botanical publication of sufficient magnificence to surpass all previous examples. The third volume, *Temple of Flora*, is one of the most celebrated flower books ever published.

Thornton (1767/8–1837) was the youngest child of the writer and humourist Bonnell Thornton and his wife Sylvia née Braithwaite. Bonnell died in 1768; Robert John may well have been born posthumously. He was an inquisitive child, interested in natural history from an early age. As a boy, he kept a small botanic garden containing wildflowers he had picked from the fields, also an aviary holding bats, birds of prey and an assortment of pigeons. He studied at Trinity College, Cambridge, originally intending to become a clergyman. However, while at university, he turned his attention to medicine and botany; he graduated as Bachelor of Medicine in 1793. As a student, he had been particularly influenced by Thomas Martyn's botanical lectures; in particular Martyn introduced him to Carl Linnæus's sexual system for plants.

Thornton spent several years travelling in Europe and then established himself as a physician in London in 1797. By this time, his mother and elder brother were dead, and he had inherited the family fortune. He used this to publish his lavish work, *A New Illustration of the Sexual System of Linnæus*. He stated his aim in his prospectus, 'to trace in as perspicacious a manner as possible the philosophical principles of botany from the earliest times up to the present period'. His completed book was to be comprised of three parts: a dissertation on the sexual reproductive cycle of plants, an explanation of Linnæus's plant classification system illustrated with botanical drawings and *The Temple of Flora*, containing large plates of exotic plant species. Thornton's text included poetry as well as scientific botany, and examined a range of political, religious, social and emotional issues. Thornton was a conservative and a royalist; he believed that the study of botany produced a love of order and proper feelings of awe for divine providence. In particular, the mathematical, logical character of taxonomy made it highly suitable for training the minds of the young, who were all too easily led astray by pastimes 'that inflame the passions'. He believed that the earth's botanical diversity gave strong support for the pursuit of free trade rather than military conquest and perpetual warfare. His model of peaceful civilization was that

TREASURES
The Special Collections of the
University of Wales Trinity Saint David

Philip Reinagle and Abraham Pether,
The night-blowing cereus, 1800,
engraved by R. Dunkarton

Martin Hoffman, *Linnæus in his Lapland dress,* 1805, engraved by R. Dunkarton

of Britain under its sovereign. Thornton dedicated the work to Queen Charlotte, the wife of George III and a 'bright example of conjugal fidelity and maternal tenderness'.

The illustrations in the first two volumes included portraits of eminent botanists, including Linnæus in Sami dress, and elaborate allegories, such as '*Cupid inspiring the plants to love*'. Volume two also includes botanical drawings. However, the third volume, *The Temple of Flora*, is a unique accomplishment, containing what Kemp describes as the most overtly dramatic illustrations in the history of botany.[1] Initially, Thornton had wanted more than seventy plates; in the event, thirty-one were produced. Thornton employed a variety of artists, selecting the plants, flower symbolism and background himself. By this means, he managed to maintain a remarkable homogeneity of style throughout. At least twenty-eight artists were involved, including Philip Reinagle, Abraham Pether and Andrew Henderson. Some of these were women, for instance Maria Cosway who painted the frontispiece depicting the goddess Flora. Thornton himself contributed the picture of the rose. Four separate techniques were used in the engraving of the plates: aquatint, mezzotint, stipple engraving and stippling with line engraving. The forty-three engravers included Richard Earlom, James Caldwall and Thomas Burke.

Each flower is shown against a background of scenery designed to represent its habitat. As Thornton commented, 'Each scenery is appropriated to the subject.' However, the settings are not always ecological; they play to the plants' aesthetic potential, their exotic origins, and their emotional and socio-political associations. The earliest plates to be finished depict the American aloe and the tulip. The aloe is shown against a landscape of mountains; the height and shape of the whole plant can be seen in the background. The tulip is placed in a Dutch setting of flat land and canals, with a windmill in the distance. Possibly the most famous illustration is that of the 'night-blowing cereus'. Reinagle's extravagant

Philip Reinagle, *Tulips,* 1798, engraved by R. Earlom

TREASURES

The Special Collections of the
University of Wales Trinity Saint David

depiction of the Jamaican flower almost fills the page. However, it is set against an incongruous moonlit landscape of church tower and 'dimpled river', painted by Abraham Pether. The plant could not possibly have flourished in this cold British setting! Thornton wrote the text to the plates, closing each part with some edifying lines of poetry. Most of the plants are exotic, newly imported from America, Africa or Asia. Thornton considered eight of the plates, including the illustrations of roses, tulips, hyacinths and snowdrops, to be of flowers native to Europe.

The printing of *A New Illustration of the Sexual System of Linnæus* was fraught with difficulties and its publication history is complex. It was issued in parts, first at a guinea and then at twenty-five shillings each. Although the plates were printed in colour, they were finished by hand. This means that each plate can be a different 'state' of that particular image. Every copy of the book is distinct therefore and it is impossible to tell if any set is complete. Eventually, Thornton was forced to abandon his project and the three volumes were issued in book form in 1807.

The exorbitant production costs combined with a shortage of subscribers ruined Thornton. The war with revolutionary France and the associated economic difficulties meant that it was not a good time to issue such a lavish publication. Thornton himself commented, 'The once *moderately* rich very justly now complain that they are exhausted through *taxes* laid on them to pay armed men to diffuse *rapine, fire,* and *murder,* over *civilised* EUROPE.' Alongside this, fashions were changing; in 1808, Sir Joseph Banks commented, 'I cannot say that botany continues to be as fashionable as it used to be.' Attempting to promote his work, Thornton exhibited the originals of his plates in 1804 at 49 New Bond Street. Then, in 1811, he launched a 'Botanical Lottery'. The top prize was to be his set of original paintings, 'paintings of the choicest Flowers, Allegorical Subjects, and Heads of Botanists, executed by the most eminent Painters'. However, Thornton failed to sell enough tickets. When he died in 1837, he left his family on the edge of poverty.

The Roderic Bowen Library's copies of the three volumes were given by Thomas Phillips in 1844 and 1850.

Ruth Gooding

1 M. Kemp, 'Thornton, Robert John (1767-1837)', in *Oxford Dictionary of National Biography* (Oxford: Oxford University Press, 2004).

Fruit of Fascinating Travel

William Alexander, *The costume of China, illustrated in forty-eight coloured engravings* (London: Published by William Miller, 1805)

By the late eighteenth century, Britain had become China's largest trading partner. The drinking of tea meant that China played a part in the lives of almost everyone in Britain. In 1786, Britain bought £1,300,000 worth of tea in Canton, (now Guangzhou). The upper and middle classes were used to purchasing luxury Chinese goods, including porcelain, silk, lacquer and wallpaper. Alongside this, British manufacturers were seeking in China a potential market for their range of new consumer products. However, they felt fettered by the system in which all maritime foreign trade was limited to Guangzhou. The guild of Chinese merchants, the Cohong, insisted that the British could only operate from suburban 'factories', using licensed boatmen and agents.

Plans were made to send an embassy to China, to carry George III's congratulations for the Qianlong emperor's eighty-third birthday. The party hoped to achieve a new era of diplomatic relations with the Qing court, and to introduce a new permanent ambassador in Guangzhou. In addition, they would appeal for more ports and markets to be opened to them and for trade restrictions and tariffs to be reduced.

Led by George, Viscount Macartney, and financed by the East India Company, the expedition set sail on 26 September 1792. Its members included George Staunton, John Barrow and the President of the Royal Society, Joseph Banks, along with a group of scientists and two doctors. However, the two interpreters, priests from the Collegium Sinicum in Naples, spoke Latin but no English. The only Briton who could speak Chinese was Macartney's page, twelve-year-old Thomas Staunton. William Alexander (1767–1816) was appointed junior draughtsman. He was one of the four children of a coachbuilder, Harry Alexander, from Maidstone. He had only recently graduated from the Royal Academy; it seems likely that he was recommended by the painter, J. C. Ibbetson. Alexander's visit to China was to provide inspiration for the rest of his career.

The embassy took ten months to reach China, going via South America. Ironically, its members spent less than three months in the interior of China. They reached the Bohai Sea in July 1793, where they disembarked at Tianjin. They then moved onto Chinese junks to sail north to Beijing. William Alexander commented of cruising up

TREASURES
The Special Collections of the
University of Wales Trinity Saint David

William Alexander,
A Chinese comedian, 1801

London Published Aug.t 13.th 1801, by G.a and W. Nicol Pallmall.

W. Alexander fec.t

William Alexander,
A group of trackers, 1797

the Pei-Ho River, 'the constant succession of new objects makes this mode of travelling the most novel & interesting that can be conceived.'[1] The group travelled by road for the last twenty miles to Beijing, using uncomfortable horse-drawn carts. They entered the city in procession on 21 August 1794, by now unwashed, tired and dishevelled. Macartney's valet, Æneas Anderson, later wrote, 'our cavalcade had nothing like the appearance of an embassy, from the first nation in Europe, passing through the most populous city in the world.'[2]

The audience was to take place not in the Forbidden City, but in the emperor's summer residence at Chengde in Manchuria, 120 miles to the north. William Alexander was among those left behind in Beijing, to set up the display of British 'gifts' to the emperor. He wrote:

> To have been within 50 miles of that stupendous monument of human labour, the famous Great Wall, and not to have seen that which might have been the boast of a man's grandson, as Dr Johnson has said, I have to regret forever. That the artists should be doomed to remain immured at Peking during the most interesting journey of the Embassy is not easily accounted for.[3]

However, Macartney's audience with the emperor was a failure. The Chinese saw the British embassy as similar to the regular tribute-bearing missions they received from neighbouring states. Macartney aimed to become accredited as an ambassador on equal terms with China. Furthermore, he refused to kowtow to the emperor, agreeing only to drop on one knee as he would to his own monarch. The emperor declared that there would be no British ambassador to China and that China had no

TREASURES
The Special Collections of the
University of Wales Trinity Saint David

need of British goods. Three months later, the British expedition set sail for home. Despite its lack of success diplomatically, it had gathered a great deal of information and did at least spark a renewal of British interest in China.

William Alexander had produced a vast number of sketches – in complete contrast to the official artist Thomas Hickey. Three folio volumes containing 870 of his drawings, in pencil, pen and ink, wash and watercolour, are now owned by the British Library. If necessary, Alexander used the sketches of other members of the embassy to record things he had missed. For the visit to the emperor's residence at Chengde, he worked from sketches drawn by Macartney's artillery officer, Lieutenant William Henry Parish. However, Alexander's best- known works at this time are his drawings of the return journey as he sailed south from Beijing. Recording scenes of ordinary life and ordinary people, he created a uniquely evocative portrait of China in the 1790s. He depicted the rivers and canals, captured views of towns, and produced studies of boats, architecture and people going about their daily life.

After he returned to Britain, Alexander used his drawings to produce finished paintings, exhibiting thirteen watercolours at the Royal Academy between 1795 and 1804. Alongside this, his illustrations were used for the official record, George Staunton's *An Authentic Account of an Embassy from the King of Great Britain to the Emperor of China,* (W. Bulmer and Co., 1797). Then, in 1805, Alexander brought out his own book, *The Costume of China* (William Miller), containing forty-eight aquatints alongside commentary on each illustration. He wrote these captions using a mixture of memory, diary entries and brief descriptions he had added to his original sketches. In some cases, he now combined figures and scenes from separate sketches.

For instance, in 'View of a burying-place', he depicted close together very different tombs found in north and south China. The finished illustration is a geographical impossibility!

Most of the plates were printed by George Nicol, who had also produced the plates for Staunton's book. The engravings are brilliantly coloured, skilfully reflecting the effect of the original watercolour. The later plates were engraved by William Miller; these have a softer line and a brownish tinge not found in Alexander's paintings.

Alexander's influence on the visual arts was significant. Frederick Crace used several images from *The Costume of China* in the decoration of the Brighton Royal Pavilion. For instance, Alexander's Chinese comedian can be found on the landing of the North Staircase and on the large chandelier in the Music Room. Designers of pottery at the Wedgwood factory used Alexander's images too.

In June 1808, the British Museum appointed Alexander assistant librarian and first keeper of prints and drawings. He died on 23 July 1816 at his uncle's house in Maidstone.

The Roderic Bowen Library's copy of *The Costume of China* was given by Thomas Phillips in 1846.

Ruth Gooding

William Alexander,
View of a castle, 1799

1 S. Sloboda, 'Picturing China. William Alexander and the visual language of Chinoiserie', *British Art Journal,* 9/2 (2008), pp. 28–36.

2 Æneas Anderson, *A Narrative of the British Embassy to China, in the Years 1792, 1793, and 1794; containing the various circumstances of the embassy, with accounts of customs and manners of the Chinese; and a description of the country, towns, cities, &c. &c.* (London: Printed by J. Debrett, 1795), p. 101.

3 Alice Rylance-Watson, *William Alexander Pictures China* (London: British Library, 2019). Retrieved 19 April 2021 from *www.bl.uk/picturing-places/articles/william-alexander-pictures-china.*

A Founding Father Makes a Fictional Appearance

Hannah More, *Cœlebs in search of a wife*, tenth edition (London: Printed for T. Cadell and W. Davies, 1809)

Hannah More (1745–1833) was a prolific writer, an advocate of women's education and a friend of Bishop Thomas Burgess, the founder of St David's College. She also has the dubious distinction of being one of the writers most admired in her own day, but least read in ours.

Hannah and her four sisters grew up in and around Bristol. Their father, Jacob More, was a schoolmaster. His daughters were educated to be able to earn their own living; eventually, they too ran their own school. However, after the breakdown of Hannah's six-year engagement to a local landowner, William Turner, she decided to devote herself to writing. Having accepted an annuity of £200 from Turner, she now had the means to visit London every year. She was quickly drawn into the celebrated bluestocking circle of literary women.

More was a much-published author of religious, moral and educational books, and of chapbook stories aimed at the lower classes. Described as a 'conservative Christian feminist', one of her central concerns was to do with the education of women. She believed that women had been short-changed by a trivial and superficial education system that left them poorly equipped to be effective wives or mothers. Criticizing the contemporary emphasis on accomplishments, she wrote to her friend Elizabeth Bouverie, 'Dancing and music fill up the whole of life, and every *Miss* of fashion has *three* dancing, and a still greater number of music masters.' Still seeing women as confined to the domestic realm, More wanted them to be educated as Christians. For her, the ideal woman possessed rational intelligence, modesty and chastity, and Christian commitment.

John Opie, *Hannah More* (1834), engraved by W. Finden, from W. Roberts, *Memoirs of the life and correspondence of Mrs Hannah More*

TREASURES
The Special Collections of the
University of Wales Trinity Saint David

CŒLEBS

IN SEARCH OF A WIFE.

COMPREHENDING

OBSERVATIONS

ON

DOMESTIC HABITS AND MANNERS, RELIGION
AND MORALS.

————————

For not to know at large of things remote
From use, obscure and subtle, but to know
That which before us lies in daily life,
Is the prime wisdom. *Milton.*

————————

THE TENTH EDITION.

IN TWO VOLUMES.

VOL. I.

LONDON :

PRINTED FOR T. CADELL AND W. DAVIES,
IN THE STRAND.

1809.

Cœlebs in Search of a Wife, (T. Cadell and W. Davies, 1808) was More's only novel. She aimed it at 'the subscribers to the circulating library' as an alternative to the standard romantic novels, 'to raise the tone of that mart of mischief and to counteract its corruptions'.[1]

Unusually, the plot features the hero rather than the heroine's search for a partner. The story is narrated by Charles (Cœlebs or celibate), a twenty-three-year-old bachelor, said to have been based on More's close friend and fellow Bristolian, John Scandrett Harford. Harford was later to donate the land for St David's College, Lampeter.

Charles's ideal wife resembles Milton's Eve in her character and embodies his dead mother's views of a proper Christian education. In addition, these opinions exactly mirror More's own:

> For my own part I call education, not that which smothers a woman with accom-plishments, but that which tends to consolidate a firm and regular system of character; that which tends to form a friend, a companion, and a wife.

The first twelve chapters describe Charles's visits to London, and his encounters with a range of fashionable women and their daughters. More based the character of Lady Melbury, the 'acknowledged queen of beauty and of ton' on Georgiana Cavendish, the recently deceased duchess of Devonshire. She is described as 'warm-hearted, feeling, liberal on the one hand; on the other, vain, sentimental, romantic, extravagantly addicted to dissipation and expence'. In contrast, Lady Bab Lawless 'knew by instinct when a younger son was in the room, and by a petrifying look checked his most distant approaches'. Having failed to find a wife in London, Charles visits Mr Stanley, a close friend of his late father. Stanley's eldest daughter, the eighteen-year-old Lucilla, is hard-working, practical and unselfish. She is a Sunday School teacher, a good household manager, active in caring for the poor, and, like More, a keen gardener. She is also a good scholar, having learned Latin. The novel ends with Charles and Lucilla's engagement, as they contemplate the 'rational scene of felicity' to come with their marriage. Thus, More presents her view of the ideal, companionate marriage.

Cœlebs was first published in December 1808 in two octavo volumes. Like most of More's books, it was originally anonymous. However, her writing style and opinions

were too well known for her identity to remain hidden for very long. The critical reception was mixed. *The Edinburgh Review* commented:

> Events there are none; and scarcely a character of any interest. The book is intended to convey religious advice; and no more labour appears to have been bestowed upon the story, than was merely sufficient to throw it out of the dry, didactic form.[2]

Cabinet wrote of More 'endeavouring to turn the tea-table into the communion-table … endeavouring to turn every person into a polemic, and every thing into religion'.[3] However, *Cœlebs* became a bestseller. The first edition was out of print after only a few days; ten more impressions were sold in the first six months. More received £2,000 in profits in the first year; in contrast, Jane Austen earned only £150 for *Sense and Sensibility* (published in 1811). The Roderic Bowen Library holds a copy of the tenth edition, issued in 1809 and previously owned by Thomas Burgess.

More was an early supporter of St David's College. She commented:

> I hardly know so pressing a cause. There will, unavoidably, to save credit, be mixed with it a little too much High Church, but we must be glad to do something if we cannot do all that is wanted.

An early list of benefactors, dated 1810, lists More's donation of £10, noting that it was her fourth gift. The University's archives include a letter to Thomas Burgess written on behalf of More by her friend Mary Roberts. She mentions her subscription of £4 for the college, as well as a donation of £2 for the Literary Society. More also bequeathed £400 to the Exhibition Fund; this provided an open scholarship, bearing her name, of £12 a year.

Ruth Gooding

1 William Roberts, *Memoirs of the Life and Correspondence of Mrs Hannah More*, 2nd edition (London: R. Seeley and W. Burnside, 1834).

2 Francis Jeffrey (ed.), 'ART. XI. Cœlebs in Search of a Wife; comprehending Observations on Domestic Habits and Manners, Religion and Morals', *The Edinburgh Review*, 14/27 (1809), pp. 145–51.

3 Anon. 'Cœlebs in Search of a Wife, comprehending Observations on Domestic Habits and Manners, Religion and Morals', *Cabinet*, 4/1 (1809), pp. 347–55.

Hazard Warnings Offshore

John Smeaton, *A Narrative of the Building and a Description of the Construction of the Edystone Lighthouse with Stone: to which is subjoined, an appendix, giving some account of the Spurn Point, built upon a sand,* second edition (London: Printed by T. Davison . . . for Longman, Hurst, Rees, Orme, and Brown, 1813)

Although lighthouses are one of the oldest forms of technology, it was only in the seventeenth century that European countries started to construct them in earnest. At that time, the city of Plymouth was becoming increasingly important, due to American trade as well as the foundation of the naval dockyard. However, the Eddystone rocks, fourteen miles south-south-west of the city, were hazardous for ships. The reef is made up of three jagged and inclined ridges of red gneiss; the rock extends a considerable distance under water. Enormous seas break on the west; swell from the south throws up spray over thirty metres.

In 1664, two Plymouth merchants petitioned the lighthouse authority, Trinity House, to build a light there. However, Trinity House pointed out that no one had yet built an offshore light. Still, requests continued to come. Eventually, Henry Winstanley, an engraver and inventor, accepted the challenge, possibly because one of his own ships had already been lost there. Work began in June 1696, only for it to be destroyed a year later by a French privateer. However, the project was completed in 1700, with an overall height of around thirty-five metres. Waterhouse[1] has described it as 'a fantastic erection, largely composed of wood bound with iron straps, the stonework of the base being bound with copper or iron'. It survived only three years, before it was swept away in a violent storm on 26 November 1703. Winstanley died with his creation; he had gone to the tower to supervise some repairs. John Smeaton later suggested that one of the reasons for his failure was his inadequate knowledge of cements.

The second lighthouse was designed by a silk merchant, John Rudyerd, between 1708 and 1709. Again, it was constructed of wood with granite ballast. It was thought that timber would move under the action of the waves rather than resisting it. This time the tower stood for forty-seven years; however, on 2 December 1755, the roof of the lantern caught fire. The conflagration continued for five days; the tower was completely destroyed.

TREASURES

The Special Collections of the
University of Wales Trinity Saint David

John Smeaton, *South elevation of Winstanley's lighthouse, upon the Edystone rock*, 1762, engraved by H. Roberts

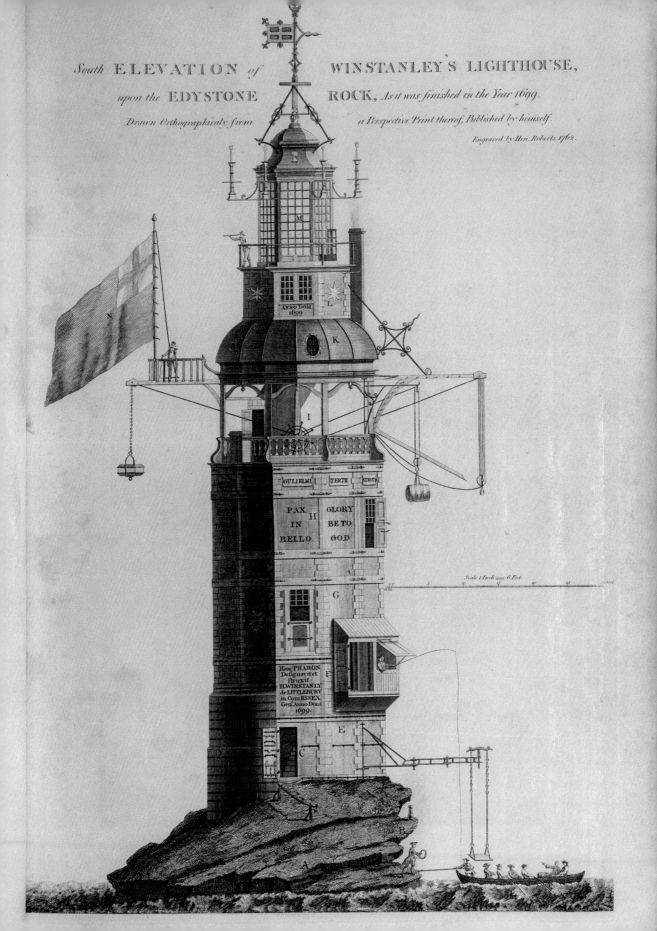

South ELEVATION of WINSTANLEY'S LIGHTHOUSE,
upon the EDYSTONE ROCK, As it was finished in the Year 1699.
Drawn Orthographicaly from a Perspective Print thereof, Published by himself.

Engraved by Hen. Roberts. 1762.

South ELEVATION *of the* STONE LIGHTHOUSE *completed upon the* EDYSTONE *in* 1759.

Shewing the Prospect of the nearest Land, as it appears from the Rocks in a clear calm Day.

Engraved in the Year 1763, by M.ʳ Edw.ᵈ Rooker, The figures by M.ʳ Sam. Wale.

The third, and most successful, lighthouse was the work of John Smeaton, eventually to be remembered as the father of civil engineering. Smeaton (1724–92) was the Yorkshire-born son of an attorney, William Smeaton, and his wife Mary. Having chosen not to follow his father into the law, he set up as a maker of scientific instruments. He developed a practical interest in the workings of machines, including water and windmills.

After the second Eddystone lighthouse burned down, its proprietor, Robert Weston, asked the President of the Royal Society, the Earl of Macclesfield, to recommend someone to design its successor. John Smeaton was appointed in February 1756. The task was demanding and the work hard. Building work could only go on during the summer months; winter was used for preparation of the masonry. Unlike his predecessors, Smeaton decided to use a structure entirely of masonry. This would be more durable, with a reduced risk of fire. The stone exposed to the sea was to be of Cornish granite, the interior works of Portland limestone. Characteristically, Smeaton spent many hours researching the nature of hydraulic limes, that would set under water. For the joints, he used a lime/pozzolana mortar of his own invention.

He based his tower on the shape of an English oak tree, with a large heavy base and a curved pillar above. The centre of gravity was low and the tapering shape provided stability and reduced wind loads. He also worked out a unique system of stone dove-tailing. The masonry was so interlocked that it was impossible to remove any stone once set, except in the reverse sequence to that in which it was laid. The outer surface was to be as smooth as possible in order to deflect the waves.

The upper part of the almost twenty-two-metre-high structure contained four floors for the lighthouse keepers and for stores. Smeaton knew that Sir Christopher Wren had used chains to resist the thrust of the dome of St Paul's Cathedral. Using this idea, he set an iron chain into a groove in the outer wall of each floor level. He then poured molten lead over the chain.

The work was finished in the summer of 1759; the octagonal iron lantern with a copper cupola roof was fitted that September. Skempton[2] points out that it was the prototype of all subsequent masonry lighthouses built in the open sea.

John Smeaton and Samuel Wale,
South elevation of the stone lighthouse
completed upon the Edystone in 1759,
1763, engraved by E. Rooker

Trinity House asked Smeaton to write an account of the building of the lighthouse, 'so that in the event of the destruction of the present edifice, they could discover the errors and imperfections'. The first edition was published thirty-five years later in 1791. In his preface Smeaton commented, 'that to write a book, tolerably well, is not a light or an easy matter ... In truth I have found much more difficulty in writing, than I did in building'. He described the construction of the two earlier Eddystone lighthouses, before offering a detailed account of his own work. He used the form of a log book, still a highly important type of document for engineers.

The finished book is a magnificent elephant folio (580 × 390 mm); Smeaton wanted to avoid the prints being spoilt as 'representative pictures' by being folded. The twenty-three plates include charts, a series of plans and perspectives of the rock, and the lighthouse with details of its construction. A plate of 'original ideas, hints, & sketches' includes a drawing of Smeaton's inspiration, the oak tree.

The volume was dedicated to George III. However, initially, only a small number of copies were printed. As Smeaton pointed out, 'the greatest real praise of the edifice, being that nothing has happened to it, nothing has occurred to keep the talk of it alive'. However, Smeaton had been unnecessarily self-deprecating; the first print run was inadequate and a second printing appeared in 1793, the year after his death. The Roderic Bowen Library holds a copy of the second edition, published in 1813; it was donated by Thomas Phillips in 1846.

In 1818, the Scottish lighthouse keeper, Robert Stephenson, reported that the lack of strength of the rock beneath might endanger the Eddystone lighthouse. Remedial work was carried out in 1838, but by the 1870s, cracks were appearing in the rocks. Smeaton's 120-year-old tower needed to be replaced. The top half was dismantled, and rebuilt on Plymouth Hoe as a monument to its builder. The base still remains on Eddystone rock.

Ruth Gooding

1 Paul Waterhouse and Mike Chrimes, 'Winstanley, Henry (bap. 1644, d. 1703)', in *Oxford Dictionary of National Biography* (Oxford: Oxford University Press, 2005).

2 A. W. Skempton, 'Smeaton, John (1724–1792)', *Oxford Dictionary of National Biography.* (Oxford: Oxford University Press, 2013).

TREASURES
The Special Collections of the
University of Wales Trinity Saint David

John Smeaton, *Original ideas, hints, & sketches, from whence the form of the present building was taken,* 1786, engraved by J. Record

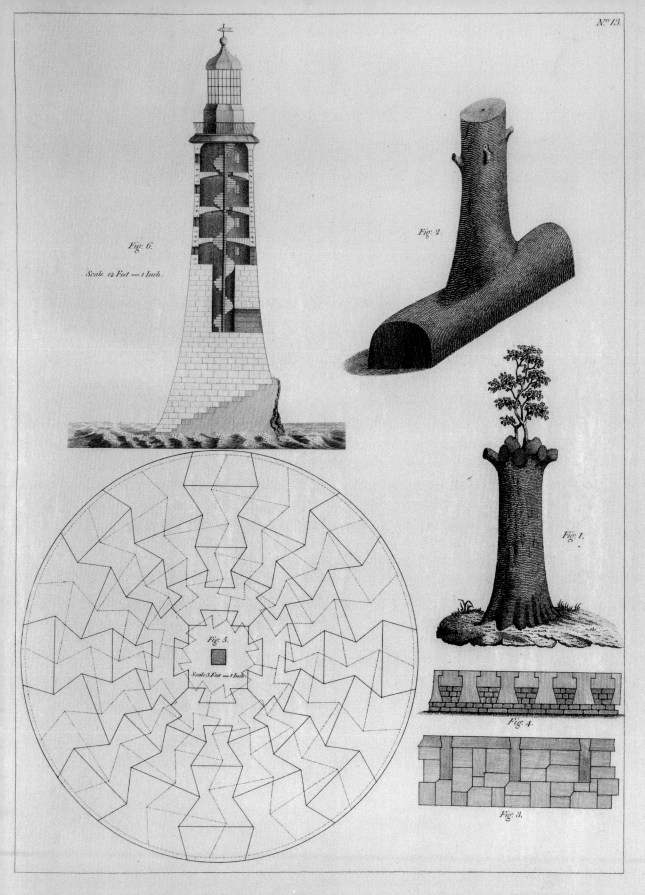

Fig. 6.

Scale 12 Feet = 1 Inch.

Fig. 2.

Fig. 1.

Fig. 5.

Scale 3 Feet = 1 Inch.

Fig. 4.

Fig. 3.

Original IDEAS, HINTS, & SKETCHES, *from whence the* FORM *of the* PRESENT BUILDING *was taken.*

An Entertaining Account of Travel in the Homeland

Edward Pugh, *Cambria depicta: a tour through North Wales, illustrated with picturesque views by a native artist* (London: Printed by W. Clowes for E. Williams, 1816)

Edward Pugh's *Cambria depicta* was the most entertaining travel account of the Wales of its day.

Pugh (bap. 1763, d. 1813) was born in Ruthin; his father, David, was a barber. Little is known of Edward's early life. Despite his lowly origins, he was well educated, probably at Ruthin grammar school. He was evidently taught in English; although he grew up speaking Welsh, he was unable to write it.

Nothing is known of how Pugh came to train as an artist. However, by 1793, he was exhibiting his work; between 1793 and 1808, he exhibited twenty-three pictures, mostly miniature portraits of Welsh gentry, at the Royal Academy. In 1794, Pugh published a set of aquatints after his own drawings, advertizing them as *Six Views, in Denbighshire.* He attempted to draw attention away from the dramatic landscapes of Snowdonia to the gentler scenes in Llangollen and Clwyd. Pugh also contributed topographical and architectural illustrations to London publications, including Henry Wigstead's *Remarks on a Tour to North and South Wales* (1799) and Richard Phillips's *Modern London* (1805). He probably spent most of his time in London, spending summers in Ruthin and working for a few weeks most years in Chester.

Pugh's magnum opus, *Cambria depicta,* arose from a conversation at the Shakespeare Gallery in Pall Mall with the publisher of prints, John Boydell. Pugh wrote in his preface:

> Mr Boydell lamented that the landscape painters, whom he had employed in Wales, confined the efforts of their pencils to the neighbourhood of Snowdon: thus multiplying copies upon copies of the same sketches, and frustrating the worthy Alderman's intention of publishing a just series of Welsh views. This practice they defended on the ground of the difficulty in which a stranger, unacquainted with the language or the country, involved himself, the moment that he quitted the high roads, and plunged into the intricacies of the mountains.

TREASURES
The Special Collections of the
University of Wales Trinity Saint David

Edward Pugh, *The perilous situation of Robert Roberts*, 1814, engraved by T. Cartwright

THE PERILOUS SITUATION OF ROBERT ROBERTS.

Edward Pugh, *Bishop's throne Anglesey*, 1813, engraved by T. Cartwright

Boydell suggested that it would be helpful to publish a small volume of direction, written by a Welsh person with local knowledge.

Although the conversation probably happened around 1800, Pugh did not start on his task until spring 1804. Over the next nine years, he walked all over north Wales, writing the substantial text and providing original drawings for seventy-two aquatints. He set out from Ruthin, accompanied by his dog, Miss Wowski, and carrying only a light knapsack, an umbrella and a small portfolio attached to his shoulder by a broad piece of tape. His whole tour must have been around 850 miles, almost all undertaken as a pedestrian. Starting at Chester and finishing at Shrewsbury, he went as far west as Nefyn on the Llŷn Peninsula and as far south as Llanidloes.

John Barrell describes *Cambria depicta* as 'long, beautifully written, amusing, and informative', and 'by some way the best of the numerous tours of Wales written around 1800'.[1] It was also very different from those that had gone before. It was

TREASURES

The Special Collections of the
University of Wales Trinity Saint David

the only tour not to be written by a member of the gentry and the only one to be written by a Welsh-speaker able to talk to the people he met. Pugh himself pointed to his 'knowledge of the ancient British language' and his 'intimacy with my native country and its inhabitants, their economy, customs, and character'. Peter Lord has pointed out that Pugh's voice was touched by a democratic spirit, quite unlike that of the other native Welsh travel writer, Thomas Pennant.[2] As well as describing Welsh history and topography, Pugh entertained his readers with interesting incidents, gossip and his own distinctive opinions. Barrell comments that much of what is best about the book is a direct result of his inability to afford the post-chaise that would have elevated him above the people he met.[3] Pugh spent time talking to the local inhabitants, rich and poor, and appreciating their many kindnesses. At this time, Britain was at war with France; there was some suspicion of strangers, particularly when monoglot Welsh-speakers were unable to recognize the English language. Occasionally Pugh pretended to be unable to speak Welsh so he could hear what people thought about him. However, Pugh was concerned to vindicate the character and behaviour 'of the different classes of the ancient Britons'. He also expressed his hopes for the improvement of contemporary Welsh culture, for instance suggesting the establishment of a national academy.

The illustrations were mainly of places off the beaten track, which had not previously been depicted in books. Pugh explained, 'I have abandoned the common practice of giving portraits of towns, castles, &c., which have been so often repeated that they now fill every portfolio.' Only about 20 per cent of the images feature the mountain scenery of the north-west. Like Alfred Hitchcock, Pugh was fond of appearing in his own pictures; however, he is always found in the middle distance. Mostly, the drawings

Edward Pugh, *Nant Francon*, 1813, engraved by T. Cartwright

Pugh provided were *en grisaille*. The majority of the aquatints were then made by Thomas Cartwright, although he sometimes called in others to help. However, Barrell[4] comments that he finds it hard to admire these aquatints as much as he would like. Although the scenes were well chosen and the composition sometimes extremely well managed, some of the aquatints lost much of the detail and texture of Pugh's drawings. Unfortunately, too, the coloured plates tend to have something 'off-key' and can sometimes be somewhat garish. The first of the two colourists also made the weather perpetually sunny. Pugh's drawing shows Nant Francon during heavy rain; the colourist adapted the image to portray a beautiful summer day!

Sadly, only five weeks after finishing his manuscript, Pugh died of a paralytic stroke in Ruthin in 1813. *Cambria depicta* was published posthumously by Evan Williams, the leading Welsh publisher in London, in 1816. As well as being lavishly illustrated, it was a costly quarto publication; Williams evidently wanted to maximize his profits.

Edward Pugh, *Llangollen,* 1813, engraved by E. Williams

The Roderic Bowen Library's copy of *Cambria depicta* was given by Thomas Phillips in 1847. In addition, the National Library of Wales holds a bound volume, containing most of the watercolour drawings Pugh made in preparation for it.

Ruth Gooding

1 John Barrell, 'Edward Pugh in modern London', *London Journal,* 37/3 (2012), pp. 174–95.

2 Peter Lord, *The Visual Culture of Wales: Imaging the Nation* (Cardiff: University of Wales Press, 2000).

3 John Barrell, *Edward Pugh of Ruthin 1763–1813: 'A Native Artist'* (Cardiff: University of Wales Press, 2013).

4 Barrell, *Edward Pugh of Ruthin.*

Illustrating the Arctic

John Ross, *A voyage of discovery made under the orders of the Admiralty, in His Majesty's Ships Isabella and Alexander, for the purpose of exploring Baffin's Bay, and inquiring into the probability of a North-West passage* (London: John Murray, 1819)

The Northwest Passage is a 900-mile sea route, lying off the northern coast of Canada and connecting the Atlantic with the Pacific. From the sixteenth century onwards, it was hoped this might provide a commercially practicable passage to China and the Far East.

After the end of the Napoleonic wars, Britain was left with a large navy, able to be used for exploration in general and for scientific surveying in particular. John Barrow, the permanent secretary of the Treasury, was an enthusiastic advocate of Arctic exploration. Furthermore, weather conditions appeared to be changing. In 1817, William Scoresby Junior, a scientifically curious whaling captain, reported that he had found the sea free of ice as far north as 80° north. Somehow, Barrow was able to gain approval for a pair of Arctic expeditions; these embarked in 1818.

In the first of these expeditions, Captain David Buchan and Lieutenant John Franklin were to sail north past Svalbard and on towards the Bering Strait and the Pacific. The second, more promising enterprise, was to be led by Commander John Ross, with Lieutenant William Edward Parry as second-in-command. They were to search for a Northwest Passage through the Davis Strait, the sea passage separating Greenland from Baffin Island. It was hoped their two ships would sail round the north-eastern point of the continent of North America, head for Bering Strait and eventually enter the Pacific. Little of the Canadian archipelago had yet been mapped.

Ross (1777–1856) was the fourth son of a Scottish clergyman, Andrew Ross, and his wife Elizabeth. He joined the navy in 1786, aged only nine. He gradually rose through the ranks to midshipman, then lieutenant and eventually commander. He was said to have been wounded thirteen times and confined in a French prison three times. Now he had charge of the *Isabella*, a 385-ton whaling ship hired for the voyage. The second ship, under Parry's leadership, was the *Alexander*. The two vessels were well equipped. They were strengthened to be able to force their way through ice; they were furnished with whatever was needed to survive Arctic winters; they contained

Henry Parkins Hoppner, *Kallie, a woman of Greenland*, 1819, engraved by D. Havell

a collection of the latest scientific instruments. The crew included an astronomer, Captain Edward Sabine, who was to determine latitude and longitude, to measure the direction and intensity of the earth's magnetism and gravity, to make careful observations and to assist in natural history. A Greenland Inuk, John Sackheouse, was to act as interpreter. Two future well-known explorers were present: John Franklin and Ross's nephew, the eighteen-year-old James Clark Ross. The ships set sail for Greenland in April 1818. On their way there, they were able to disprove the existence of the sunken land of Buss.

Early in the seventeenth century, William Baffin had discovered three large sounds, leading from northern Baffin Bay. Ross was to explore these inlets, hoping to find a passage. Ross first examined Smith Sound, naming the two capes on either side of its entrance after his ships. However, he wrongly concluded that the inlet was closed off by land to the north. He therefore went on to Jones Sound; he decided this was only a small bay enclosed by mountains and made no attempt to explore it. At the end of August, he sailed about fifty miles into Lancaster Sound. It was here that he made a mistake that was to haunt him for the rest of his life. On 30 August, at about four o'clock in the morning, Ross thought he saw a ridge of high mountains across the bottom of the inlet. He wrote:

> The land which I then saw was a high ridge of mountains, extending directly across the bottom of the inlet. This chain appeared extremely high in the centre, and those towards the north had, at times, the appearance of islands, being insulated by the fog at their bases.

Then at three in the afternoon, he again observed what appeared to be mountains to the west.

John Ross, *A bear plunging into the sea*, 1819, engraved by R. Havell & Son

He named the mountains Croker's mountains, after John Wilson Croker, the first secretary of the Admiralty. Against the wishes of his junior officers, he decided to turn back. Having been deceived by a bank of ice fog or an optical illusion of some sort, he had given up his only chance of finding the Northwest Passage. On his way south, he passed Cumberland Strait, which he thought offered a better opportunity of a passage. However, as it was already October, he did not investigate it. He arrived back in Britain in the middle of November 1818, having at least mapped several new islands and corrected some errors on earlier maps.

Initially, Ross's account was accepted and he was quickly promoted to the rank of captain. However, John Barrow, the moving spirit behind Arctic exploration, was furious that the attempt to find the 'open polar sea' had failed. He felt Ross had turned round 'at the very moment which afforded the brightest prospect of success'.[1] William Edward Parry believed that Lancaster Sound was an open strait. Edward Sabine

John Sackheouse, *First communication with the natives of Prince Regent's Bay,* 1819

claimed that Ross was the only person to have seen the Croker mountains, and that he had misrepresented some scientific results of the voyage.

Early in 1819, Ross issued his official account of the expedition. In the introduction, he listed the ships' officers, as well as giving details of their equipment and crew. However, the greater part of the book consists of his journals. He commented, 'I have here attempted nothing beyond the journal of a seaman.' Following the standard practice, the book was published by John Murray, the 'Official Publisher to the Admiralty', in an expensive quarto format. Even before it was published, Barrow wrote a long and scathing commentary on it in *The Quarterly Review.* He commented of Ross:

> he knows no more, in fact, than he might have known by staying at home; and however invidious it may seem, we cannot but contrast the indifference and want of perseverance on the present occasion with that of former navigators sent on voyages of discovery.[2]

However, Ross had produced a beautiful book, containing what are still among the most striking and attractive illustrations of the Arctic. There are thirty-two engraved plates, maps and charts, including fifteen aquatints engraved by Havell and Son. Ross himself was responsible for many of the sketches and coloured drawings, including

TREASURES

The Special Collections of the
University of Wales Trinity Saint David

that featuring the Croker mountains. One illustration, showing the first meeting between the explorers and the Inuits at Prince Regent's Bay, is based on the work of John Sackheouse, the interpreter. This is thought to be the earliest representational work by a native American artist to be so reproduced. Not surprisingly, Ross's book was expensive: the 1,250 copies sold for three and a half guineas each. The Roderic Bowen Library's copy was donated by Thomas Phillips in 1846.

In 1819, Parry returned to Lancaster Sound, leading another more successful Admiralty expedition. Ross never again worked for the Admiralty. In 1830, he made a second exploration to the Arctic, this time in a steamboat, sponsored by the gin magnate, Felix Booth. In his last journey to northern Canada, made when he was already in his seventies, he went in search of the doomed expedition led by Sir John Franklin.

Ruth Gooding

John Ross, *Cape Byam Martin, Possession Mount, and Cape Fanshawe*, 1819, engraved by D. Havell

1 John Barrow, 'ART. XI. A voyage of discovery, made under the order of the Admiralty, in His Majesty's Ships Isabella and Alexander, for the purpose of exploring Baffin's Bay, and inquiring into the probability of a North-west Passage', *The Quarterly Review*, 21/41 (1819), 213–62.

2 Ibid.

Beauty in Meticulous Detail

John Frederick Lewis, *Lewis's sketches and drawings of the Alhambra, made during a residence in Granada in the years 1833–4*, drawn on stone by J. D. Harding, R. J. Lane, W. Gauci & John F. Lewis (London: Hodgson, Boys & Graves, 1835)

John Frederick Lewis painted some of the most beautiful images ever created of the Alhambra.

Lewis (1804–76) came from an artistic family; he was taught to paint by his father, the distinguished engraver Frederick Christian Lewis. John Frederick was later to be nicknamed 'Spanish Lewis', to distinguish him from his brothers Frederick Christian (Indian Lewis), and Charles George (Swiss Lewis). He developed a friendship with the Landseers and, like Edwin Landseer, his early works were almost entirely focused on animal life. His first exhibited work was *A donkey's head*, displayed at the British Institution in 1820. From 1827 onwards, his main medium was watercolour. The same year he visited the continent of Europe, visiting Belgium, Switzerland and Italy. Gradually genre scenes began to replace animals as his main focus; travel to picturesque sites became the basis of his work.

At this time, Spain was a fashionable destination, considered exotic or even mysterious by the English. Travellers were keen to visit lesser-known cultures, and Spain, with its fusion of Arabian and Gothic customs, was particularly appealing. She was seen as a 'gateway' to the Orient. The Scottish artist David Wilkie travelled to Spain in 1827; he became a 'father figure' to many others who travelled in his footsteps.

Lewis toured Spain from mid-1832 to 1834. The trip was to be the start of a twenty-year exploration of the picturesque and exotic in Europe and the Middle East. He had some commissions from young ladies' albums and from booksellers for an illustrated edition of Byron. (Byron's *Childe Harold* and *Don Juan* had sparked an interest in all things Spanish.) After copying Old Masters at the Prado in Madrid, Lewis journeyed south to Andalusia. He spent time in Seville with the writer and Hispanicist Richard Ford and his wife Harriet. He corresponded with his fellow artist David Roberts, who was also visiting Spain. At around this time, interest in the Alhambra was reviving due to romantic writings, including Washington Irving's *Tales of the Alhambra*. In the guest book, Lewis's signature can be found on 20 October 1832. In a letter to David Roberts, he wrote:

TREASURES
The Special Collections of the
University of Wales Trinity Saint David

John Frederick Lewis, *Entrance to the Baños,* 1835, engraved by J. D. Harding

ENTRANCE TO
THE BAÑOS

I trust you may meet with the same satisfaction and delight I did in the short time I stayed there … To be in the Alhambra, under any circumstances, to you will be everything. I regretted then, for the first time in my life, that I did not draw architecture, and almost intended to commence … I wish much to see it again.

This was his first contact with the remains of a Muslim culture and with the 'gossamer perforated fabric' of Islamic architecture. The experience strongly influenced the remainder of his career. From April to September 1833, he lived with the Fords in the Casa Sánchez –now known as the Torre de las Damas – in the Partal of the Alhambra. David Ford was a skilful amateur illustrator and it is possible that his work on the Alhambra influenced Lewis.

Although Lewis exhibited numerous watercolours, the chief results of the tour were two volumes of lithographs, *Lewis's Sketches and Drawings of the Alhambra* (1835) and *Lewis's Sketches of Spain and Spanish Character* (1836).

Lewis's watercolours of the Alhambra were his first real attempt at depicting architecture to any great extent. Unlike his contemporaries, James Cavanah Murphy and David Roberts, he chose not to exaggerate the scale of the architecture. However, his scenes of the interior capture brilliantly the palace's intricate designs. It seems Lewis recognized the Alhambra's ability to inspire awe even in its more intimate spaces. He does include and even exaggerates the architecture's picturesque deterioration. In his illustration of the Courtyard of the Mexuar, large portions of the façade have been lost, showing the brickwork beneath. In the same picture, Lewis paints a pile of rubble and a door that has fallen off its hinges. He also emphasizes the irregularity of the rooflines and balustrades; these appear to have settled and buckled over time. Figures occupy a more significant place in his work than in some images of the Alhambra. He includes a number of colourful types – peasants, monks, nuns, Spanish ladies and occasionally turbaned Moorish figures. Attempting to demonstrate the character and flavour of Spain, Lewis also tends towards stereotypes. A number of images depict idleness or inactivity; several prints contain possible beggars. Lewis is anxious to emphasize the decline of the once glorious Muslim palaces; far from cherishing the historical monuments, the Spanish seem wholly unaware of their significance.

Lewis's Spanish pictures were painted in meticulous detail, using a minute stippling technique. This fastidious method anticipates the Pre-Raphaelites of the middle of

the century. However, Lewis's work does not have the same theatrical intensity and he paints standard, smiling figures rather than irregular individuals.

Lewis's Sketches and Drawings of the Alhambra consists of twenty-six prints; it includes no text, other than the dedication to the Duke of Wellington. The printer was C. J. Hullmandel, one of the main pioneers of lithography in Britain. Some of the plates were lithographed by Lewis himself; the others are by J. D. Harding, R. J. Lane and W. Gauci. The images are *c.* 280 × 380 mm.

Lewis's exposure to the Islamic architecture of Granada influenced him profoundly for the rest of his life. Later, he lived for ten years in Egypt, establishing a reputation as England's chief oriental artist. His sketches of bazaars, mosques, monuments, streets, interiors and people provided his basic imagery for the remainder of his

career. Eventually, he turned from watercolour to oil painting, attributing this to the better remuneration of the latter. He died at his home in Walton-on-Thames in August 1876.

The Roderic Bowen Library's copy was given by Thomas Phillips in 1846.

Ruth Gooding

John Frederick Lewis,
Patio de la Mesquita, 1835

The Age of Steam

John C. Bourne, *Drawings of the London and Birmingham railway, by John C. Bourne, with a historical and descriptive account by John Britton F.S.A.* **(London: Published by the proprietor J. C. Bourne . . . Ackermann and Co. 1839)**

The London and Birmingham Railway was Britain's first major rail line, as well as the initial long-distance line from the capital. The Stockton and Darlington railway, the earliest to carry both passengers and freight, had opened in 1825. Eight years later, the bill for the London and Birmingham Railway went through Parliament at the second attempt, despite the opposition of many of the relevant landowners. It was to run 112 miles from Euston to Curzon Street Station, where it linked up with the Grand Junction Railway and through that with the Liverpool to Manchester line. The chief engineer was Robert Stephenson (1803–59).

Nothing comparable had been attempted before. Stephenson's railway pioneer father, George Stephenson, believed that the ruling gradient of the new line should be no steeper than 1 in 330. However, the route went through a series of ranges of hills and intervening low ground. More than 20,000 navvies built a series of long and deep cuttings, for instance at Tring and Roade, as well as several long tunnels – Primrose Hill, Watford and Kilsby – interspersed by long and high embankments.

These navvies carried out extraordinary feats of strength and endurance, with minimal mechanization. Although they were paid relatively well, their food and lodgings were poor and they worked for up to sixteen hours a day. Furthermore, their job was dangerous; at Watford, for instance, ten men were killed when one of the shafts collapsed.

The first section of the new line came into use in July 1837. On 17 September 1838, the railway was formally opened; the final cost was £5,500,000 – an average of £50,000 a mile. The fastest trains took five and a half hours to complete the journey – compared to about eleven hours by road.

A young artist, John Cooke Bourne (1814–96) began to make a series of drawings of the construction of the railway, originally without any idea of publication. His pictures were intended merely as 'subjects of professional study, as scenes and compositions replete with picturesque effect and artistic character'. However, Bourne's work came

TREASURES
The Special Collections of the
University of Wales Trinity Saint David

John Cooke Bourne, *Entrance to locomotive engine house Camden Town; Primrose Hill tunnel*, 1839

ENTRANCE TO LOCOMOTIVE ENGINE HOUSE CAMDEN TOWN

PRIMROSE HILL TUNNEL

London. Published 1839, by the Proprietor J.C.Bourne, 19, Lambs Conduit Street and Ackermann & C? Strand

Printed by C.Hullmandel

to the attention of the writer, publisher and antiquary John Britton (1771–1857). Britton saw the possibility of a commercial publication, which could also present the railway in a favourable light. He wrote to Richard Creed, secretary of the line:

> Fully aware that we have jealous and fastidious critics to deal with, both in the houses of parliament, & out of them, I wish to remove, or at least to check, the tide of prejudice against us, & display our powers, capabilities, & efforts.

Bourne produced over fifty magnificent wash drawings, selecting thirty-six of these for publication. Although he is thought to have had no previous experience of the technique, he worked his drawings into a series of lithographs with notable success. The drawings were originally published in four parts at a cost of £1 1s. each, with the first instalment appearing in September 1838. The third and fourth sections, published together in July 1839, were accompanied by Britton's topographical and descriptive account. The Roderic Bowen Library holds the final two portions, donated by Thomas Phillips in 1847, whose home in Brunswick Square was within walking distance or a short carriage-ride from the London terminus. Later in 1839, the components were issued in a single volume, entitled *Drawings of the London and Birmingham Railway*. Its size, price and content meant it was intended mainly for the gentleman's library.

Bourne's illustrations were intended to 'gratify both the lover of the picturesque and the man of science'. He brought a trained artist's appreciation of classical composition, combined with a draughtsman's accuracy, to the subject of railways.[1] He gradually traced the route of the new track, recording its construction in intricate detail. The title page depicts the departure shed at Euston; the last illustration shows Curzon Street Station in Birmingham. Bourne emphasized engineering works: embankments, cuttings, tunnels and viaducts. Some of these are depicted in construction, others in finished form. Matt Thompson comments that Bourne gives a first-hand impression of what it would have been like to experience the first flush of railway building and the power of the Industrial Revolution.[2] He carefully recorded the machinery and apparatus used in the construction of the line, as well as the navvies swarming over the workings. Each figure has both function and purpose; every element falls into a logical place. However, Bourne also attempted to show that the railways could sit comfortably in their landscape and sometimes complement it. For instance, his view of the River Blythe depicts the new viaduct alongside the old bridge.

TREASURES

The Special Collections of the
University of Wales Trinity Saint David

John Cooke Bourne, *Tring cutting*, 1839

The reviews were uniformly excellent. John Herapath's *The Railway Magazine* commented:

> Mr Bourne seems to have adopted the method of all others best calculated for the illustration of his subject, and his drawings may fearlessly challenge a comparison with those of the first landscape painters of the day.[3]

The Gentleman's Magazine felt, 'There is perhaps, no object less picturesque … than the dull strait level of a rail-road; but in the hands of Mr Bourne, the subject seems to have lost much of its intractable character.'[4]

However, despite the glowing reviews, Bourne was to remain a relatively obscure artist; wealthy art patrons did not want to be reminded of the social and technical revolution surrounding them. Bourne published a second set of railway illustrations in 1846, *The History and Description of the Great Western Railway* (D. Bogue). After this he spent twelve years in Russia, illustrating Charles Vignoles's design for a road bridge across the Dnieper at Kiev and then working as resident artist for a number of civil engineering projects.

Ruth Gooding

1 Francis D. Klingender, *Art and the Industrial Revolution*, edited and revised by Arthur Elton (New York: Augustus M. Kelley, 1968).

2 Matt Thompson, *John Cooke Bourne: Railway Artist and Visionary* (History West Midlands, n.d.). *www.historywm.com/file/historywm/e10-john-cooke-bourne-railway-artist-visionary-42057. pdf*

3 John Herapath, 'Review of books', *The Railway Magazine and Steam Navigation Journal*, N.S. 6 (1839), pp. 266–7.

4 Sylvanus Urban, 'Fine Arts', *The Gentleman's Magazine* (1840), pp. 187–8.

A Drawing Master's Visit to Canada

John Richard Coke Smyth, *Sketches in the Canadas* (London: Published by Thos McLean, 1840)

Sketches in the Canadas is one of the great pictorial records of nineteenth-century Canada. However, its British artist, John Richard Coke Smyth (1808–82) remains a figure of considerable mystery.

Coke Smyth was the only son of Richard Smyth and Elizabeth Coke. He seems to have been a gentleman of independent means; his passport shows that he travelled widely in Europe. He was able to visit Istanbul in 1835/6, apparently as an unpaid attaché. Following this, he published *Lewis's Sketches of Constantinople, made during a residence in that city in the years 1835–6*. The volume was composed of twenty-six lithographs, produced from Coke Smyth's drawings by John Frederick Lewis, a noted artist.

Coke Smyth's next role was as drawing master to the household of John George Lambton, 1st Earl of Durham. His new employer was a member of a landed Durham family, a leading radical Whig politician and a former ambassador to Russia.

In 1837 and 1838, both Lower and Upper Canada rose in rebellion. In Lower Canada (later to be renamed Quebec), the British authorities had rejected the Patriotes' Ninety-two Resolutions, asking for constitutional change. The group quickly became an independence movement, preparing for civil war. In Upper Canada, William Lyon Mackenzie proclaimed, 'if we rise with one consent to overthrow despotism, we will make quick work of it'. However, in the one 'major' engagement, the rebels were dispersed. Both uprisings proved short-lived. Back in Britain, the prime minister, Lord Melbourne, appointed Coke Smyth's employer, the Earl of Durham, governor-in-chief of British North America and high commissioner. Like Durham, Coke Smyth sailed on HMS *Hastings*, reaching Quebec City on 28 May 1838. He wrote in his diary for that day 'very much delighted with the general appearance of the country – towards this Part, it resembles the Highlands much – Anticipate good sketching'.

Durham travelled widely during his time in Canada, so there was ample opportunity for Coke Smyth and his pupils to sketch the Canadian landscape first-hand. Among these pupils were Durham's daughters including Lady Mary Louisa Lambton, Katherine Jane Ellice (the wife of Durham's secretary) and perhaps Durham himself.

TREASURES

The Special Collections of the
University of Wales Trinity Saint David

John Richard Coke Smyth, *Moos hunter,* [1839]

However, Coke Smyth's time in Canada was to be short. Durham sailed back to Britain after only five months; it is likely Coke Smyth returned with him.

Coke Smyth brought home with him numerous lead pencil drawings; these provided the basis for the twenty-three lithographic views published as *Sketches in the Canadas*. Lithography had been invented by Aloys Senefelder in 1798. The technique is based on the fact that grease and water do not mix. It is one of the few processes in which artists' works can be presented to their public, without an intermediary other than the printing press. In Britain, it developed mainly as a medium for topography; many sets of picturesque views were published. Coke Smyth's book was published by Thomas McLean and printed by Alfred Ducôte. It was dedicated to Coke Smyth's employer, the Earl of Durham. Possibly Coke Smyth wanted to increase sales by displaying a prestigious name; possibly he was simply grateful for Durham's patronage.

John Richard Coke Smyth, *Quebec City from the chateau*, [1839]

The illustrations cover a variety of subjects: topographical views (Niagara Falls, Falls of Montmorency), genre scenes (Indians bartering, buffalo hunting), town views (Montréal, Quebec City from the Chateau) and historical reportage (attack and defence of rebels at Dickinson Landing, Engagement in the Thousand Islands). Very unusually for Quebec art, he includes one scene of an interior: the private chapel of the Ursuline convent. We can follow Coke Smyth's travels from Quebec City to Beauharnais, Montréal, Toronto and the Niagara Falls. His drawings are remarkable for their spontaneity; the vigorous style goes directly to the heart of the subject while still attempting to keep the freshness of the first impressions. A number of British artists, including military officers, had visited Canada. Although he drew many of the same scenes as these predecessors, Coke Smyth treated his subjects in a different manner. For instance, in his illustration of Quebec from the Chateau, the prominent diagonal in the foreground makes the ruins of Chateau Saint-Louis seem like an eagle's nest above the city. The mass of houses and roofs blend in with the horizontal in the background. The parapet, prominent in the foreground, is a symbol of British military power.

The Roderic Bowen Library's copy of Coke Smyth's book was donated by Thomas Phillips in 1846. In Phillips's first voyage in 1780, he had crossed the Atlantic in the *Danae* and then visited military stations along the St Lawrence. Coke Smyth's pictures of Quebec City and its surrounding area would have depicted familiar scenes for him.

On his return to Britain, Coke Smyth continued his career, with a focus on portraiture and on architecture. He developed a particular interest in painting costume and historical dress and in 1842 Queen Victoria commissioned him to illustrate a commemorative volume of her masked ball. He also exhibited at the Royal Academy between 1842 and 1855 and at the British Institution and Society of British Artists up to 1867. Examples of his work can be found in a variety of collections in Britain and Canada.

Ruth Gooding

John Richard Coke Smyth, *The private chapel of the Ursuline convent, Quebec* [1839]

Special Collections and Archives in the Future

So, what of the future? As we look back over the first 200 years of University of Wales Trinity St David's (UWTSD) Special Collections and Archives, what might the next decade hold? Ours was the first major library in Wales and our collection is of national importance. Our collections reflect a sense of national identity, and our materials have many compelling stories to tell. We can give the university a way to reach beyond its campuses into its surrounding communities and then into the world at large.

Ever more sophisticated technology will enable us to serve an audience that never enters a library building, and indeed may never visit Wales. Digitization, the process of converting an analogue original into a digital format, provides surrogate versions of rare and often unique materials. As well as protecting fragile originals, it enables us to share our collections with people all round the globe. It may also be possible to add extra functionality to the original, so the reproduced version is something more than merely a facsimile. For instance, an image can be magnified, allowing a user to see tiny details otherwise invisible to the naked eye. In many cases, digitization will be accompanied by transcription. Handwritten records, for instance, early lists of students, are not generally searchable unless the original text is separately inputted. This sort of task is time-consuming, laborious and potentially costly, meaning it is often best done through crowd-sourcing. Volunteers can add huge value to special collections services, alongside gaining experience in working with primary sources.

We need to consider new approaches in the way we collect archive material, as technology is reducing the quantity of ephemera that brings life to an archive. Personal letters have been replaced by texts and newspaper cuttings by online newspapers. Photographs are now stored on phones rather than printed. Over recent decades, many records have been stored on formats soon to become obsolete, (for instance, video and cassette tapes as well as floppy disks). One of the duties of an archivist is to ensure that significant material is converted into a digital medium and thus preserved for posterity.

By their nature, items in special collections are often highly visual. Increasingly, images of our treasures will be displayed through library catalogues and online repositories.

Core special collections work has always included curating and running exhibitions. These have enabled us to teach, to reach out, to celebrate milestones, to advocate and to share. Traditionally displays were physical. Although often stunning, the constraints of a display case meant that they were limited both in time and space. As most items are fragile and precious, moving volumes outside their home in Lampeter has always been problematic. More recently, we have supplemented physical displays with online exhibitions. As they are available to anyone with access to the internet and easy to promote via social media, they have huge potential to augment the profiles of our collections. (Our latest statistics cover a ten-month period in 2020 and 2021; the most popular exhibitions were viewed over 1,300 times each.) Online displays can also be more flexible. We can display many images from the same volume, instead of showing only one double-page spread. We can draw attention to a tiny detail, by magnifying the relevant image. We can include links to other resources. It may be possible to curate joint exhibitions with other libraries, museums or galleries with complementary collections. (For instance, it would be feasible to compare two manuscripts thought to be written by the same scribe or potentially from the same workshop.)

We hope to draw attention to some of our exhibitions by holding launch events. These could either be physical, held in Lampeter, Swansea or Carmarthen, or electronic. There is certainly the potential to start exhibitions off with a virtual talk. We might also promote our collections and educate our community by holding lectures, whether physical, online or hybrid. Traditionally, Lampeter has seen itself as geographically isolated and with only a very small surrounding community. In a post-pandemic world, we can communicate virtually with a global audience.

However, even in a digital world, original artefacts will not lose their significance. As the information in early volumes becomes available through other means, the study of books as physical objects will become increasingly important. Just being able to hold a copy can be stimulating, providing unique educational opportunities. In many cases, scholars will be interested in individual items. Every copy of a book from the hand-press period (1450–1800) is unique. In many cases, people arranged for their acquisitions to be bound after their purchase, or pasted in their bookplate. This means that every binding will be different. Often a book will have been signed by its former owner(s). Thomas Bowdler II, the major accumulator of Lampeter's tract collection, often annotated his purchases with his dates of acquisition, as well as the names

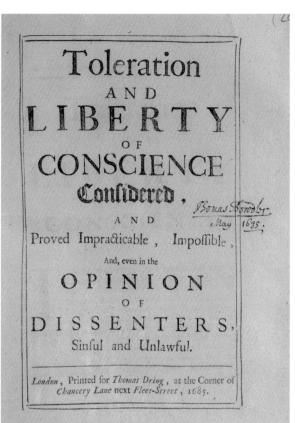

of authors of anonymous works. His notes offer a great deal of evidence to counter or corroborate modern scholarly conjectures. Researchers may well be interested in books owned by significant individuals. An academic working on John Locke would want to consult Locke's copy of Antonii van Dale's *Dissertationes de origine ac progressu idolatriæ et superstitionum*, held in UWTSD's collections.

Tract signed by
Thomas Bowdler II

Reading Room of the Roderic Bowen Library

As a nation, Britain is struggling to come to terms with the legacy of the transatlantic slave trade. Between the late sixteenth and early nineteenth centuries, over eleven million Africans were transported to the New World. By the mid-eighteenth century, the British had come to dominate Atlantic slavery. UWTSD's rich collection of primary source material will enable us to support research into slavery and, more generally, into colonialism. We hold volumes from a variety of perspectives. The three Thomas Bowdlers are not listed in the Legacies of British Slavery database as possessing enslaved people. However, their collection of pamphlets includes material written by plantation owners; for instance, Edward Littleton's *The Groans of the Plantations* (published by M. Clark, 1689), and Robert Robertson's *A Detection of the State and Situation of the Present Sugar Planters, of Barbadoes and the Leeward Islands* (printed and sold by J. Wilford, 1732). Three hundred years later, some of this material appears truly horrific; (for instance, balance sheets list the price of enslaved people brought from Africa alongside the sums paid for food and wine). On the other hand, Bishop Thomas Burgess was an abolitionist, whose library included anti-slavery material. Rather revealingly, we possess very little representing the enslaved peoples themselves. The main work we hold is Olaudah Equiano's classic, *The Interesting Narrative of the Life of Olaudah Equiano : or Gustavus Vassa, the African* (the first internationally famous slave narrative and the prototype for later works). Despite this limitation, the blend of viewpoints means we have ample resources to support research into slavery and, more broadly, into Western representations of history.

Nevertheless, we openly acknowledge that our collections only reflect a Western and Global North representation of the historical context of slavery, and indeed the colonial landscape more broadly. As with the wider heritage sector we recognize we need to do far more work in ensuring that the voices and stories of those excluded from this narrative are heard far more clearly in our collections, exhibitions and wider services. The absence of these voices means that our collections do not reflect accurately the colonial legacy of the institution, or indeed the complex and diverse narrative of the institution as it is today.

UWTSD must also recognize its own past. Like many of Lampeter's founders, Thomas Scandrett Harford, the donor of the college site, was an active abolitionist. However, much of his family's wealth came from transatlantic commerce; furthermore, his business partner, Philip John Miles, owned sugar plantations in Jamaica and Trinidad. More

significantly, Thomas Phillips, the donor of over 22,000 volumes between 1834 and 1852, owned a sizeable sugar plantation in St Vincent. After emancipation, he received £4737 8s. 6d in 1836 for the loss of his 167 enslaved people. This is equivalent to *c.* £670,000 at current values. We have no means of knowing how much of this he used to fund his gifts to Lampeter. In the past, university historians have tended to skate over the darker side of Phillips's activities. Such a stance is becoming ever harder to justify. Already, undergraduate teaching modules explore some of the influences behind what was collected, including the strong colonial legacy. In addition, UWTSD is working to put in place reparative justice, establishing links with educational institutions and academics in St Vincent. It is hoped that this relationship can be led by the community of St Vincent so that they can inform the institution's approach to justice and reconciliation.

UWTSD aims to 'contribute to the vibrancy of Welsh culture, visual arts, heritage and language'. The Small World Theatre at Cardigan has previously taken inspiration from our collections, for instance, in creating their mythological sea monster, Cragen. We hope to be involved in similar projects in future, still with a strong environmental message. We hold the texts of many Welsh ballads; we hope a gifted folk artist will be able to compose music for the written words. Some things are best done in collaboration with other libraries; for instance, most Welsh special collections and archives departments produce an annual adult colouring book, *Colour our collections*. There will be more we can do; UWTSD's bicentenary has given us a spur to seek out new opportunities.

Clean Seas Cragen created by Small World Theatre, Cardigan, 2019
Photo © Small World Theatre

It is said that the experience of higher education makes a person's brain a better place to live in for the rest of their lives. Special collections materials are often beautiful, often fascinating, often unique. They contribute hugely to the experience of university life.

Alison Harding
Ruth Gooding
Nicky Hammond

Peter Charles Henderson, *Vegetable Monsters,* 1802, engraved by J. Hopwood the elder, from R. J. Thornton, *A new illustration of the sexual system of Linnæus*

TREASURES
The Special Collections of the
University of Wales Trinity Saint David

Select Bibliography

This bibliography is not intended to be exhaustive, but lists most of the principal printed works that are referred to in the text.

Abbey, Charles J. and Overton, John H., *The English Church in the Eighteenth Century* (2 vols, London: Longmans, Green and Co., 1878)

Ackroyd, Peter, *Blake* (London: Sinclair Stevenson, 1995)

Acworth, Bernard, *Swift* (London: Eyre & Spottiswoode, 1947)

Anderson, Æneas, *A narrative of the British Embassy to China: in the years 1792, 1793 and 1794 …* (London: printed for J. Debrett, 1795)

Backhouse, Janet, *Books of Hours* (London: British Library, 1985)

Barański, Zygmunt G., *Dante, Petrarch, Boccaccio: Literature, Doctrine, Reality* (Cambridge: Legenda, 2020)

Barrell, John, *Edward Pugh of Ruthin 1763–1813: 'a Native Artist'* (Cardiff: University of Wales Press, 2013)

Beer, A., '"Left to the world without a Maister": Sir Walter Ralegh's *The History of the World* as a public text', *Studies in Philology*, 91/4 (1994), 432–63

Bentley, G. E., jnr, 'Richard Edwards, publisher of church-and-king pamphlets and of William Blake', *Studies in Bibliography*, 41 (1988), 283–315

Bryant, Julius, *Robert Adam 1728–92: Architect of Genius* (London: English Heritage in association with the National Library of Scotland, 1992)

Byrne, Paula, *Jane Austen and the Theatre* (London: Hambledon and London, 2002)

Colish, Marcia L., 'Scholastic Theology at Paris around 1200', in Spencer E. Young (ed.), *Crossing Boundaries at Medieval Universities* (Leiden: Brill, 2011)

Cook, Andrew S., 'Alexander Dalrymple (1737–1808), hydrographer to the East India Company and to the Admiralty as publisher' (3 vols, unpublished PhD thesis, University of St Andrews, 1993)

Coppola, A., '"Without the help of glasses": the anthropocentric spectacle of Nehemiah Grew's botany', *The Eighteenth Century*, 54/2 (2013), 263–77

Culpin, D. J., *Catalogue des Ouvrages du Fonds Français 1601–1850, conservés dans la 'Founders' Library', Université du Pays de Galles, Lampeter* (Cardiff: University of Wales Press, 1996)

Davis, Natalie Zemon, *Women on the Margins: Three Seventeenth-Century Lives* (Cambridge, Mass.: Harvard University Press, 1995)

Duffy, Eamon, *Marking the Hours: English People and their Prayers 1240–1570* (New Haven; London: Yale University Press, 2006)

Eaves, M. (ed.), *Cambridge Companion to William Blake* (Cambridge: Cambridge University Press, 2003)

Ehrenpreis, Irvin, *Swift: The Man, his Works, and the Age* (2 vols, London: Methuen, 1967)

Ford, Brian J., *Images of Science: A History of Scientific Illustration* (London: British Library, 1992)

Ford, E., 'Some early Australian medical publications', *Medical History*, 16/3 (1972), 205–25

George, Frank, *Anchovy Paste, by Appointment: The History of John Burgess & Son and a Guide to Collecting Victorian Fish Paste Pot Lids* ([Orpington]: published for the author, 1976)

Gilson, David, *A Bibliography of Jane Austen* (Winchester: St Paul's Bibliographies, 1997)

Harford, John S., *The Life of Thomas Burgess, DD* (London: Longman, Orme, Brown, Green and Longmans, 1840)

Harris, J., *Sir William Chambers: Knight of the Polar Star* (London: A. Zwemmer, 1970)

Harris, L. J., 'The missing number of Defoe's *Review*', *The Library*, 5th series, 28/4 (1973), 329–32

Hewerdine, C. V., 'A study of the hours of Charles Boddam' (unpublished MA thesis, University of Wales, 1981)

Hewerdine, C. V., 'Symbolic decoration in a fifteenth-century book of hours', *Trivium*, 18 (1983), 49–54

James, Brian Ll., *A Catalogue of the Tract Collection of St David's University College, Lampeter* (London: Mansell, 1975)

Ker, N. R., *Medieval Manuscripts in British Libraries*, vol. 3: *Lampeter–Oxford* (Oxford: Oxford University Press, 1983)

Keuning, J., 'The history of an atlas. Mercator-Hondius', *Imago Mundi*, 4 (1947), 37–62

Klingender, Francis D., *Art and the Industrial Revolution*, edited and revised by Arthur Elton (New York: Augustus M. Kelley, 1968)

Margócsy, D., 'The camel's head: representing unseen animals in sixteenth-century Europe', *Nederlands Kunsthistorich Jaarboek*, 61 (2011), 61–85

Marx, William (ed.), *The Founders' Library, University of Wales, Lampeter; Bibliographical and Contextual Studies. Essays in Memory of Robin Rider* (Lampeter: Trivium, 1997)

Nicholls, Mark and Williams, Penry, *Sir Walter Raleigh: In Life and Legend* (London: Bloomsbury, 2011)

O'Malley, A. (ed.), *Literary Cultures and Eighteenth-Century Childhoods* (London: Palgrave Macmillan, 2018)

Pennant, Thomas, *The Literary Life of the late Thomas Pennant, Esq., by himself* (London: for Benjamin and John White, 1793)

Popper, Nicholas, *Ralegh's History of the World and the Historical Culture of the Late Renaissance* (Chicago: University of Chicago Press, 2012)

Price, D. T. W., *A History of Saint David's University College, Lampeter. Volume 1: to 1898* (Cardiff: University of Wales Press, 1977)

Price, D. T. W., *A History of Saint David's University College, Lampeter. Volume 2: 1898–1971* (Cardiff: University of Wales Press, 1990)

Robbins, Keith and Morgan-Guy, John and Thomas, Wyn (eds), *A Bold Imagining: University of Wales, Lampeter: Glimpses of an Unfolding Vision: 1827–2002* (Cardiff: University of Wales Press, 2002)

Roberts, W. (ed.), *Memoirs of the life and correspondence of Mrs Hannah More*, 2nd edition (London: R. B. Seeley and W. Burnside, 1834)

Rupp, Gordon, *Religion in England 1688–1791* (Oxford: Clarendon Press, 1986)

Scott-Stokes, Charity (ed.), *Women's Books of Hours in Medieval England* (Cambridge: D. S. Brewer, 2006)

Sloboda, S., 'Picturing China. William Alexander and the visual language of chinoiserie', *British Art Journal*, 9/2 (2008), 28–36

Solly, N., *Memoir of the life of David Cox* (London: Chapman and Hall, 1873)

Stones, Alison, *Gothic Manuscripts 1260–1320* (London: Harvey Miller, 2013)

Taylor, Jeremy, *A vindication of the sacred order and offices: divine institution, apostolical tradition, and Catholick practice of episcopacy* (London: for Austine Rice, 1660)

The Charters, Special Statutes and Ordinary Statutes of St David's College in the County of Cardigan (Lampeter: Welsh Church Press, 1913)

Thomas, J. R. Lloyd, *Moth or Phoenix? St David's College and the University of Wales and the University Grants Committee* (Llandysul: Gomer, 1980)

Valiant, S., 'Maria Sibylla Merian: recovering an eighteenth-century legend', *Eighteenth-Century Studies*, 26/3 (1993), 467–79

Watkin, David, *The Life and Work of C. R. Cockerell* (London: A. Zwemmer, 1974)

Wildman, Stephen, Lockett, Richard, and Murdoch, John, *David Cox 1783–1859* (Birmingham: Birmingham Museums and Art Gallery, 1983)

Wilkins, Ernest Hatch, *The Trees of the Genealogia Deorum of Boccaccio* (Chicago: Caxton Club, 1923)

Wilks, Austen (ed.), *The Foundation Stone of Saint David's University College* (Llandysul: Gomer, 1977)

Woodbridge, E., 'Boccaccio's Defence of Poetry; as contained in the fourteenth book of the "*De Genealogia Deorum*"', *Publications of the Modern Language Association*, 13/3 (1898), 333–49

Young, Spencer E., 'Parisian Masters of Theology, 1215–48: a biographical register', in idem, *Scholarly Community at the Early University of Paris: Theologians, Education and Society, 1215–1248* (Cambridge: Cambridge University Press, 2014)

Zuber, M. A., 'The armchair discovery of the unknown southern continent: Gerardus Mercator, philosophical pretensions and a competitive trade', *Early Science and Medicine*, 16/6 (2011), 505–41

…tum pr…
…ante ad…
…gis aff…
…istl' capt…
…giones…
…se hebreo…
…mav. Si…
…l' lectio…
…aduenti…
…annūciat…

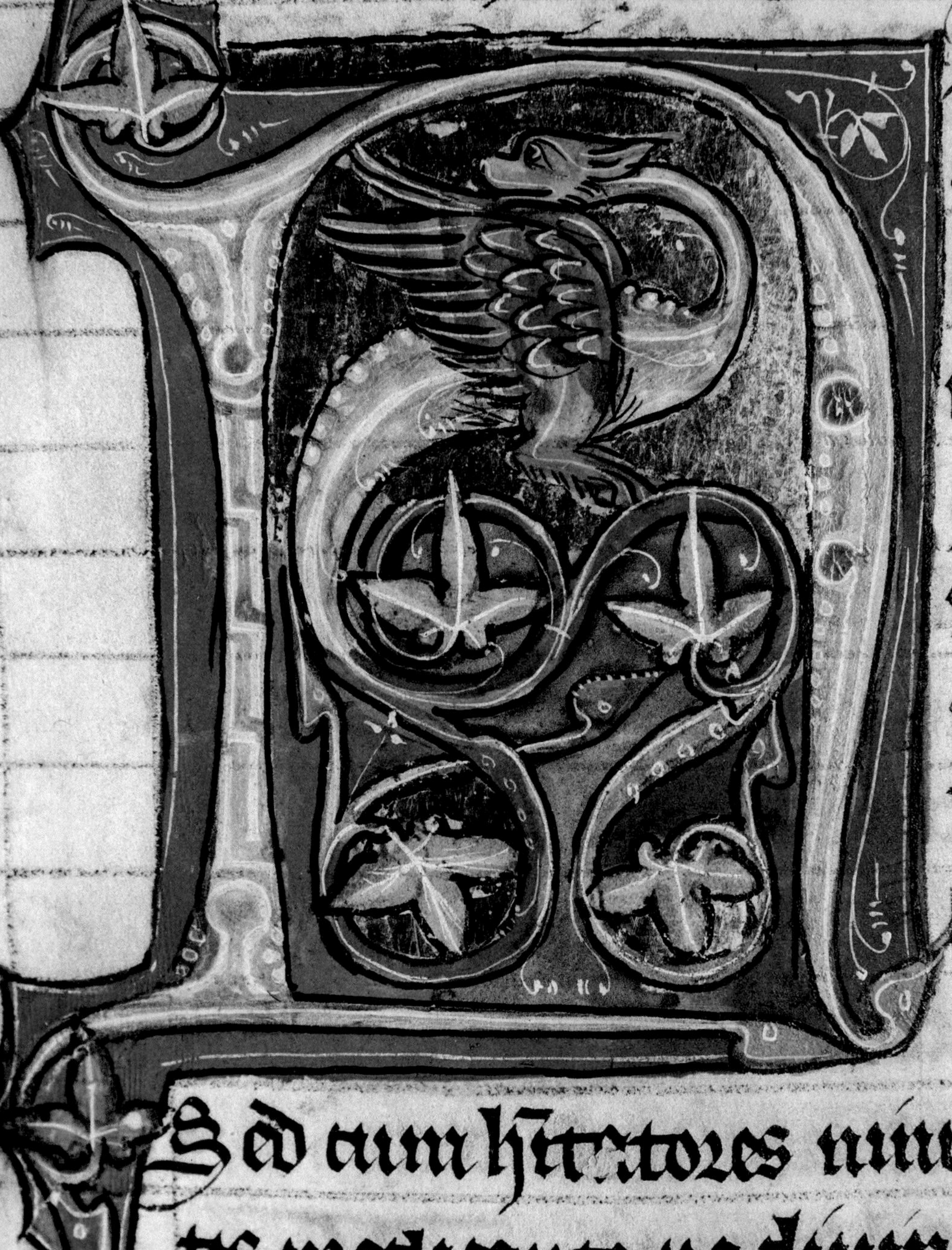

Sed cum hītrtores nīniue iona
tis prelicante ne diuina ira det…
sustinerent peccox & impietat…
sentr? accepta dei nra gratio…

Index

Page numbers for illustrations are shown in **bold**.

Initial from the Lampeter Bible

Illustration from William Chambers, *Desseins des edifices,
meubles, habits, machines, et ustenciles des chinois*, 1757